Virtuous Magic

Virtuous Magic

WOMEN SAINTS AND
THEIR MEANINGS

Sara Maitland and Wendy Mulford

MOWBRAY

Mowbray

A Cassell imprint

Wellington House, 125 Strand, London WC2R 0BB

First published 1998

British Library Cataloguing-in-Publication Data
A catalogue record for this book is available from the British Library.

ISBN 0–264–67386–7

Designed by Geoff Green
Typeset by York House Typographic Ltd, London
Printed and bound in Great Britain by Bookcraft (Bath) Ltd,
Midsomer Norton, Somerset

Contents

Acknowledgements

Thanks are due to:

Garland Publishing Inc., New York, for permission to use material from their reprint of *An Autobiography: The Story of the Lord's Dealing with Mrs. Amanda Smith, the Colored Evangelist*; originally published by Meyer and Bro., Chicago, 1893.

The Mina Loy Estate (courtesy Roger Conover) and the Jargon Society, for the epigraph, which is taken from 'Illuminations', from '*Anglo-Mongrels and the Rose 1923–1925*', in *The Last Lunar Baedeker*, pp. 163–4. © Mina Loy, Jargon, Corinth, USA.

Floris Books, Edinburgh, for permission to use material from their reprint of *Carmina Gadelica*, edited by Alexander Carmichael.

Coleman Barks for his translation of lines from Lal Ded, 'Lalla: Naked Song', reprinted in Jane Hirshfield (ed.), *Women in Praise of the Sacred* (HarperCollins, 1994).

Dr Oliver Davies for permission to quote from his translation of 'The Life of Melangell', from the seventeenth-century Welsh manuscript, first published in A. M. Allchin, *Pennant Melangell: Place of Pilgrimage* (Gwasg Santes Melangell, Oswestry, 1994).

Every effort has been made to contact other copyright holders and the authors would be glad to know of any mistakes or unintentional omissions.

NOTE

My sections of this book could not have been written without the co-operation of the texts of some of the saints and their authors, living and dead. The writings of Amanda Berry Smith, Jean Donovan and the El Salvador sisters, Sor Maria of Santo Domingo and Sor Juana Inés de la

Cruz in particular have been 'borrowed' from the main sources listed at the end of each section. In each case I have freely adapted and interwoven these sources with my own words, and in the latter two cases I have transformed the prose sources into verse.

I made a similar transformation of the liturgy of St Hild from the Northumbria Community.

The material in the text for Jean Donovan and the El Salvador sisters is taken either directly or indirectly from Ana Carrigan, *Salvador Witness: The Life and Calling of Jean Donovan* © Ballantine Books, New York, 1984), which introduced me to the work of the sisters in El Salvador and moved me to compose the whole piece from it.

WENDY MULFORD

... The high skies
have come gently upon her
and all their
steadfast light is shining out of her

She is conscious
not through her body but through space

This saint's prize
this indissoluble bliss
to be carried like a forgetfulness
into the long nightmare

Mina Loy, 'Illumination', from *Anglo-Mongrels and the Rose 1923–1925*

Man as a moral being hungers and thirsts after justice, and man as artist hungers and thirsts after form, and although these two are ultimately one, because of the truth of that best of all sayings, 'the beauty of God is the cause of being of all that is', nevertheless for us they are not one, not yet, not by any means.

David Jones, *Art in Relation to War*, p. 134

Introduction

I drag a boat over the ocean
with a solid rope.

. . .

Like water in goblets of unbaked clay
I drip out slowly
And dry.

. . .

. . . Let me
discover my home

Lal Ded of Kashmir, fourteenth-century mystic and dancer, trans. Willis
Barnstone, in J. Hirshfield (ed.), *Women in Praise of the Sacred*

These words point up something of the enormous distance between contemporary consciousness and that of the time of the saints. The solid rope
– the records, legends, images, monuments, buildings – that connects us, in
1997, to the starting-point of this journey, the century of the birth of Jesus
Christ, seems far from solid across the changes in consciousness and belief
through the centuries. What is material evidence to one age is immaterial to
another.

Historically, from the earliest centuries the saints were woven into the
fabric of people's lives, through the rituals of the church year, the extraordinary and holy days of feasts, the 'red-letter days', the presences of
patron saints and protectors in church buildings, communities and organi-
zations such as the medieval guilds.

Pilgrimages and relics, like stigmata, exercise a curious fascination on the modern mind. Television documentaries have investigated all three. Withered hands, bog-lined but still evidently fleshly skin, eyes and toes encased in jewelled caskets, before which tapers burn and masses are said: all these offer a great deal to contemporary curiosity and the desire for the 'way out'. So does the curiosity of reaching into the medieval mind's explicit obsessions with putrefaction and its devotions to the odder parts of the holy body: Christ's foreskin being perhaps the most extreme example.

But nothing divides the medieval from the modern so clearly as all the *business* of relics, the marketing of the metonym, which is the relic or part which stands for the whole. The modern mind shrinks from the hacking up of the saint's body, the haggling, scheming, manipulating and downright robbery, and the economic power of well-attested and spiritually valuable relics of saints. All of which appears today to be little more than a fairly cut-throat branch of the antiques trade overlaid with a smear of piety. Perhaps pilgrimage itself is the acceptable modern face of the relics business.

The pilgrim who sets out to follow the way of the saints, whose goal is to arrive at the earthly location of their spiritual power, in whatever place or form that may be held to inhere, hopes to draw on that power for herself and attain a closer relationship with God. That the Turin Shroud and Veronica's handkerchief have been shown to be medieval fakes does not alter the need of the believers to establish a material link with the sources of their belief, any more than the absence of original certified fragments of the True Cross (see **Helena**) destroys the symbolic efficacy of the millions of crosses worn and venerated by Christians around the world.

As an archetype of underlying patterns of motivation in human beings the quest or journey is a familiar form in the literature of most cultures. Going on a pilgrimage today combines elements of these mythical journeys, of inner journeys of self-discovery and of faith, with traditional testing of the self through the exploration of one's resources over time and space in a venture which is open to unforeseen developments through the evolving partnership between pilgrim, saint and Holy Spirit. While the ostensible aim of the pilgrimage may be to follow the saint's tracks, to mark the holy places of her life and work, the actual outcome of the pilgrimage may be entirely different.

If faith is after all, as many would now argue, a performative practice, whose power is guaranteed precisely by the measure to which the adherent engages *in* that practice, the value of pilgrimage is that it offers a coherent space and shape to one such practice. Coincidentally and importantly, it also meets the need of contemporary searchers to encounter spiritual reality at first hand, not to receive it via the (often damaged) authority of texts and institutions.

We are arguing that saints today are *potentially* spiritual resources whose presences through the traces they have left behind in the minds of the whole community of the faithful can be tapped by contemporary searchers. Pilgrimage, the making of a journey through a definite time and over a definite amount of space, is one form of access.

Pilgrimage is at once profoundly concerned with the search for the (divine) Other, and the search for the transforming of the Self. It is an opening up, a prising apart of closure, of familiarities and securities and easily acquired knowledge, in pursuit at one and the same time of the unknown and the known.

These ideas of pilgrimage have become, in the two years we have been working together on this book, an implicit metaphor of our endeavour. The 'ardures, adventures, difficulties and delights' of this pilgrimage – in research; in fury at the lost or damaged channels of transmission; in recognition of the known and implosion of the unknown; in asserting self (there are always two quite distinct and sometimes quarrelsome selves here) and acknowledging other; in negotiating between the material landscapes of history and the equally real but non-material marks of meaning – have informed even the structure of the book.

We could not get away from the necessity, to us, of exploring both the material and the metaphorical meanings of the women we wanted to write about. We have used the word 'meaning' in the sub-title of this book: we mean to. It is not a book about who are, or might, or should be saints. It is an exploration of what saints mean to us. Our argument is that as minds gradually slough off the constraints of the Enlightenment, there are new ways in which we can be challenged by the saints' narratives, and addressed by their search. Our aim is to make usable, actual, visible, the lives of saints who have touched us; to recreate some particular saints and their meanings.

Hagiography – the writing-up of saints – has taken on for us the metaphorical shape of a pilgrimage, a chronology and a geography of the boundaries, the borders, and of the unboundaried, the wild space beyond the boundaries. It is a hard terrain to map.

After various compass errors, wrong turnings and failed explorations, we have developed the double texts that you will find in the body of this book.

Each of the saints we have looked for, we have looked for at two levels – the level of 'history' (which means both the 'factual' basis of their lives and the way, over time and within social construction, these have been developed, used, mapped, manifested, exploited, recorded, evaded) and the level of imaginative interiority. Our own acts of recreation – which take several different forms: poems, stories, sermons, quotations, combinations – appear for the most part on the left hand of each double-page spread. This is technically called the verso page, which has a pleasing double meaning in this context. The right-hand, or recto, pages contain our commentaries on our own texts, references, sources, useful background information or anything else we thought was interesting or made the women, or our creations, more accessible. We are both literary, wordy writers, dependent on intertextuality, history and language for our own work. Consequently it has not always been clear which side of the entirely artificial line some of the material belonged; in some cases it would not break down properly at all – so, when we felt that the weight of parallel texts could not work for us, we have juxtaposed the two in slightly different ways. The point we needed to make was that neither level should be given priority over the other. The overall intention has been to make transparent, or translucent at least, the idea that our texts are interpretations of interpretations and that the reader is free to interpret further. Hopefully the layout will permit the reader to weave from one discourse to another as we feel the saints weave.

A few further points may asssist the reader. Our selection of saints has been entirely personal and therefore arbitrary. They are saints with whom we have engaged in this literary sense: they are probably therefore those who have touched our imaginations in particular ways (or occasionally we have to say, the imagination of our publisher, who has put in a few specific requests). Exactly what has engaged us has varied pretty widely. Sara has tended to be more attuned to the biographical and hence to ethical dilemmas, the nature of 'holiness' as a liminal (foot in two camps) condition. Both of us would see the imaginative effort to find a link across the centuries as central to these texts, but Sara would define that more, perhaps, as a declaration of friendship, which Wendy has found almost impossible. For Wendy that link has been searched for through these women's writings, through their images and churches, through the material context.

What this difference means is not entirely clear to us. It may just be the difference between a poet and a fiction writer, or it may, we suspect, indicate theological differences, or at least differences in theological traditions:

traditions which deliver up the sense of a holy life for Wendy through word and context, for Sara through sacrament and performance. We have wondered whether this has something to do with the fact that the Church and its authority and traditions have been significantly meaningful to Sara, who regards herself as central to them, but not in the same way for Wendy, who sees her position as peripheral and provisional, oblique like Anglicanism's own relationship to the saints. Crudely, we have labelled this difference Celtic and Roman: the Celtic Church saw its integrity in shared images and rituals, while the Latin Rite was more credal and dogmatic, more centralized, but less personalist. This may not be quite the right way to put it, but we have discovered, with more interest than distress, a real though shadowy division which we cannot articulate properly, and which the process of fictionalizing has not teased out. Perhaps if we had written about the same saints we would have made things clearer for ourselves – but, equally, if we had been drawn to the same saints, perhaps we would not have discovered the differences. The alert reader will notice, however, that we have both engaged with Mary Magdalene. Comparing the two may explicate this point.

Maybe all we can say at this point is 'Look!' 'Look, I stumbled over this one; I stubbed my toe on her; somehow, somewhere, a corner of her grabbed hold of a corner of me, provoked me, made an impress on my flesh.'

Each of the verso pages is the work of one of us alone, although we have read critically and suggested textual changes to each other. The recto pages have been the responsibility of whoever wrote the parallel verso material, but occasionally this responsibility has been delegated.

Before the thirteenth century there was no formal canonization process and we therefore make little apology for the fact that not only are not all of our women formally canonized, but a few have actually been declared heretical, or in the Church's terms sacked (the revision of the calendar in 1968 reduced the status of noticeably more women saints than men, even though 90 per cent of the official saints were men).

The one thing that all our saints have in common is gender: this is a text about women saints, and therefore about women. This was not an arbitrary decision – it was the one stabilizing factor from the very start of our collaboration. It could be defended on the grounds that women have had their meanings more consistently distorted and their lives more consistently obscured; that the ethics of female sanctity raise more particular problems in a religion that has been so predominantly sexist; that we are more identified with women than with men saints; or that setting some limits was helpful. We, however, would justify it on grounds of delight.

Our saints also have, we would tentatively suggest, four other things in common — or perhaps, rather, four other things have become part of the themes or objectives of our pilgrimage towards them:

1. We wanted to write about them. They have touched the writerly affections, imaginations, sensibilities, of two contemporary Christian women writers who identify themselves as feminists.

2. They have helped us to come to terms with, or at least to recognize, submerged parts of our own faith stories — assisting us, in a sisterly way, to excavate our own meanings from the mine of history.

3. They demonstrate a readiness to go into the abyss of the self and confront the inner darkness or emptiness there. We would understand this abyss as the French philosopher Luce Irigaray expresses it, in her meditations on risk and the relinquishment of the self, in the direction of 'horizonless ends'. 'Who goes not into the abyss can only repeat and restate paths already opened up that erase the traces of the gods who have fled.'[1] Because these women have ultimately not been intimidated, because they have not dodged the interior obstacles to surrendering the self, they are often the ones who can irradiate the everyday with the gleam of the extraordinary. They unmask another, uncomfortable kind of truth.

4. They display the risky joy of the uncalculable lavishing of the Self upon the Other. Saying 'yes' with a high-hearted certainty — but without any guarantee of safety — to what calls beyond: which is for them, us and all the religious, saying 'yes' to the call of God.

Praise: they are all devoted to praise and glory.

---

1. Luce Irigaray, 'He risks who risks life itself', in M. Whitford (ed.), *The Irigaray Reader* (Blackwell, Oxford, 1994).

So, who cooked the Last Supper?
A story for Martha

❧

One lamb – the kid lamb, which was a nuisance. She'd hoped to rear that one, she needed a new billy-goat. But there were too many of them for a sheep lamb. It would help if he could tell her how many.

Herbs.

Wrapping cloths for the bread; she would have to wash some. But, damn the rules, she was baking here, in her own oven, wherever they ate.

Wine.

Blessing cup.

Hyssop.

When Martha got tired she got cross. To be honest, she got cross when she wasn't tired too. But mainly when she was tired. She was tired most of the time, so she was cross most of the time and it was not fair.

He was so arrogant. Thoughtless.

She heard his voice, 'Lazarus, come out.' And her brother had walked out of his own grave. She felt guilty. That wasn't fair either.

Dishes.

Water vessels.

They hadn't even got the donkey back yet. Come to think of it, where was the donkey? If they had just turned it loose and forgotten about it, she really would be angry. It was a valuable donkey and, as it happened, it was *her* donkey.

And, without a donkey, she was going to have to go to town at least twice. Today she would have to go down and persuade some friend to lend them a room. And how could she, how could she put some poor woman and her household at risk? And there would be a risk . . . a flicker of fear raised her irritability further . . . there would be a risk.

Martha of Bethany: 1st century
Friend of Jesus
Feast: 29 July

Martha, with her sister Mary and her brother Lazarus, lived in Bethany (a village a few miles from Jerusalem), which seems to have been both home and headquarters when Jesus was in Judaea. The three biblical scenes (Luke 10:38–42; John 11:1–46; John 12:1–2) in which Martha appears are the only 'domestic' details we have of Jesus' life.

The Jewish Passover, celebrating the escape of the Hebrews from slavery in Egypt, was appropriated by Christianity very early, for obvious symbolic reasons, as the occasion of the Last Supper. Like many Jewish festivals it involved a household meal, the Seder: the idea that women were not present at the Last Supper as Seder is ridiculous. Exodus 12 and 13 contain instructions for keeping the Passover, though the ritual has developed since, including the idea that Passover is most properly kept in Jerusalem.

The account of the raising of Lazarus (John 11:1–46) is a key episode in John's Gospel, and presents a very different portrait of Martha from that in Luke 10. It contains some of Jesus' most explicit self-definitions and leads Martha (*before* Lazarus is restored to her) to one of the first epiphanic moments – the recognition that Jesus of Nazareth is both Messiah and Son of God. It also shows a moving and profound friendship between Martha and Jesus.

The donkey on which Jesus rode in triumph into Jerusalem on what is now called Palm Sunday (Matthew 21:2; Mark 11:2; Luke 19:30) was collected from Bethany. Nothing else biblical links it with Martha.

See Mark 14:12–16 and Luke 22:8–15 for the complicated arrangements employed.

Then, when she'd exploited the affection of her friends, she was going to have to cart all the stuff into town and she knew that none of them would help. They'd be laughing and singing, high as kites on Kingdom and Freedom and the Spirit. And her sister would get all mystical and dreamy and just sit there looking holy and sweet and beautiful.

She tasted the bile of her jealousy and was appalled. That did not improve her temper.

No one seemed to realize that if you had about thirty extra guests, it made more than thirty times as much work.

'How many for Passover?' she had asked him.

'Oh Martha, I don't know. The hungry must be fed.' And then, 'Oh, Martha, how much I have longed to eat this Passover with you.' Who could snarl at such a smile?

'All right,' she'd said, 'I'll get the big barn cleared.'

'Oh, no,' he'd said, 'we have to do it in Jerusalem.' He saw her face. 'We have to, Martha, that's the whole point.'

He was her friend, but she was sulky in her fury. She said only, 'I can't. It's too dangerous.'

He didn't smile then, he said, 'Nothing is too dangerous now, Martha – except not getting it right.'

She had given him a hug then, and with her arms round him she had learned that he was as scared and anxious as she was. So she said, 'Well, I'll see what I can do. But you might have told me sooner.'

'Oh,' he said, 'I only just thought of it. But you can manage, can't you?'

'No, I can't,' she said crossly, but he had only grinned. Bloody men!

Oil.

Fruit.

Cooking fuel. She was not borrowing off her friends; and she was not paying Jerusalem prices either. She'd tell him tonight. Though they probably would not get in till midnight. They'd get back dirty, tired and hungry. Noisy, over-excited. Tense.

Nard.

Rubbing ointment.

Lentils. They must be set to soak tonight.

Oh, no, really; she could not do it on her own.

And she would not ask her sister to help.

From the gospel accounts it appears that Bethany was Jesus' base throughout the week preceding his death, and that he and the disciples walked into Jerusalem each day, and returned at night. However, the Last Supper itself was held in a borrowed upper room in Jerusalem.

All four Gospels make the schedule of Jesus and his disciples during Holy Week – from the arrival in Jerusalem to the resurrection – sound gruelling. Based on these accounts, the disciples falling asleep in the Garden of Gethsemane on the Thursday evening seems unsurprising.

John 6:35ff.

Luke 22:14 – though there addressed to all the apostles gathered for the Seder, immediately before offering the bread and wine of the Passover meal to them as his body and blood.

Because of the Luke 10 episode, where Martha gets 'reprimanded', she has become the patron saint of housewives, and her usual attributes are a ladle or a bunch of keys. However, there was a medieval legend that, with her brother and sister, she was responsible for the evangelization of Provence, where she tamed a dragon (cf. **Margaret of Antioch**). Her feast day, 29 July, was chosen for the first 'non-canonical' ordinations of eleven women deacons in the Episcopal Church of America in 1974.

There. There she hit the kernel of her crossness.

Once she had asked him to tell Mary to help. Mary had been sitting on the floor at his feet looking soulful and beautiful while a dozen hungry travellers needed supper. He'd said, 'Martha, calm down. You're fussing. Mary has chosen the best job and no one will take it away from her.' You just run along and organize me a whole Seder and don't moan. Mary is too sweet and holy and pretty to have to work. Be like Mary. Mary is best. Mary is just wonderful. Mary looks so lovely when she's crying that she can't be expected to get her hands dirty. Mary's the youngest, the pretty one. Martha's the oldest, the sensible one.

How dare he? How dare he tell her one minute not to fret, and the next minute demand she gets this dangerous, stupid and unnecessary dinner party on the road?

'I won't,' she told herself. 'I just won't. Then he'll see.'

But she had to laugh at herself, a little bitterly, because even as she spoke she was adding to her list.

A sharp knife.

A dish for the blood.

She found she was crying.

That night, though, they were all in time for dinner; and grateful, even in their tension.

'Martha,' he said when they had eaten all her delicious food, 'I told a story for you in the Temple today. Do you want to hear it?'

'You can come out in the yard and tell me while I do the washing,' she said. 'I haven't got time for stories.'

He left the others then and came out with her, just the two of them, alone in the fading of the light. She knelt over her scrubbing stone and he said, 'This is how my story went. I didn't tell it quite this way in town, but this is the real version. There was this man and he had two daughters. He said to the first one, "Girl, go and work in the kitchen today." And she said, "I won't." But later she went and got on with it. Then he went to his other daughter and said the same. She answered, "Yes, of course, dear Father," but she didn't. Now here's the question: which of the two daughters really did the will of their father?'

She threw back her head, her hands still in the water, and roared with laughter. He knew her too well. 'Don't be cheeky,' she said, still

Luke 10:38–42. This episode has been so formative in the construction of women within Christianity that it is now extremely difficult to decode. The polarization between Martha and Mary (the active and the contemplative) has borne on women very particularly. Even the revision of the canons for religious after the Second Vatican Council in the 1970s re-stressed the division between types of women's orders (splitting up such orders as the women Dominicans, who had succeeded in eliminating the distinction – one unknown in male orders). The Martha/Mary split not only polarizes women's lives, it does so punitively: women simultaneously are told that Mary has chosen the better part *and* are expected to *act* like Martha: no father of the Church, nor parish sermon, ever seems to have suggested that what Jesus might have done is have helped with the cooking himself – or instructed the men to do so. This impossible exhortation seems to me to have had more, and more negative, effect on women's lives than the far more often instanced Virgin/mother dichotomy.

Matthew 21:28–31. But here the parable has sons in a vineyard rather than daughters in the kitchen.

laughing. 'You, dear boy, are not my father. Flattery will get you nowhere.'

He climbed off the hay bale and came to stand beside her.

'Oh, Martha,' he said, 'what would I do without you?' He bent down to give her a kiss, and suddenly she was a child again, irresistibly. Under the soapy surface she cupped her hands and, as his face came tenderly towards hers, she scooped out a double handful of water, and chucked it, neatly, splash, straight in his face.

For a second he was stunned, silenced, his beard and nose both dripping, and then the two of them collapsed into laughter, infantile giggles, helplessly hugging each other until the others came out to see what on earth was going on. And when Mary saw them she looked quite shocked.

Much later that night, when Martha finally got to bed, she found herself thinking of a different list.

I am the way.

I am the truth.

I come that you may have life, life more abundantly.

I am the good shepherd.

Anyone who believes in me shall never die.

Lazarus, come out.

Martha, I am the resurrection and the life. Can you believe this?

But it was not his wisdom that she remembered last, on the edge of sleep, but her own:

'Oh yes, dear friend, I believe you are the Christ, the Son of God, he who is coming into the world.'

John 14:6.
John 14:6.
John 10:10.
John 10:14.
John 11:26.
John 11:46.
John 11:25, 26.

John 11:27.

Many women in the past have found considerable comfort in the humble service of Martha — content with the knowledge that Jesus 'loved' her, and gladly sharing that ministry. Martha has been a particular patroness of lay-sisters, for instance, whose contribution cannot be measured. However, it is interesting to note that **Teresa of Avila** — with her particular concern about class privilege and personal 'honour' and dignity — was worried by the Martha/Mary division and at times in her writing definitely 'sides' with Martha. Contemporary liberal exegesis constructs this story as revealing the anti-sexism of Jesus — who here authorizes women as disciples (Mary 'sitting at the feet' (Luke 10:39) being the language of the student or disciple in relation to a rabbi). This seems optimistic! *Some* women are so authorized at the expense of other *women*. The command of Jesus that each should be 'servant of all' is isolated from this episode rather deftly so that men are ritual servants (offer the sacramental meal) without having to do the cooking. At the same time women (in contrast to the Judaic tradition) are not freed from external religious duties because of their domestic religious duties. At some level the unwillingness of men to take on such 'degrading' responsibilities, in relation to this text, must have assisted enormously in the valorization of virginity (and enclosure) for women: if you want to be free to pray properly (like Mary), you must not deprive a man of domestic (Martha) services, and meanwhile he can dismiss these services as being inferior to those of 'consecrated' contemplatives. If, however, this episode is read in rigorous connection with the raising of Lazarus story, it is possible to see a bond of intimacy between Martha and Jesus, which may allow the reader to see the Luke story as (a) specific to their relationship (rather than a universal truth for all women at all times and in all places) and (b) as 'occasional': Martha has got a bit over-the-top and could stop now and come and sit down for a while — after all she knows who he is, even though most of the people gathered haven't yet got the point. If this is coupled with the medieval tradition that sees her activity as both evangelical and heroic (dragon-slaying), a glorious dignity as Jesus' closest woman *friend* can be returned to her. Perhaps.

Vera Ikon

You hold the cloth
carefully fingers and
thumb by each
corner as if to
hang it out on
the line to dry some
gentle breezy April day
of sun and shower
the image weighs
the cloth in
folds hair and
cloth hang down

Veronica: 1st century
Woman of pity, patron saint of washerwomen
Feast: 12 July

❦

The poem is inspired by *Saint Veronica with the Sudarium*, by the Master of Saint Veronica, *c.* 1420, in the National Gallery, London.

Legend relates that when Christ fell as he was carrying the cross to Calvary, Veronica wiped his face with her handkerchief (*sudarium*). The image of Christ's face was then miraculously imprinted on it.

The earliest version of the story comes in a late Latin interpolation to the Gospel of Nicodemus (fourth to fifth century). A cloth supposed to be Veronica's, known as her 'veil', has been preserved at St Peter's in Rome since the eighth century. Arousing great popular devotion in the Middle Ages, because of the increase of devotion to Christ's humanity, it was last exhibited in 1933.

> *. . . it seems likely that the story of Veronica is a delightful legend without any solid historical basis . . . invented to explain the relic. (ODS)*

The Church, however, has never suppressed her cult.

In the revelations or 'showings' that **Julian of Norwich** received on 13 May 1373, she was reminded of the veil or vernicle, during her second revelation of Christ hanging on the cross and of the mockings he endured:

> *. . . a figure and a likeness of our foul black deed, which that our fair bright blessed Lord bare for our sin. It made me to think of the holy vernacle of Rome, which he portrayed with his one blessed face, when he was in his hard passion, wilfully going to his death, and often changing of colour . . .*
>
> E. Colledge and J. Walsh (eds), *A Book of Showings to the Anchoress Julian of Norwich*

The vernicle (veil or handkerchief) was a source of great veneration to pilgrims, who were assured of three thousand years of indulgence from their sins if they came from Italy to St Peter's to revere it, increasing to nine thousand years if they had come from the Alpine regions, and to twelve thousand if they had actually crossed the Alps.

An indulgence was a specific commitment by the Church's authority to remit not only the sins for which the pilgrim sought absolution but also the time that would be spent in Purgatory as a consequence of the sins committed. It was the particular target of reformers as the sale of indulgences became a regular practice and a key part of the economy both of the Church and of places of pilgrimage (cf. **Wendreda**).

Accounts of the vernicle in England included one by Capgrave in his *Solace of Pilgrims*. By the time of **Julian**'s showings, Franciscan devotion to the stations of the cross, which incorporated the original legendary incident of Christ's fall, had increased the popularity of the legend, and the image of the vernicle and texts about it were plentiful in the West.

Bernadette of Lourdes

✦

The candles flicker in the night – the air is warm and thousands of flecks of fire dance in the dark, processing up and around the hill. The long trite song winds on and on; on and on.

There are too many people – nuns with sharp elbows and incomprehensible accents push and shove their way to the front. Priests saunter, oblivious, oblivious and sleek, and the crowds are dense, dense, and the sick, the very sick, whose place this is, are wheeled through the crowds by over-enthusiastic, smiling and often self-righteous teenagers, who try not to notice they wish they had opted for the family holiday on the beach instead. Around the shrine there is a market-place of vulgarity. In the centre of the shrine is a huge church, a small grotto and a complicated queuing system for both the secular toilets and the miraculous baths.

Everywhere there is religion – religion and the ill: the sick, the crippled, the deformed, the dying. The children, the old. The barren, the desperate, the agonized, the hopeful, the serene, the outraged, the resigned. There are also the carers, both professional and emotional, competent or incompetent, loving or bored.

There are miracles. Often there are small miracles, of hope and faith and love, little miracles of joy. Occasionally, very occasionally, there are big miracles – miracles of healing outrageous enough to be investigated by the Competent Authorities. Always there is the enormous miracle – this is the place where the last are first; the place where the ill, the disabled, even the freaks come first and are central. The place of the gospel. The place of prayer and penance and grace.

It is a throw-back, Lourdes, a throw-back to a more primitive faith, here where the market-place and the sacraments, vulgarity and sublimity are united, mixed, stirred together. It is medieval, without

Bernadette Soubirous: 1844–1879
Visionary
Feast: 16 April

❧

Bernadette Soubirous was the oldest of the six children of a miller, from Lourdes in the foothills of the Pyrenees in southern France. The family were extremely poor, which probably explains her general ill-health, although in addition she suffered from asthma. In 1858, over a period of six months, she received eighteen visions of Mary, the mother of God, which she described in very straightforward terms. Since she was often told the date of the next vision, people were able to watch her – and large crowds gathered to do so. Although no one but she saw anything remarkable, her behaviour during these events *was* remarkable. On the most famous occasion she was seen lapping at a patch of mud which gradually turned into a small puddle and subsequently a spring of fresh water.

The ecclesial authorities instructed her to ask the vision to identify itself (Bernadette referred to it only as 'The Lady'), and she reported that it declared 'I am the Immaculate Conception', a phrase she claimed to have no prior knowledge of. The Lady wanted penance, prayers and a church built.

Bernadette's startling unshakeability led to full investigation and considerable curiosity and publicity. Eight years after the apparitions she joined the Sisters of Notre-Dame of Nevers, an enclosed order; and died in the convent from tuberculosis at the age of thirty-five.

Lourdes very quickly became, and still remains, a major place of pilgrimage. The water from the spring which The Lady had opened for Bernadette is believed to have miraculous healing properties; so a Commission has been appointed to test all cases. The criteria are strict and medical notes, X-rays and the mental stability of the 'healed' are all taken into account. The Commission has recognized surprisingly few (five) cures as 'miraculous' in the fullest sense of the word. However, Lourdes is deeply attractive to the sick, and even to the healthy, and has developed a strong spirituality of its own which is highly physical (sacramental), including a bathing ritual of

the visual charm – by all imaginable aesthetic criteria the Basilica is hideous and the surroundings kitsch. It is also joyful, noisy, passionate, hopeful, alive.

At its core there is a silence.

Bernadette Soubirous.

Poor, stable, stupid, devout – it was noticed later – brave, obedient, asthmatic, unshakeable, tubercular as it transpired, calm. Tedious, really, and she led a tedious life. This is not a silence of the mystic, not the silence of the heroically stubborn, but a silence because really there is nothing to say. Nothing.

Except that during six months in 1858 (conveniently just as the railways developed to make cheap transport possible) The Lady appeared to her eighteen times and chatted of this and that. Prayer, penance, church-building. 'I am the Immaculate Conception,' The Lady said in response to a direct question someone else had told Bernadette to ask. And The Lady opened a spring where there had been none before, which has pumped out nearly 4,000 gallons of water a day ever since.

Boring. No mighty deeds, no great thoughts, no complications. She was born, she chatted with The Lady, she reported her conversations when asked, she became a nun – mainly because no one, including herself, could think of anything better. She endured her painful disease bravely. She died.

Not a sign of hysteria, over-excitement, mental instability. Very little for psychiatrist or theologian to get their teeth into; very little for the faithful and the sceptical to fight over. Pubescent, of course, but so are most of us at one time or another and we do not start mass popular pilgrimage movements. She did not even leave her convent to attend the consecration of 'her' Basilica.

Tedious. Unclassifiable. Balanced somehow and certain. Unshakeable. Unusable by anyone. Except God, perhaps.

Infuriating.

total immersion, mass processions by candlelight, and an extraordinary centring on the ill as 'hero'. For the more middle-class observer, the kitsch and vulgar elements of Lourdes' aesthetic tend to overwhelm the corporeality and humility of its ethos.

The medieval atmosphere of Lourdes is indicated by a curious error in David Farmer's *Oxford Dictionary of Saints*, in which the saints are arranged 'in alphabetical order: up to the end of the fifteenth century under their Christian names, after that time under their surnames'. The sole exceptions appear to be Bernadette, who is found under *B* rather than *S* for Soubirous, and Thérèse of Lisieux, two nineteenth-century women saints who seem so conspicuously unmodern.

The claim that The Lady declared 'I am the Immaculate Conception' baffled Bernadette's investigating theologians, as this belief was not dogmatized at the time; and it remains odd (and annoying to many of us, given the particular dislike that feminist theologians have for this dogma: see Mary Daly's *True Lust* (Beacon, 1989)), especially as Bernadette insisted she had never heard the expression before. Nonetheless she remained unshakeably certain that this was what she had been told.

It is this blankness in Bernadette which draws me to her in curiosity – and, oddly, faith. She is not a saint I would choose. She has so little going for her in any ordinary sense: her conscious or unconscious (almost certainly the latter) bid for fame and immortality has proved so preposterously successful against the most appalling odds imaginable that she cannot but speak for the hope of all the oppressed.

The sentimental film *The Song of Bernadette* makes narrative drama out of the idea that Bernadette went reluctantly to her convent. At a more serious level there seems no evidence for this – nor that she had a deep desire for the contemplative life. That that was what happened next to visionaries in the nineteenth century seemed the universal attitude. One of the Fatima visionaries emigrated to the USA and married; a number of the Medjugorje visionaries have also gone on to more average secular adulthoods. The Mexican visionary of Guadeloupe was already married when the Virgin Mary appeared to him. None of these, however, have been canonized.

Bernadette is an example of a woman who did not 'use' her voices or visions for any self-authorization whatsoever; although equally it is hard to read her as a passive victim of ecclesial needs. She really does 'dodge' categorization, analysis, modernity and even 'femininity'.

Clare's Garden, San Damiano

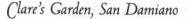

Holy poverty, lady poverty
clear light shine out
the darkness this world
pattern of purity
illumine our way
holy poverty, lady poverty
give us your abundance
dedicate of perfection
consoler companion
joy in simplicity

three tunics and a mantle
to wrap the dear body
Christ-hallowed
born of Mary
three tunics and a mantle
a small cloak for convenience
in serving and working
the Umbrian winter
shoes to go out
into the world
barefoot and fasting
following with joy
the Cross of love

Clare of Assisi: 1194–1253
Franciscan, abbess, founder of the Poor Clares
Feast: 11 August

The following are extracts from *The Rule of St Clare, c.* 1250: the first rule of the religious life to be composed by a woman, it was finally guaranteed by Pope Innocent IV on 9 August 1253, two days before her death. The other document that Innocent finally granted to Clare was the *Privilege of Poverty*, which incorporated her order's right to refuse all forms of property, and to subsist on alms and their own labours, which she had striven all her life to maintain and defend as the hallmark of the Poor Clares' distinctive way of life and the guarantee of their autonomy.

Chapter I
1. *The form of life of the Order of the Poor Sisters which the blessed Francis established, is this:*
2. *To observe the holy Gospel of our Lord Jesus Christ, by living in obedience, without anything of one's own, and in chastity.*

Chapter II
1. *If, by divine inspiration, anyone should come to us with the desire to embrace this life . . . [and if, on examination, she believes the Catholic faith and the sacraments of the Church] and is willing to profess them faithfully and to observe them steadfastly to the end; . . .*
3. *and if she has no husband, or if she has [one] who has already entered religious life . . . and has already made a vow of continence . . . let the tenor of our life be clearly explained to her.*
4. *. . . let the words of the holy Gospel be addressed to her: that she should go and sell all that she has and take care to distribute the proceeds to the poor. If she cannot do this her goodwill suffices.*
5. *And let the Abbess and her sisters take care not to be concerned about her temporal affairs, so that she may freely dispose of her possessions as the Lord may inspire her.*

compline
the psalms spoken
in the darkness nightly
become flesh
release into sleep

lauds strikes daybreak
facing the sun she
makes her unspoken
orison
deo gratias
      the dawn breaks
      from on high

prime
praise without ceasing
our helper defender
engage our weakness
let not the torrent
wash over me nor
      the pit of the deep
      swallow me

terce, before sext, before
none, the workday
lift the mind
teach me your statutes
centre this heart
to work is to pray

❧

6. *Afterward, once her hair has been cut off round her head and her secular dress set aside, she is to be allowed three tunics and a mantle.*

7. *Thereafter, she may not go outside the monastery except for some useful, reasonable, evident, and approved purpose. . . .*

10. *The sisters may also have small cloaks for convenience and propriety in serving and working. . . .*

11. *Indeed, the Abbess should provide them with clothing prudently, according to the needs of each person and place, and seasons and cold climates. . . .*

15/16. *The sisters who serve outside the monastery . . . may wear shoes. . . .*

18. *For the love of the most holy and beloved Child who was wrapped in the poorest of swaddling clothes and laid in a manger, and of His most holy Mother, I admonish, entreat, and exhort my sisters that they always wear the poorest of garments.*

Chapter III

1. *The sisters who can read shall celebrate the Divine Office according to the custom of the Friars Minor; . . . they may have breviaries, but they are to read it without singing. . . .*

7. *The sisters are to fast at all times.*

8. *On Christmas . . . they may eat twice.*

9. *The younger sisters, those who are weak, and those who are serving outside the monastery may be dispensed mercifully . . . .*

10. *In a time of evident necessity the sisters are not bound to corporal fasting.*

11. *At least twelve times a year they shall go to confession . . . .*

13. *They should receive Communion seven times a year . . . .*

Chapter IV

7. *[The Abbess] should strive . . . to preside over the others more by her virtues and holy behaviour than by her office . . . .*

9. *She should console those who are afflicted, and be . . . the last refuge for those who are disturbed . . . .*

10. *She should preserve the common life in everything . . . .*

16. *To preserve the unity of mutual love and peace, all who hold offices in the monastery should be chosen by the common consent of all the sisters.*

Chapter V

1. *The sisters are to keep silence from the hour of Compline until Tierce . . . .*

Chapter VI

4–6. *. . . as I, together with my sisters, have ever been solicitous to safeguard the holy*

Neither a house nor a place
nor anything at all
no stream no wood no dell
no copse no rill no pool
no slope no marsh no
bluff no gravels chalks
granites marls no clays
no gentle hills no stern
cliff no brows no cloud-
capped mountains no
olive groves no terraces no
winding fertile river valleys
no cypress shade nor poplar
the sisters shall not hold
but live enclosed as
pilgrims to this world
strangers to the heart's
affections fastened to
their only Beloved Lord
and gentle master

❧

poverty which we have promised the Lord God and the Blessed Francis [the Abbesses and sisters to follow] . . . are not to receive or hold onto any possessions or property . . . except as much land as necessity requires for the integrity and proper seclusion of the monastery; and this land [is] not to be cultivated except as a garden for the needs of the sisters.

Chapter VII
1. *The sisters . . . are to work faithfully and devotedly, . . . after the Hour of Tierce, at work which pertains to a virtuous life and to the common good. They must . . . banish idleness . . . but not extinguish the Spirit of holy prayer . . . .*

Chapter VIII
1. *The sisters shall not acquire anything as their own, neither a house nor a place nor anything at all; instead, as pilgrims and strangers in this world . . . let them send confidently for alms. . . .*
10. *Those who are ill may lie on sackcloth filled with straw and may use feather pillows for their head; and those who need woolen stockings and quilts may use them.*

The Rule of St Clare, in R. J. Armstrong and I. C. Brady, *Francis and Clare: The Complete Works*

Clare was born into a 'truly noble family', the Offreducci, part of Assisi's 'urbanized aristocracy', and into a courtly culture: her father was a knight, a *miles*, and she spent her whole life near Assisi, which at the beginning of the thirteenth century was 'a small town of medium importance'.

During that turbulent period, when civil war between the patrician *maiores* and the *minores* (other citizens) was raging, the house of such a family was in fact a well-defended castle, and the women lived in a separate part of it. Clare's mother, Ortolana, was a well-travelled woman typical of the religious renewal of the end of the twelfth and beginning of the thirteenth century, who had been to all the major pilgrimage centres – Rome, Compostella, the Holy Land – in company with other women of her household and her friends. Clare would have been surrounded by well-informed, spiritually questing, older women, and made friends amongst her own generation of their daughters. Surrounded by the courtly values for women of prudence, silence, reserve and humility, and facing an arranged marriage when still young, Clare showed an independent spirit early on, wearing unbleached wool in place of richer clothing and saving part of

through the courtyard
tended stooping
through the pilgrims
up narrow stairs
rich wood polished
small casement wide
pressed behind
the curious craning
Clare's sweetbriar
narrow terrace
opening to gentle
descending olive groves,
almonds, ochre-red
farm-buildings, cypresses
still the sweet
briar flowering, still
high hills above, Francis'
tree, acorns falling

her food to give to the poor. The information on her early life comes from the canonization process, which testifies to Clare's good reputation: for example, how she kept herself hidden, not showing herself at the window, in other words, obeying the precepts for gentlewomen of her time.

The key figure in transforming Clare's life from its conventional path was Francis of Assisi. Clare herself says that 'a little after his conversion . . . I promised him obedience'. Clare was in touch with him after his conversion in 1206, when he gave up his own comfortable background to live according to the gospel and become a penitent, stripping himself of all his clothes in front of the Bishop of Assisi as a symbolic break. Francis used to preach to her, having heard of her holiness many times, probably unbeknownst to her father, who was to oppose violently her decision to become a nun.

Before she fled from her family, Clare was known for her works of charity around Assisi. Her family's opposition to her choice of the religious life was extreme, so that she had to escape from the house in secrecy at night. She was received by Francis and his companions at the church of St Mary in the Portiuncula, and he cut off her hair and consecrated her, even though he was only a layman. The breach was final when she sold her inheritance – the dowry which would have secured her a noble husband – for the poor. The family, when they discovered her flight, over several days tried physically to drag her out of the monastery of San Paolo delle Abbadesse where the brothers had taken her, but were defeated by her determination.

Here she lived as a servant – not as one of the nuns from her own class, the nobility, since she had already given away her dowry. In this Clare was following Francis' own precedent, although unsupported by him at this time.

Clare left the rich and powerful Benedictine monastery where she was safe from her family to join a relatively unprotected group of women at St Angelo in Panzo, living an unregulated life of retirement, prayer and penance, like many others all over Europe at this time (see the note on the beguines, pp. 167–71).

The first half of the thirteenth century saw a great demand for religious life on the part of women who did not find sufficient outlets through the traditional monastic channels . . . an upsurging of experiences of prayer, of love and the life of penance which were to come to their full flowering in the great Beguinages of Northern Europe.

Marco Bartoli, *Clare of Assisi*

Il mezzo giorno. Lightly tap. Small bells pressed.
Clear air echoing, traverse. Unpeopled hillside,
    olive, almond, sweetcorn, rooting. Muted light,
    jutting terraces. Stones raked and packed, juicy
    veins.
Long-ago saints live in the twisted branches,
    faded potflowers, hollowed wayside offerings,
slip out from springs and walls
dedications their
tranced eyes, luminous bodies,
call, frequent the
heavy midday sleep, watching, lightly maybe to the
brow's arch touch
their breath. Songs
scoop out a ledge of air precisely unfold in this our
cave the hand presses
obedient. Single. Steady. Line
phrasing by heart falls still.
Awaiting sister death
or pressed
like their dear founder
cheek to ochre earth
deathjuice mingling
with the Umbrian dust
feeds the straggling
briar or crabby olive-root

Renewed attacks by the family followed the flight of Clare's sister Catherine to join the church. There was physical violence involved in their attempts to remove her which very nearly succeeded, but again the family were frustrated by Clare. On Francis' advice, Clare and Catherine, now given the religious name of Agnes, left Mt Subasio and the community to found their own women's religious community, after the pattern of the Fratres Minores and under the special loving 'care and solicitude' of Francis himself (Bartoli, p. 51). Clare had served her novitiate, her determination had been tried and tested, and they settled at San Damiano, the small ruined church close to Assisi where Francis had first heard the injunction to repair the Lord's Church. Within three years of Clare's conversion and renunciation of worldly life, in about 1215, Francis made her abbess, responsible for all the sisters who had come to join the new community, a responsibility which she reluctantly accepted.

(In some of the new religious communities, the head or prioress was secondary to the priest in charge; the old established monastic model used the term 'abbess', but the difference in the new Franciscan model was that the community was extremely poor, whereas the title conferred power and autonomy.)

One of Clare's first and most radical acts was to petition Pope Innocent III for the 'Privilege of Poverty':

> . . . *you have renounced the desire for all temporal things . . . to dedicate yourselves to the Lord alone . . . you have sold all things and given them to the poor, you propose not to have any possessions whatsoever, clinging in all things to the footprints of Him, the Way, the Truth and the Life, Who, for your sake, was made poor. . . . The left hand of your heavenly Spouse is under your head to support the weakness of your body . . . we confirm with our apostolic authority . . . your proposal of most high poverty granting you by the authority of this letter that no one can compel you to receive possessions.*

The document is the oldest text to refer to the Franciscan community or *fraternitas* and communicates clearly the radical nature of Clare's vision. Not only did she as a woman demand of the Pope this juridical authorization of her community's way of following Christ and the Poverello by renouncing *all* possessions – no dowries, no bequests, no lands or rents – but she tenaciously hung on to this Privilege granted by Innocent III. This was in the face of Pope Gregory IX's later move to bring the Franciscan women's communities into line with the other newly established communities of women and the existing monasteries, and later efforts by Pope Innocent IV and others to legislate that *all* monasteries must have land or goods in common at least to support them. It was to prove an ongoing problem, many centuries later.

Clare's vision went further than living the life of absolute poverty, central as that was to the Franciscan way which she had made completely her own, for it also included most importantly the right of her communities to determine who should be their spiritual advisers amongst the brothers, and the right of open access for those who helped the community practically, brought their food from the town and did other services.

The *Privilegium* document was kept with great care – 'honoured with great reverence and kept well and with great diligence since she feared to lose it'.

The significance of this matter of the *Privilegium* is that it shows that the path Clare had chosen was one towards the building and maintaining of her own community according to her vision. Numerous depositions in her canonization testify to her great love and care for her sisters and that she worked as hard as any of them weaving and spinning and making altar cloths and chasubles for others. Nothing the sisters did was for money: all was to be given away, and they depended entirely on alms for their support. That they worked, living on the most bare and frugal of diets, when often there might not even be bread to eat, and supported by their small vegetable garden, was in line with the vision of sharing the lot of the poor – the choice of a life absolutely shorn of all security, dependent upon the generosity of their fellow-citizens and passers-by – 'working in order to give away and begging in order to live'.

Clare's special calling was not to the life of the visionary – though she did have visions – the hermit or the reformer of the Church, but to the building of a new type of radical religious women's community. The outcome of her vision was that the community, although enclosed, was in fact open to the widest influences of its time, since the brothers who came to preach and to seek spiritual guidance and retreat with Clare and her sisters were working in far-flung places – in Africa, the Middle East, even China.

Clare herself never wrote about enclosure as such – for her the community was a limitless horizon. Groups or individual lay women who lived apart within the city – cf. *Julian of Norwich* – were common in thirteenth-century Tuscany, following a life of prayer and intercession and supported by the wider community of their towns. By 1300, probably as many as seven thousand were living in this way in this part of Italy alone. The community at San Damiano was representative of this movement in women's spirituality, but Clare's radical vision marked it out in the tenacity with which it clung to its defining characteristic of poverty – even the buildings remained poor and simple, with mud and straw huts for the changing group of brothers who came and went – and in its open character.

The hallmark of the San Damiano community, lived out daily, was its literal following of the gospel – 'seeking first the kingdom of God and His justice' – in a life set apart. There was no need for the discussion of enclosure since the character of the life followed by Clare from the beginning in turning her back on her life as a noble Tuscan lady had been to serve God by going apart from that life. However, she did not apparently choose or intend to remain at San Damiano for the rest of her life, for her sisters recorded that after some years she was filled with the desire to follow her martyred Franciscan brothers to Morocco and there sacrifice her life in trying to convert the Muslims. As it happened, soon afterwards she became ill, and never wholly recovered. She spent the last twenty-seven years of her life at San Damiano, bearing her sufferings with great cheerfulness and fortitude. She was revered as one of the great medieval contemplatives. Such was the strength of her popular following, and the belief in her miracles, that she was tacitly recognized as a saint even before her death – San Damiano had become a shrine with a constant stream of pilgrims, and even Pope Innocent IV came to her bedside. On 10 August, before she died, the monastery received Innocent's papal bull guaranteeing their privileges and the Rule: Clare pressed the seal of the letters to her mouth. She had won her long-fought battle to maintain the integrity of her vision. The following day she died.

The thronging crowds who came to San Damiano required soldiers and cavalry to control them and to guard Clare's body. At the funeral the Pope, who had stayed on in Assisi, celebrated the Office of Virgins rather than the office of the day, indicating she was considered to be a saint already. Her body was translated to San Georgio within the city walls. She was canonized within two years, by Pope Alexander IV. The Poor Clares still exist as a contemplative order in many countries and cherish the same Franciscan ideals.

When she was nearly sixty, Clare wrote in one of several letters to Agnes of Bohemia, who had founded a monastery at Prague modelled on that of San Damiano, that she was running to meet her beloved:

I will never grow tired until you lead me into your wine-cellar, until your left hand

is under my head and your right hand embraces me so joyously and you will kiss me
with the most joyful kiss of your lips.

In the last testament of Clare, and in the testimonies given by the sisters in the canonization process, Clare's particular feeling of identity and closeness with the women saints is underlined. She calls for the intercession of all the saints and, specifically, '*Sanctarum*', the women saints; one of the sisters, Benvenuta, saw in a vision a procession of women saints accompanying Mary to Clare's deathbed.

One of Clare's most noted miracles involved her defence of the monastery against the Emperor's Arab-Sicilian army in 1240 (the Saracens of popular legend and hatred) by holding up the pyx or box containing the Blessed Sacrament. When the soldiers fled, this was seen as a triumph of the Catholic faith against the heretical Emperor and his Saracen allies – Emperor Frederick II had, so the papal side maintained, entered into a treaty with the Sultan of Egypt.

A year later, the attack was renewed, directly against the city. As a result of the prayers and intervention of Clare, who made the city's cause her own, the siege failed. Afterwards the cult of Clare became, even more than that of Francis, 'a symbol of the unity and concord of the whole city'.

CLARE'S BLESSING

I bless you during my life and after my death as much as I can and more than I can,
with all the blessings that the same Father of mercies has blessed on earth and will bless
in heaven every one of his spiritual sons and daughters, and with all the blessings which
a spiritual father and mother have blessed and will bless their spiritual sons and
daughters.

SOURCES

R. J. Armstrong, OFM Cap, and I. C. Brady, OFM, *Francis and Clare: The Complete Works* (Paulist Press, 1982).

Marco Bartoli, *Clare of Assisi*, trans. Sister Frances Teresa, OSC (Darton, Longman & Todd, London, 1993).

Inner darkness, inner light

❦

Mary Fisher, spinster, though not of this or any other parish, was a vagabond woman, bound to the road as a bondsman is bound to a master, or a husband to a house. She was never quite sure how this had come about.

But she had been weaned on politics and religion and had come to womanhood in a vagabond time. Her father, with the authority of the Bible in his hand and the stirrings of change coming down on the wind from Scotland, would doff his hat to no man. Such a small thing it seemed, but it was that she brought with her from the morning of knowledge; that she was free-born and should doff her hat to no man, nor bend her knee to curtsy when the great ones walked by. There had been other things, long ranting and shouting meetings, part Bible and part bile. There had been little gentleness in the making of the Commonwealth of God. She had not understood those; what she had understood was the solid obduracy, the clear pride with which her father would keep his hat upon his head. And as she grew that obduracy cost him his work, his comfort, his liberty and his ears, but not, oh never, his bell-like sense of himself as righteous, as justified, and as free-born.

Inevitably, inevitably as the pulling of the tide or the waxing of the moon, he had marched off to join Cromwell's army and the only time in all her life that she saw love in his eyes was when he said the name *Oliver*.

And she, she had seen him go rejoicing, for his pride and his willingness to die for it would bring in the time of Jubilees, the acceptable year of the Lord; and their land would be called Beulah, and spears and swords would be beaten into pruning-hooks and ploughshares, and each man would sit under his own fruit-tree in freedom and equality.

'Oliver, Oliver,' they had shouted in the streets when he rode through. She had seen the light of Pentecost shine on his brow when

Mary Fisher: 1623–1698
Missionary of the Society of Friends (the Quakers)

For the basic outline of Mary Fisher's adventures I have used Frances Anne Budge, *Annals of the Early Friends* (London, 1877), pp. 187–92. However, nothing is known of her life before she joined the Society of Friends. The political picture in this representation of her childhood owes a good deal to Mary-Lee Settle's novel *The Long Road to Paradise*.

Without pursuing a religious history of the English Civil War it is important to recognize how on the radical wing, beyond the Parliamentarians, there was a utopian, millennialist and biblical egalitarianism, which was unquestionably used by 'moderates' like Cromwell and Halifax for their own ends.

> *In these boisterous times the British Protestant people formed three great sections . . . neither the Episcopalians, the Independents, nor the Presbyterians were men of peace. Each of their Churches, where it had power, persecuted the other for not conforming to their religious rites.*

Maria Webb, *The Fells of Swarthmore Hall*, pp. 29, 30

The New Model Army, which Cromwell raised initially in the Fens and East Midlands (he came himself from Huntingdon), was composed entirely of volunteers, and so full of a passionate enthusiasm; at the same time it was highly trained and rigorously disciplined. The political-religious education the army received, especially at the outset, was remarkable.

The political rhetoric of the anti-royalist parties in England was deeply influenced by the Authorized Version (the King James translation) of the Bible, which was both a political and a religious text for many radicals, who were often ill-educated or indeed illiterate. I have tried to catch something of this spirit in this text – rather than a literal seventeenth-century discourse.

he led the Lord's army out from the fen country with Liberty as his banner and Freedom of Conscience as his battle cry.

Under that glorious banner, and leading free-born men, he had ridden to Naseby and had fallen on the Man of Blood as the wave of the Red Sea had fallen on Pharaoh and all the horses and chariots of the Egyptians. A wave had risen up in England that day, a wave of freedom. A tide of God – and, filled with the Spirit, the army of the people of Freedom had rejoiced and prophesied the coming of the end of the ages.

Oliver had taught his soldiers freedom. They took it from him as a gift of love. And he betrayed them. He used them to winnow Parliament; to put down the King and throw out the popish Prayer Book. He used them to set himself up in the King's place; to abuse the rights of the free-born army he had created; and to impose the preachings of the presbyters. He gave them neither liberty nor freedom of conscience and said the land could not be ruled by those without property or interest.

And those, like her father, who would not go to Ireland to kill and murder a poor people and still further steep their hands in innocent blood, the Levellers, Oliver invited to Burford to treat with them; and he shot their leaders and broke their high hearts and stubborn wills.

Oliver had taken her father in his pride and sent him home, five years later, defeated, broken, ashamed. Oliver had betrayed her father. Her father had betrayed her.

'I do not permit a woman to speak in church,' said the cold minister who had invited questions. He shamed her in front of the congregation. 'Brother,' he said, 'take your daughter home and teach her respect. Respect for the word of God and the good ordering of His holy church.'

Even while they walked home she had still believed that as he had taught her, so would he justify her.

He said to her only, 'I'll not have you shame me.'

She said nothing.

'It's out of Paul, daughter, a woman must not speak.'

She did not, but slowly she turned to look at him straight.

'You lack respect,' he said, a voice so weary.

'I plead the Liberty of my Conscience,' she said calmly. 'As you taught me, I'll doff my hat to no man.'

The Battle of Naseby in eastern Northamptonshire in 1651 was a significant turning-point in the history of the English Civil War. It was the first major engagement of Cromwell's New Model Army, which arrived on the field rather late, after a forced march, and completely turned the battle, to the immeasurable enhancement of Cromwell's personal prestige. Naseby wrenched the centre of politics away from the aristocratic Parliamentarians who wished to reprimand, rather than abolish, the monarchy and who certainly did not set out to execute Charles I or establish a 'republic'. One of Cromwell's greatest strengths was the passionate devotion that he elicited from his troops; his army's personal commitment to *him* as the symbol of their cause made him immensely powerful.

As his own power increased, Cromwell was to find this army which he had trained both to fight and to think politically something of an embarrassment. In particular they wanted representation in the new state. The most radical elements refused to disband and return home. They expected to reap the social rewards they had learned to treat as their birthright. (This included a redistribution of property and the vote. A Leveller petition is the first known record of a desire for *women's* suffrage.) In addition the English Parliament was unable to pay them. After marching them round England for some months Cromwell introduced his Irish campaign, partly at least to get them out of the country. This led to a mutiny. ('Wherefore go we to Ireland to kill and murder a poor people and still further steep our hands in blood?' as a Leveller pamphlet said.) The radicals argued that, as they had volunteered for a moral, domestic cause, they had no obligation to obey an order to fight elsewhere. At Burford, Cromwell had three ringleaders shot, and kept all the rest locked in the parish church for four days while he – and various clergy – preached at them. Their nerve broke and they 'repented' *en bloc*.

The conduct of Cromwell and his army in Ireland later that year still has political ramifications today. Nonetheless the breaking of the Burford mutiny in effect ended the serious threat from the radical wing in English Civil War politics. The failure of this movement and the disillusionment that followed were deeply influential in the forming and the success of the quietist Quaker movement, which turned away from active politics and war.

This episode is based on one recorded by George Fox, describing the process that led to the founding of the Society of Friends. He defended the woman's right to speak: 'He [the minister] ought to have answered it, having given liberty for *any* to speak' (George Fox, *Journal*, p. 14).

So he beat her.

She left his house the next morning and never returned, because she knew her love for him would betray her if he pleaded with her.

Soon afterwards she heard Elizabeth Hooton preach and she joined herself to the Friends. She was moved to do so because they let women preach and meet without men set over them and pray together; and they stood for Liberty of Conscience, against all the principalities of the world. They held all people free-born, children of God, by the power of the light within them, and they set no one in authority over another.

In the power of her Inner Light she became a vagabond woman – blessed in persecution. In Cambridge, where she went to discourse with the students and to preach, she was honoured, with her friend Elizabeth Williams, to be the first, the first of the Friends to be publicly scourged. From the day her father beat her with his bare hand she was not afraid of any rod. In York, in Selby, throughout the north, she was whipped and imprisoned and abused.

'I am called,' she told one Meeting after another. 'I am called to go North . . . South . . . to Boston . . . to Virginia . . . to the islands of the Carib Indians, the Barbados . . .'

'I am led,' she announced calmly, 'to cross the sea again; I have a clear call to go and preach to him who is called the Sultan of the Pagans.'

The Meeting had not been unduly surprised, and why should they have been? They did not question her call, nor she theirs to stay at home. They made such preparations as they could and prayed her on her journey.

It was not altogether true. She had not been led; she had been driven. Driven by the need to get away; to flee from all the places of childhood and safety, to trust no one and nothing for fear of betrayal. She took the wings of morning and fled to the uttermost ends of the earth.

But on the long road to Adrianople she was alone. She reached Smyrna safely, but owing to the excessively paternal care of the Ambassador there, she was put on a ship back to Venice. Undaunted, she persuaded the captain to let her disembark in Greece and all alone she walked through Macedonia and Thrace, with the vibrant blue

Elizabeth Hooton (b. 1600) was Fox's first convert — although she had been a preacher before their meeting. Her ministry and friendship were acknowledged by him as instrumental in his understanding of the full ministry of women within the Friends, which in turn was instrumental in the enormous success of early Quakerism (60,000 people became Friends in the first forty years of the movement).

The Cambridge episode was in 1653. The same year Cromwell declared himself Lord Protector; and John Liburne, 'Honest John', the Leveller spokesman, joined the Quakers.

Mary Fisher and Ann Austin were the first Quakers to visit Boston. Their reception was extraordinarily hostile: as well as being arrested and whipped, they were pricked for witches, and then taken out into the wilderness and left. Boston puritanism had already developed an ambivalent understanding of the 'freedom of conscience' in whose name they had founded the city.

Of her visit to the Barbados it is recorded that 'she proved very serviceable' — meaning useful, of service — 'to the brethren'.

The Society of Friends (the Quakers) is of the greatest importance in exploring a central question that this whole study of women saints has raised: the question of self-authorization — what Rosemary Ruether and Ellie McLaughlin have called 'radical obedience':

> *It is difficult for persons to remain sane and mature from a stance of radical rejection of and by the normative culture ... it is women acting from a stance of 'radical obedience' rather than dissent who are likely to make the greater impact on their male colleagues for their claims cannot be so easily rejected.*

Aegean at her right shoulder and the great dry mountain range on her left. It was enormously silent. She was vouchsafed a word against the silence and she proclaimed it aloud to the gold-brown hills and the bright blue sea:

. . . neither death, nor life, nor angels, nor principalities, nor things present, nor things to come, nor height, nor depth, nor anything else in creation can separate us from the love of God.

A word is not given without a purpose, but this one gave her no comfort.

Walking, sturdy, through the long dawns and dusks, resting in the hollows from both the day and the night, she realized that Paul had left something out.

It is in Paul, daughter, a woman may not speak.

Paul had left something out. It worried her, more insistent than hunger. She worried at it. Frightened but determined. Baffled. Tough. The devil was near. The devil was her fear. Her inner light, her own flame, flared up to meet her fear; and they wrestled in the lonely desert, as He had wrestled.

One bright dawn she woke knowing. She knew what Paul had left out. It was the past. The past had separated her from the love of God. She turned, and this was the bravest moment, she turned to her past and walked there, down into her own darkness, alone, and a year's walking away from home, and friends, and comfort. Alone. She was free-born, and she could not live enslaved even to her own fear. So she plunged, leapt, dived into herself. Her courage was rewarded. The truth would set her free.

Led and driven were not different ways: they were different responses. If she had walked in love and forgiveness she would have walked the same road as she had walked in pain and bitterness — she would just have had more fun. More joy.

She compassioned her father now and wept for him. For his bold light put out and his heart broken. She wept for him. His woe was greater than hers. He had loved her. He had failed only to love himself.

Or it may be simply that we are more likely to know about them, they are more likely to have their lives mentioned, at least in the annals of their churches.

> *Such loyal dissent typically takes its stand on a vision of the 'true meaning' of the Gospel that at the same time rejects its patriarchal deformations. It is characteristic of the leadership roles in Christianity claimed by women that they derive their authority from person charism rather than from office . . . so that it was in those areas where roles based on 'gifts of the Spirit' were recognised that there was likely to be space for women.*
>
> R. R. Ruether and E. McLaughlin (eds), *Women of Spirit*, p. 19

Many of the women we have written about in this book found individual sources of self-authorization. In particular, for Roman Catholic women, visions (direct interventions from the *same* source as that from which those who are forbidding your actions claim to draw their authority) proved immensely enabling in the laborious task of freeing oneself (allowing God to free one) from societal prescriptions. This self-authorization is particularly important in relation to human people whom you love, or whose authority you respect, who suggest that you are separating yourself from the God you love: **Joan of Arc** is a very obvious example of someone who learned to trust her own interior authorization over and above that of the Church authorities, whose right to judge her in these matters she did not question.

All such women, however, have been obliged to find their strategies on an individual basis. Even charismatic movements speak of special gifts, recognizable by the whole community, flowing from the Holy Spirit into chosen, individual vessels. Quakerism breaks away from this by locating the only source of authority *within* the individual: the Holy Spirit is not 'outside' being poured in, but starts and remains within each person completely and singly. The 'Inner Light,' the spark of holiness which is the birthright and absolute possession of every individual, is the only source of authority and is also the ultimate arbiter of conduct. Thus self-authorization becomes, curiously, the institution, the hierarchy. This is something far stronger than the Lutheran and Anglican understanding of conscience as the final location of judgement. It is interesting that in the case of the Society of Friends this actually worked. The whole early Quaker movement is shot through by an extraordinary number of highly active, highly independent,

She forgave him. It was simple, now she knew what it meant. It was simple because, truth was, she liked being a vagabond woman.

She arrived eventually in the palace of Adrianople and became the first Christian woman to preach to the Sultan.

Then she went back to England again. Her heart was more restful now, though no one noticed. Restful and joyful. She was a free-born woman who need doff her hat to no man – not even to her own fears. Free. Joyful.

highly communally supportive women. Mary Fisher was by no means the only travelling Quaker missionary — although her adventures are particularly wide-ranging and well recorded. The first generation of women Friends clearly did receive the doctrine of Inner Light as self-authorization and so used it.

Although this story of Mary Fisher is meant to suggest that her profound belief in both radical equality and self-authorization did not spring from nowhere, but had a clear historical root, it is important to recognize the remarkable effect that such faith could and did have on individual women and groups of women.

It does seem likely, though, that the Quaker emphasis on the bogus and worldly nature of all authority — the belief that meant that while magistrates, kings, bishops, etc. were to be treated politely as human beings, they should be accorded no other honours — must have been helpful to women in the face of their own menfolk!

In 1219 Francis of Assisi met and talked with the Sultan of the time. Apart from him, Mary Fisher is the only Christian known to have attempted such a conversion. In both cases the individual Sultan expressed interest and admiration (though not conversion), which, in comparison to the Christian Church's attitude, speaks well of Islamic tolerance.

After this adventure Mary Fisher married. She was widowed. She married again. She emigrated to Carolina. She was still preaching there, serviceable to her community, well into her seventies when history loses touch with her.

'Mamma'

Timid I do not think.
Where she met the
weight of the Church it
crushed her. Where she went forth
beguiled, persuaded, illumined
at such cost thereafter
she dreamed, took ill
and joined their communion whose life
she had long practised
exemplary to the band of catini
her far-flung followers in
Siena. In the dream the
stone of the church
toppled over upon her
earthed her in paradox.
She could rise no more.
Is this defeat? we can't know.
She never spoke again.
An independent woman
following her own path
woven into Christ's.
Six hundred years ago her ministry
like Christ's
ended against the power of the
church. She was just thirty.

Catherine of Siena: 1347–1380
Doctor of the Church, mystic, diplomat
Member of the Dominican Third Order
Feast: 29 April

৶

Like **Joan of Arc**, Catherine of Siena is a boundary-transgressor. On the one hand a mystic, who recorded a large amount of writing, mainly through devoted male amanuenses, about complex interior states of being, the most famous being the account of her 'mystic marriage' to Christ, she was at the same time a much-travelled, much-respected, and much in demand international diplomat, thus bridging the opposition between active and passive in religious life.

The youngest of more than twenty children of a Sienese dyer, a member of the skilled working classes who became the personal friend of popes and princes, she never entered an enclosed religious order: the Dominican third order, like the Franciscan (founded by Francis in the early thirteenth century, to enable people to live out the Franciscan way of life in the world), was a lay order and its members were living in the world.

Both Catherine's inner spiritual life and her penitential practices were marked by an extreme character: Christ exchanged hearts with her and gave her the jewelled ring she wears in most of the paintings in which she features. By the end, her ecstatic experiences so dominated her life that she barely ate or slept. At the same time she had a vibrant gift for friendship, an openness to both men and women, and enormous charm. Obedience for Catherine of Siena was complex, since the strength of her character and her strong prophetic visions precluded any easy compliance.

The political project of her life was to persuade the Pope to return the papacy to Rome from its 'Babylonian captivity' in Avignon and thus to counter the excessive influence – from the Italian point of view – of France. The first step was to reconcile Florence and the papal states.

She travelled to both Avignon and Florence, with a papal mandate to act independently in the cause with the latter, almost unheard-of for a woman who was not herself of royal status. Indirectly her intervention, which succeeded in persuading Gregory XI to return to Rome in 1376, led to the

'my teacher told me one thing
live in the soul

when that was so
I began to go naked
and dance'

'You would come back to the soul
to fill her with your blessedness.

There the soul dwells –
like the fish in the sea
and the sea in the fish.'

'Mamma' was Catherine's nickname, used by her closest followers.

The quotations are from Lal Ded, fourteenth-century mystic of Kashmir, translated by Coleman Banks, and from Catherine's prayers, translated by Suzanne Noffke, OP, both in Jane Hirshfield (ed.), *Women in Praise of the Sacred*.

greatest schism in the history of the Roman Catholic Church. (On Gregory's death a rival papacy was set up in Avignon for the next two centuries, as his successor, Urban VI, was unable to unify the cardinals. The struggle was joined by half of Northern Europe.) This political failure, however, never affected Catherine's standing, which rests securely upon her reputation as a visionary and luminous inspirer of a servant community in Siena. She was created Doctor of the Church in 1970.

Her letters, like **Teresa of Avila**'s, are a curious blend of admonition and charm. One of her last was written to Urban VI at Christmas. She sent him three oranges – then still a rarity in Italy – which she had gilded and sweetened herself. The letter to the supreme pontiff is an intriguing mixture of poetic allegory, theological reprimand and encouragement – and includes her recipe for the oranges – like its sender, at once beguiling and complex.

SOURCE

Jane Hirshfield (ed.), *Women in Praise of the Sacred* (HarperCollins, New York, 1995).

Radegund, patron of learning

※

She knew she was dying. She knew it with contentment and peace. Three score years and ten almost precisely measured out and it was time to go.

'Tonight you will walk with us in paradise', sing the angels, and if it were not too much of an effort for an old woman she would smile. Her heart is smiling, her soul is praising. Thanking her God for a life so smilingly lived, against what seemed preposterously and improbably long odds.

It was high summer and they had carried her into the chapel to die. High above her, hazy and shadowed now, the great roof, the ark that had carried her through so many storms, still offered a protection she no longer needed. The altar which she faced still offered beauty and serenity; the reliquary containing the piece of the True Cross, a gift to her from the Pope himself, shone in glory in the chapel. Her sisters, her daughters, her nuns watched with her so that she did not feel lonely. Out in the guest house the Frankish Ambassador fretted, needing answers to his now so unimportant questions about the peace treaty, so that she did not feel useless. Her dear sweet lover-son, poet-priest, waited tearfully, silly boy, to give her the wayfarer's food, ready to hand her from one love to another. She rejoiced, for 'the children of the barren woman were more than the children of her who was married'. She was the barren wife and the fruitful virgin, and God was gracious.

Underneath it all, through the tiredness and the little joys, was the long swell of excitement – for she was on the move again, on the road, kidnapped again, travelling free again, and going home again, she who had never stayed still.

Radegund, daughter of Berthaire, King of Thuringia. Not a childhood

Radegund of Poitiers: 518–587
Foundress, politician, queen
(but not virgin, nor martyr, nor mother)
Feast: 13 August

❧

Radegund's biography is fairly straightforwardly laid out here. She was kidnapped from her father's home by the Franks at the age of twelve – and brought up in Clovis's household. The Thuringians were pagan, but the Franks Christian. Betrothed to the heir to the Frankish kingdom, she was baptized in her early teens and married at eighteen. By all accounts, even his contemporaries found Clothaire's behaviour extraordinarily offensive – not just in relation to his wife. This may, of course, be why Radegund initially was able to gain such an extraordinary level of support when she left him: there was no question of them coming to any accommodation. On several occasions he tried to reclaim her forcibly. The marriage was childless.

She left him after six years of marriage and took the veil at Noyon – where she was consecrated as a deaconess (although this was by no means usual, it is an interesting precedent), mainly for her own protection and that of the local church which had decided to sponsor her: although Teutonic law was not as heavy-handed in relation to wives' rights as many seventh-century societies, her husband did want her back and they were perfectly properly married. Later she founded the monastery of the Holy Cross at Poitiers under the Rule of St Caesarius of Arles. The monastery was a centre of northern scholarship – her Rule was unusual in that it laid down two hours a day of study for all the nuns – and patronage of the arts. Radegund herself was a principal peace-broker in Northern Europe. Her insistence on the rights of the Church earned her the gratitude of the Pope.

Isaiah 54:1–2. A specific prophetic celebration of the barren.

After her death miraculous cures were reported from her tomb, and her feast was celebrated in France, particularly Tours, from at least the ninth century. She also had a following in England: along with five parish churches, the Cambridge college now called Jesus was originally dedicated to her. There is a fifteenth-century life, by Henry Bradshaw (ed. F. Brittain, 1926).

to encourage sweetness in any woman — that household of banditry, brigandry and intrigue and violence. Her father's war bands did not disperse throughout the fighting season: they sat down to eat and they stood up to fight — and when there was no readily available enemy they happily murdered each other. An exciting home for a royal child. Her long pigtails had bounced with glee at the tensions in the High Hall and more than one night she had been woken when the whole clan was on the move again — in fear or in aggression, depending on the turns of power and politics. She remembered her father with a thrilling passion — so it would be in the Court of Heaven, where a God who was like her fierce father would excite her dreams.

Nothing in her childhood had prepared her for a gentle eternity and she did not anticipate one now.

She was twelve the night of the great raid, when the Frankish soldiers descended on the household, their pine torches smoking and glowing, catching the light of horned helmet, round shield, short sword and bright eye. They carried her off to Clovis's court, where she was held first for a ransom never paid, and then as promised bride of Clothaire, heir of Clovis: prisoner and queen. Slave and lady. Child and politician. Loathed pagan and beloved convert.

As it happened, Clothaire — even by the abysmal standards of his contemporaries — was a thug.

He raped her.

He abused other women and made her watch.

He mocked her in public — for her beauty and her barrenness.

He killed her brother, in her presence.

He burned her books — laughing at her faith and her learning.

She offered it up. She united her sufferings with the sufferings of Christ. She followed the instructions of Paul and was obedient unto him.

Until one day she had had enough. Then she left. She was twenty-three.

Nothing in her adolescence had prepared her for a boring eternity and she did not anticipate one now.

She took the long road to Noyons, where, shamelessly, she used her intelligence and her beauty and her piety, and the threat of the Thuringian war bands, and her own wealth, and her husband's

The clans, tribes or even households of northern Europe were still expanding in the sixth century: Angles, Saxons, Jutes, Huns and Vikings had overrun much of post-Roman Britain, and Christianity, except in Ireland, had only the most tenuous claim on the people. Radegund was almost exactly a contemporary of St Columba of Iona (*c.* 521–597), who started the reconversion of northern Britain. On the Continent, while some areas were Christianized (e.g. the Franks), large areas were not; and culturally Christianity had very little hold on an unstable, but enormous, land mass along what had been the northern and north-western frontiers of the Roman Empire. The networks of kings, overlords and military commanders were complicated: war on various scales was endemic. To be a peace-maker, or even peace-broker, was no light office here on what southern Europe saw as the boundaries of civilization (not without cause from their point of view – Rome itself was sacked by Northern tribes, first in AD 410 and repeatedly thereafter). 'Patron of the Arts' and such-like phrases, even the idea of women having any access to civilization, must be seen in the light of her chaotic times; Europe was still unreconstructed since the invasions from the east and the withdrawal of the Roman legions (see her biography by L. Schmidt, 1956).

From the contemporary *Lives* of Radegund by Baudovinia (one of the nuns of her foundation) and Venantius Fortunatus. Farmer in *ODS* makes the rather odd comment that he carried on like this even 'though Radegund united beauty with piety' – presumably it is all right to treat ugly pagan women in this way.

Colossians 3:18. The passage continues: 'Husbands, love your wives and do not be harsh with them' (3:19).

instability and the long, tenuous, attenuated networks of kinship and influences, and eventually obliged the bishop to make her a deacon so that the Church needs must protect her from Clothaire's increasingly deranged attempts to recapture her. Later she took a longer road to Poitiers where she made her foundation. A house of prayer where women studied, wrote, thought, worked and laughed; and that was part of their prayer. Where the makers of beautiful things – whether peace or paintings – were welcome. A beacon in the Frankish darkness. And she, wily as a serpent and gentle as a dove, following the instructions of her Saviour, spun out the threads of dependency, of dowry, and border balances, of alliance and compromise, that made her peace-broker of the North, beloved ambassador of the papacy, refuge of oppressed women, centre of hope.

Nothing in her adult life had prepared her for a humble eternity and she did not anticipate one now.

When love came to her late and sweet everyone smiled and was pleased for her. She was beyond reproach. Venantius Fortunatus, the poet of little joys and sunny delights, 'the halcyon on the dangerous Frankish sea', came troubadouring into her guest house and never left. *Vexilla regis prodeunt* he wrote for her, the great song of joy to welcome the True Cross into France, but he wrote it from his love and she loved him. If he loved good cheer he loved goodness more; he loved her goodness, and she loved his lightness. Young enough to be her son. Lovely enough to be her lover. And no one either sniggered or gossiped. She had earned the sweetness by then. Purged into purity. Revirginated by her own energy. And a love more delightful than the little princess with the long plaits could even have thought of.

Nothing in her ageing had prepared her for a cold eternity and she did not anticipate one now.

Three score years and ten, surrounded by two hundred daughters, a chosen son, a princely court, a lovely church, power, riches, pleasure, learning, beauty, honour and authority . . . and a long afternoon of sunlight – all earned by disobedience to Paul. And in obedience to a higher authority, her own, she slipped anchor, slid out from the harbour in the small craft of her own self and travelled into the dark night into a further sea.

Poitiers had, apart from its nuns – 200 of them by the time Radegund died – a particular claim to fame: at the command of a grateful pope, Radegund was sent a piece of the True Cross from Constantinople. Although the enthusiasm for relics had not fully developed in Europe by the sixth century, this was a gift of enormous significance (as can be seen from the fact that the convent was dedicated to the Holy Cross). (See **Helena**.) It was for the arrival of this magnificent sacred object that Venantius Fortunatus (see next note) wrote the song *Vexilla regis prodeunt*, which was to become the marching song of the Crusaders and is still sung today.

The tender and passionate and, obviously, chaste relationship between Radegund and Venantius Fortunatus (*c.* 530–603), the poet, is charmingly recorded by Helen Waddell in *Mediaeval Latin Lyrics*, pp. 309–11; and rather more imaginatively in *Women in the Wall* by Julia O'Faiolin. He was born in Trieste, and got his learning 'as gay and perhaps as shallow as mosaic' in Ravenna. He was on pilgrimage to Tours, in his thirties, when in 567 he arrived in Poitiers, 'which her living presence had already made a shrine', and never left.

> *Her influence fell on him like a consecration. Sensitive to all beauty, of the spirit or the flesh, and capable of strange and high exaltations, he settled down beside her, took holy orders, and in his old age was consecrated Bishop of Poitiers . . . Radegund indulged him, with the tolerance that sometimes accompanies great personal austerity.*
> Waddell, p. 310

Waddell is always a romantic; but in fact there is a relationship that develops between women of known – public – chastity ('great personal austerity') and younger men which is apparently a privilege of sanctity: **Teresa of Avila** with Father Gracian; **Josephine Butler** with James Stuart; **Catherine of Siena** with a long string of people; **Martha** or **Mary Magdalene** with Jesus perhaps, where the devotion is publicly acknowledged but outside of 'gossip'. A relationship passionate, dependent and

Dear Sisters, let us celebrate together the life of one who left her violent husband, without his blessing; who deserted her wifely duties;
and who became famous, not for the ladylike virtues of obedience
and humility, but for scholarship, patronage of the arts and political
astuteness in the cause of peace.

We have too often been taught that in gentleness, in submissiveness, there is power, in giving power up, in throwing it away. We have
been taught that love is simply the ability to suffer and to suffer and
to suffer.

From her high place in heaven, her hand still clasping her sliver of
the True Cross, Radegund – Queen of the Franks, Deacon of the
Church, Foundress of the Convent of the Holy Cross at Poitiers –
utters the Old High German equivalent of 'Pah'.

She says, 'You have been too often deceived. There is another
power. Anger has two lovely daughters: courage and hope.'

maternal – acknowledged by both parties and beyond naming: the original fag-hags. (A similar relationship also arises between women, but in social arenas where lesbianism is less likely to spring to mind people are less curious, simply because close intimate friendship between women is unlikely to arouse prurient interest the way heterosexual relationships constantly did.) I would like to understand this particular mode of love better, and there seem few points of access to it in current discourse. Frustrated, childless women at menopause does not seem an adequate explanation.

'Anger has two lovely daughters: courage and hope' is, surprisingly enough, a quote from Augustine.

St Wendreda and the daughters of King Anna

❧

A long hot late day in dead July
I went to stand under your roof
to peer up at you amongst the angels
already rustling their outstretched wings
your secretive image blessing the dark, yours and
that of Etheldreda.

I am thinking too about your sister saint – Withburga
here in East Anglia there are wells named for you both
some people muddle you
and give you her royal ancestry,
daughter of King Anna and sister to
Etheldreda.

I suppose you're used to that. Etheldreda
our only acknowledged English virgin founder
of the Anglican calendar
first-league saint, patron
of the cathedral of the fens her
abbey church of Ely

self-sure in her vision she excused herself
from a royal marriage and preserved
her virginity, relinquished
the affairs of the world and
dedicated herself to Christ, the only
true king, she would never
wear linen but only woollen garments, would
seldom take a hot bath, rarely
ate more than once a day

Wendreda of March: c. 9th century
East Anglian foundress

Wendreda is reputed to have secured the conversion of Canute to Christianity and to peace. Her relics, after much wandering, are finally hidden, it is believed, beneath the stones of her medieval church of March in the fens (see below). The entry for Wendreda in *ODS* reads: 'Obscure Anglo-Saxon female saint . . . presumably the foundress of a nunnery at March, Cambs where a fourteenth-century church with magnificent angel-roof is dedicated to her.'

The other female saints recognized in the Anglican calendar are all early martyrs, including the mythical **Margaret of Antioch** and **Katherine of Alexandria**.

The confusion between Wendreda and Withburga is made in T. A. Bevis, *The Story of a Famous Fen Church: St Wendreda, March*. Material and quotes for Etheldreda are drawn from Bede's *Ecclesiastical History of the English People*.

The gold of Wendreda's name has vanished; the repute of Etheldreda, and the writings of Bede and the hagiographers, have assured the memory of the Queen Abbess of Ely, and of her sisters, including Withburga. Like many of the Anglo-Saxon, European and Celtic saints, royal descent ensures the continuity of remembrance, for the history of these saints forms part of the history of the country.

Etheldreda, after Hild, is perhaps our most important English female saint. She has inspired writers today, and continues to exercise her patronage in Ely, despite no longer being the Cathedral's patron saint. There is a simple tablet bearing her name in the floor of the chancel, and in the north chancel aisle a few remains of crocket capitals beneath a 'superstructure of unknown purpose', once thought to be part of a fourteenth-century casing of the shrine. (See N. Pevsner, *Cambridgeshire*.) Her feast day is 17 October; 23 June is also kept as her feast.

Etheldreda was a royal Saxon, the daughter of King Anna of East Anglia. She was first married when very young *c*. 652 to Tondberht, ealdorman of

at home amongst masons and princes of the Church
founder of a great company of virgins
builder of a long-enduring monastery
worthy contemporary of Hild

I think Etheldreda probably had pizazz.
To survive two husbands and
without a stain on her character
still get her foundation
shows a talent at the very least
for ecclesial manipulation.
Etheldreda the austere the incorrupt
abbess and penitent.

In the chancel I stood on her plaque.
Her spirit kept its counsel.
In the lofty spaces nothing moved.

I am silenced by this Aethelthryth/
Aedilthryd/Audrey of whose virginity
after twelve years Bishop Wilfred told
the chronicler he had most perfect proof
first-league subject of fictions
annotated admirable
and whose flesh in her wooden coffin
would not corrupt
— token and proof of her uncorruption
by contact with any man, even two husbands —

and after sixteen years they got into a boat
and came to a small deserted fortress not far away
        which is
called Grantacaestir in English
and near the walls of the fortress
they soon found a coffin
beautifully made of white marble
with a close-fitting lid of the same stone

South Gyras, who died *c.* 655. She retained her dowry of the Isle of Ely in the fens and in 660 was married against her will to Egfrith, king of Northumbria, when he was only fifteen. Despite agreeing to her condition of perpetual virginity, twelve years later he wished to consummate the marriage. Supported by Wilfrid, bishop of Northumbria, Etheldreda left in 672 to become a nun under her aunt Ebbe at Coldingham on the Scottish border; a year later she founded her double monastery at Ely.

For seven years she lived an austere life of penance and prayer to atone for her previous lifestyle, eating one meal a day, wearing wool only and keeping watch between Matins and dawn. She died in 679 of a tumour of the neck due to the plague. Her body was found to be incorrupt seventeen years later, the linen cloths fresh and the tumour healed.

Her sister Sexburga, who succeeded her as abbess, placed her body in a Roman sarcophagus brought up river from Grantchester, and translated it to the shrine in the abbey at Ely on 17 October 695.

This was one of the most popular of shrines and Etheldreda the most revered of Anglo-Saxon woman saints.

Grantacaestir is Cambridge (see Bede).

Her sister Withburga, who died c. 743, the youngest of the four daughters of King Anna, lived as a solitary at Holkham, Norfolk, where the church is dedicated to her. Later she moved to East Dereham and founded a community. Her well in the churchyard there may still be visited.

and so they reburied her, the
tumour beneath her jaw healed, the
linen grave clothes as whole and fresh
as on the very day of her burial
ah perfect Etheldreda

but you Wendreda you in your
spacy incognito   you incite my
curious imagination
your unsigned existence somewhere
ruffles my thought, colours
the drift of my dreaming
searching for you amongst the
gorgeous gregariousness of angels
amongst the lofty rustling wings
in your fenland memorial church
you drop me into the unscripted dialogue of
poetry

for I am pondering still who you may be you
saints   about
human beings   about
un-recognition   about
our absconding time and
the fullness of yours

about these identities we carry like
heavily-inked stamps
in the passports of our genes. I am thinking
about settlement and dispersion –
not clever stuff – about what happens if, like you,
you give up home and history, becoming only the
passage of your grace, the conduit of
altruism, dedicated to the other. If you bear
suffering with desire, with love,
good humour and contrition
(you)
if
as if

Withburga is said to have died before the buildings for her community at East Dereham were finished. As she was too poor to feed her labourers, two miraculous white does appeared out of the forest to give their milk (a not uncommon saintly theme). The does appear with Withburga on several Norfolk screens.

Buried in the churchyard, her body was exhumed after fifty years and found to be incorrupt. The spring is said to have sprung up then, and in the twentieth century was still held to have healing powers. Her relics, stolen by order of the abbot of Ely in 974, are enshrined at Ely. Her feast day is 17 March.

THE RELICS OF ST WENDREDA

Wendreda's name is absent from most menologies. The most significant fact about her is the church. The medieval cult is attested by a series of transactions with regard to her relics, beginning with their brief 'removal' in the tenth century by one Abbot Elsin to the newly restored abbey church of Ely, whence they were taken into battle against the Danish invader, Cnut (Canute); after his conversion – which he credited to their power – he gifted them to Canterbury; finally they returned to March in the fourteenth century, at the time of the Papal Indulgence. The wealth created by the pilgrims visiting Wendreda's shrine enabled the construction of the unique angel-roof and the beauty of the church built to house the shrine.

The peregrinations of Wendreda's and Withburga's relics, while not matching those of Cuthbert, before his body finally reached entombment in Durham, are characteristic of the time and indicate the significance accorded to the possession of relics – a significance which is not restricted either to Christianity or to the Middle Ages.

The story of Wendreda's relics being taken into battle and converting Canute catches a trace of remote paths of transmission like footpaths long since occluded or wiped bare by agribusiness, leisure parks and motorway links. Relics were *for use*, they offered protection, they were effective in guarding the community and ensuring prosperity and health.

In the case of powerful and foreign saints the relic might be extremely small: a tiny splinter of bone, a toenail clipping, or a piece of cloth, a fragment of the True Cross that had touched the dead saint, would be placed in a reliquary and carried where it was needed, to give forth its actual power.

(you)
unhindered by our mortal conditions
(time without recovery)
(you)
weighing here in heavy mid-August (you)
(as the sap drops)
(you)
in this saintly labour-intensive work
(you) dart off do you see? how you
reverse (as they say) time's
arrow?

(and then are you a 'you'?
Is this your bag, your
category?)

It is not for whom I write but where I write from
It is not for whom I pray but out of where I pray
Whether the angels lightly dust her cheek

I am wondering about your saints' tears
— *sympatheia, idiopatheia* —
about the time of the Other that is yours
to receive this unfaltering flow of petition.
They tell us —
some, like Mamma — not you — they say they fell
into ecstasy and
we believe them, they enter into the wounds of
          Christ
unerringly to their union replenished with divine
          substance, dizzy
like bees drowning in their senses.

Was/is it so for you?
How does one ask a saint such questions?

At Canterbury the relics rested, objects of veneration and of pilgrimage, for three hundred years. Whether they continued steadily to accrue value we cannot know, for fashions in saints shifted rapidly in the Middle Ages. Some three hundred years later, the small Fenland settlement of March finally and painfully secured their return, after enlisting the aid of the Pope, through a papal indulgence obtained in 1343.

It seems that there was common cause in the community to achieve the return of Wendreda's relics to their rightful home, although the 'translation' of relics to a more holy and august shrine was commonplace throughout the early and high Middle Ages. A wealthy March family led the campaign for the relics' return: a Papal Indulgence was no cheap matter.

In 1343, Pope Clement VI (of Avignon – there were two popes at the time), 'being desirous that the Chapel of the Virgin St Wendred at March in the diocese of Ely should be frequented with condign honours, and held in continual verification by Christ's faithful people,' granted an Indulgence to all who came to the 'Chapel of March, for devotion, prayer and pilgrimage, especially for the feast of St Wendreda'.

Interestingly, on the translation of Wendreda's relics back to March, most of the bishops who attended the ceremony were foreign: two archbishops and ten bishops attended – a measure of the event's significance at least to the Vatican. Was that significance primarily religious, or was it also political?

The Indulgence and the return of the relics were part of one process in the building of March as an important pilgrim centre – without the Indulgence the relics would not have been given up by Canterbury; without the actual possession of the relics the shrine would have attracted no worshippers. The added dimension of political implications of foreign concern in an apparently relatively minor Saxon saint suggests that the procedures became caught up in papal politics – possibly acting as a focus for those of Clement's party to rally support for their Pope against the one in Rome.

Documents show that one hundred years later, in the mid-fifteenth century, the tomb of the saint – which, like many others in Britain, has been lost since the Reformation – was in need of improvement in keeping with the sumptuous new fittings of the church. The furnishings and appearance of the whole church had been lavishly transformed thanks to the flow of pilgrims visiting March while travelling the route of the sacred sites in the fens – Peterborough, Thorney, Crowland, Ramsay and, above all, Ely. Now yet more expenditure was under way.

One late needy night I tried — in Paris —
wired up to a cardiograph
in the bums and vagrants hospital of my quarter —
destitute I recognized my guardian saint, a
Russian painter returned to earth — practical,
    approachable —
she gave me the answers of her craft — how
to start, to
stretch and prime, mix and choose
from the gamut of fine to coarse, how to
work with light. Of herself this only.
For the next three days I wrote the
dialogue of our talk. To reconstitute her.
There was no point.
Only my destitution summoned her.

Perhaps it is so for you?
Do the needy call you into being?
I am talking to a you, wanting a
saint-as-friend, a voice
in conversation —
perhaps you are a hushed voice in my throat or
where the next fickleheart-beat stops —
Perhaps you are not an intellectual fantasy?
project of the creative imagination or
after all only — only — friend-as-saint?

Perhaps some unmapped energy shoots through
    the universe
to rouse you? Does some angelic bell
in a far-off servants' hall ring? to summon you
into your being, your
saintly servitude? replenishing
my lack?

Looking back to the time of the saint's life, it is clear that over the succeeding five or six hundred years, Wendreda's status and influence have, in common with the great majority of saints, been transformed, and her influence has diffused widely out from the local and parochial sphere where it was centred. As saint, Wendreda is now implicated in the networks of international Catholic power and policy. In a small way she has entered the political relations between Rome and Canterbury, and the settlements in which she chose to make her home and found her community have been transformed alongside her. In a very real way her fortunes are their fortunes, and their fortunes are hers.

This was the tangible, material dimension of the saint's protection to a community, and that much wealth and effort were expended in keeping the shrine gilded, the wax tapers burning, and the church lit and cared for was only one aspect of the material compact between people and saint that blurred irreducibly the lines between sacred and profane.

UNKNOWN WOMEN SAINTS

Some saints only come to life after death.

Of course saints do not live until after their death. That is the paradox. But the impact of their lives on the societies in which they lived, as given in their hagiographies, is, at least for the formally canonized, crucial.

Against that scrupulous weighing of good deeds, and equally scrupulous attention to the visionary and miraculous, some saints arrive into the canon as it were free of the delineation. To my mind they are equally, if not more, fascinating.

The medieval historian Caroline Walker Bynum points out that the stories of most medieval women saints' lives were not wildly exciting. Whereas the male saints' lives from the twelfth to the fifteenth centuries are told as a drama, the woman saint's life is presented as a life in which:

> *nothing happens . . . a story of very undecisive change . . . with homely imagery . . . women's dramas were incomplete — [there were] no abrupt conversions or renunciations . . . what women's images and stories expressed most fundamentally was neither reversal nor elevation but continuity. . . . [For them] . . . Christ on the cross expresses not victory nor humility but humanity.*

Caroline Walker Bynum, *Fragmentation and Redemption: Essays on Gender and the Human Body in Medieval Religion*

The more I think about you saints the more I am sure
that settlement, authority, power
(the two are not the same after all)
are not where we reach you for
in the absences of your life
the emptiness of your history I address you
my sister name-saint
Wend/reda

There was something I wanted to say
in the dull mid-afternoon of the dulled
middle of the month before Autumn
– You are a quiet saint
You have lived solitarily
founded a small community of nuns
(perhaps this was so)
your sanctity grew from small acts
quietly lived in remote fenland settlements –
But no matter; let it rest.
Saint Wendreda
obscure female saint of the ninth century –
what is your gift for us?
Is there a face in the dark of this encounter?
When faith, reason, imagination fall away
is there a conduit to saintly grace?

While this view excludes those female saints whose lives were certainly full of drama (including Etheldreda), of whom **Joan of Arc** is just the most notable, it certainly includes, from the little we know, a Withburga or a Wendreda. In their saintly lives all the drama occurs with their relics.

A less flamboyant but equally striking example might be Margaret of Cortona, a Franciscan tertiary of the thirteenth century, whose life exhibits quite as dramatic reversals. After living for nine years with a knight who had seduced her and with whom she had a son, Margaret dramatically undertook a life of penance when he was murdered (her family refusing to forgive and take her and the child in). Like **Rose of Lima**, Margaret went in for extreme self-mortification, apparently mistreated her child (who himself became a tertiary but who bore the psychological scars of his upbringing all his life), but, nevertheless, 'admitted to the third order of St Francis . . . and later to the Franciscan novitiate, she advanced steadily in prayer and holiness . . . she died at the age of fifty after spending twenty-nine years in penance . . . Formally canonised 1728 . . . her incorrupt body rests in the church at Cortona' (*ODS*).

Bynum stresses that in order to understand women saints' stories today we need to 'stand *with* those whom we study'. 'Standing with' is clearly a prerequisite in any imaginative engagement with a character. Whether we can make any connection with the saint, find any relevance to our own lives and problems, 'drag' her into our contemporary framework, is another question, and we have argued that with some of the, to us, more extreme lives and practices, our responses have been more in the nature of shock, recoil – followed by questioning and requestioning of the meanings involved.

If we have few or no known facts around which to weave our understanding, the temptation is to project our desires and needs limitlessly onto this figure, and something of this predicament is explored in the verso text here. But it is just possible to operate the process in reverse, as it were forensically, from the material evidence of relics, or in the case of Wendreda, of her church, and of her cult.

To infer what the reality of the saint was to the faithful who regarded her as their protector and intercessor from the remains she has left behind, however indirectly, is one way into the experience of participating in the saint's life. What we can and do know about the saint's life after her death – through its re-presentation whether in text or stone and glass and wood – is arguably for us the most meaningful part of that life, because it

Indulgence

❦

In 1389 in the small town of March
before her altar two candles burn
in honour of the saint and one
at the elevation of the host
on her feast and all festivals
Wendreda virgin saint who here
has been translated

for the Pope has decreed
that the Chapel of the Virgin Saint
Wendred at March in the diocese of Ely
should be frequented with condign honours,
and held in continual verification
by Christ's faithful people –
for devotion prayer and pilgrimage

and after three hundred years
Canterbury yielded up the relics
whose grace forsook the Saxons
in the battle of Ashingdon
but the power of their truth
procured the conversion
          of the invader Cnut

is that in which 'successive generations have lodged their imaginations of their best perfection' (André Vauchez, 'The saint').

THE CHURCH OF ST WENDREDA

While with some saints we may receive that best perfection through known, historical data or through their writings (as with **Hildegard of Bingen**, **Julian of Norwich**, **Catherine of Siena**, **Teresa of Avila** or **Edith Stein**), for many, even the well-known early ones like **Brigid of Kildare** and **Hild** of Whitby, the process is one of post-historical reconstruction in which the imagination is key. The processes of interpretation, decipherment, construction of meaning are at once as elusive, as exacting and as complex as those involved in the reading of the Scriptures, and, I would argue, no less substantial, for the community of saints is part of our Catholic belief:

> *[The art of reading] . . . is the interpolation of the text . . . into the reader's experience and the reader's experience into the passage . . . not haphazardly or according to rigid values but tactfully and experimentally.*

> Richard Niehbuhr, quoted in D. Chitty, *The Desert a City*

The fairly scanty material about Saxon virgin saints of the ninth century could be read as the stuff of picturesque legend, as minor byways of social and ecclesiastical history or of topographical and antiquarian interest. But we can read the material, and its silences, 'otherwise', which is to allow into the texts, into the gaps between the texts, processes of imaginative reconstruction. And where there are no texts, or the texts are dubious – 'a tantalising mixture of the true, the dubious, and the notably incredible', as Brian Lehane expresses it *(Early Celtic Christianity)* – there are the other material sources: the churches, relics, shrines, wells, wall-paintings, inscriptions, stained glass, statues and so forth; and, in some areas, the memory of a community, the oral legends still passed down, especially in rural Ireland.

And amongst these material remains, the church or shrine is one of the most potent expressions both of community and of continuity.

What remains still alive today of the obscure Anglo-Saxon Wendreda (about whom even so sensitive a writer as M. R. James could pronounce dismissively 'nothing is known') is the glory of her church. When, in the fifteenth century, all the finest skills of medieval stonemasons, carvers and craftsmen were brought in to create the lovely Perpendicular building and its astonishing, supererogatory, redundant glory, the double hammerbeam angel-roof, it was the culmination of six centuries of a life still circulating, still meaningful.

In the beginning was the life; in the beginning was the word. Both. Somewhere, at some time, as with the early Celtic saints, there was a life of simple holiness, affection, an association with healing that accompanies the holy, which transfixed the imagination of her contemporaries – and the memories were passed down.

From the beauty and the power of the church of St Wendreda at March we can infer something of the strength of feeling attached to the sanctity of her relics. For, without a legend built upon a reputation for great holiness, would the cult ever have gained the sway it held? Political considerations certainly entered into the processes of canonization in the Middle Ages, but to confer the papal indulgence on an unknown Anglo-Saxon saint assumes, beside political calculation, already a popular cult.

That the cults of saints' relics were demand-led, as were most 'causes', or initial stages of canonization, is clear from the way that the relics continued to be manufactured into the seventeenth and eighteenth centuries, demand far outstripping supply. As well as being in demand for healing, protection, blessings and victory in battle, they were used for swearing oaths, and were carried around to promote the 'laws' of the saint and to promote the work of evangelizing.

To read these narratives 'otherwise' is to view them not as simply fanciful, as legendary and adventitious, but to stand alongside the Celtic, the Saxon and the medieval mind, to enter into

> *the early Christian belief in the communion of saints and angels [that] there is a great cloud of unseen witnesses who surround us with their love and prayer, and guard us on our way.*
>
> A. M. Allchin, *Pennant Melangell: Place of Pilgrimage*, p. 18

Such reading involves us in giving ourselves to the narratives, and reading within the gaps, as well as questioning the authorized, authoritative versions, hagiography itself. The process might be compared with that creative power Keats named 'negative capability'. Negative here has no pejorative value, but rather lies in the capacity to allow ourselves to remain suspended in the midst of doubts, promptings, uncertainties, mysteries, giving ourselves up to the work of the imagination.

For another five hundred years Wendreda's church has drawn people from far afield, long after Wendreda's tomb has vanished, maybe buried in order to avoid the same fate as the shrine, the gild altars, the rood and church treasures taken and destroyed by the fanatical Dowsing and his men in the seventeenth century.

Unlike the faded screens and barely visible images of East Anglia's favourite martyr-virgins in their far-off fragments of medieval glass, the angel-roof of St Wendreda's remains wholly visible in all its proud intricacy of detail.

The roof bears witness to the faded and tangled coils of the saint's little-known life which, through the fact of her death, became the stuff of transformation for those who came into contact with her.

Saints too offer us an experience of resurrection.

SOURCES

Bede, *Ecclesiastical History of the English People*, B. Colgrave and R. A. B. Mynors (eds) (Clarendon Press, Oxford, 1969).

T. A. Bevis, *The Story of a Famous Fen Church: St Wendreda, March* (Chatteris, Cambs, n.d.).

M. R. James, *Norfolk and Suffolk* (Dent, London, 1930).

R. O'Floinn, *Irish Shrines and Reliquaries of the Middle Ages* (Country House, Dublin, 1994).

N. Pevsner, *The Buildings of England: Cambridgeshire*, 2nd edn (Penguin, Harmondsworth, 1970).

André Vauchez, 'The saint', in Jacques Le Goff (ed.), *The Medieval World*, trans. Lydia Cochrane (Collins and Brown, London, 1990).

C. H. Westlake, *The Parish Gilds of Medieval England* (London, 1919).

Joan the Maid

M ay morning and early, before cockcrow even, before sunrise and still grey, cool, half dark, and the moon, as transparent as heaven, dipped towards its setting. In the apricot-coloured east the Lady Star shone, cool, bright, distant, beautiful, heralding the birth of the sun.

She did not wake with the first pre-light for she had not slept, but she surfaced from a more pleasurable if less real stupor to the horrible knowledge that she was going to be sick again, like some mewling pregnant housewife.

The pregnant woman is sick and then she craves, she craves a particular food. Joan was sick and then she craved the bread of heaven; she wanted, needed, desired; her stomach-heart-soul clamoured for the sacred bread, for communion, for the Holy Mass.

For Joan it had always been simple. Simple child, simple woman, on her own terms: Joan the Maid, the pure child-woman warrior, the one for whom the gap between heaven and earth was filled with church bells and voices and everything was simple. Now it was not simple. She was torn apart.

In Domrémy it had been simple. The voices had told her what to do; the bishop had acknowledged her calling and financed her adventure. She did as she was bid.

In Poitiers it had been simple. She had been shown into the court, the glittering, moving, tides of people, and the King's kingliness, like Christ's, had called out to her in simplicity and she had greeted him, and he had known her simple truth. She had come to relieve Orléans, and lead him to Rheims for his coronation. So simple.

Her armour was white. She was Joan the Maid, and no man would offend God by touching her and she relieved Orléans in April, and in July to the sound of trumpets and clarions she had stood beside her

Joan of Arc: 1412–1431
Canonized, as virgin, 1920
Feast: 30 May

❦

Joan, a peasant girl from Champagne, started hearing voices, which she identified as those of **Margaret of Antioch** and **Katherine of Alexandria** and the Archangel Michael, at the age of thirteen. The voices directed her to assist Charles VII to regain his crown and drive the English out of France. Throughout her life she was regarded with both suspicion and veneration. In a spectacularly successful campaign in 1429 she led the recapture of Orléans and the victory of Patay. By July she was standing beside the king as he was crowned in Rheims. However, a subsequent attack on Paris failed, and the following year she was captured outside Compiegne. She was betrayed by her king, sold by the Burgundians to the English and tried in Rouen, by her Church, for witchcraft and heresy. In the spring of 1431 she made a public recantation, including a commitment to abandon male dress; but four days later she reversed this decision and on 30 May 1431 was burned in Rouen market-place. Her ashes were thrown into the Seine.

Less than twenty years later, led by her mother, the process of vindication had already started. However, since she had been condemned by an ecclesial court it proved difficult to get the Church to reinstate her. It took almost exactly 500 years.

Joan has always attracted an immense amount of complicated and complex attention. Marina Warner, in her excellent cultural study, *Joan of Arc: The Image of Female Heroism*, notes (p. 6) that although Joan is a 'universal' female figure, she fits none of the available feminine archetypes, not

> a queen, nor a courtesan, nor a beauty, nor a mother, nor an artist of one kind or another, nor — until the extremely recent date of 1920 — a saint. She eludes the categories in which women have normally achieved a higher status that gives them immortality, and yet she gained it.

king, her banner spread, in the great cathedral of Rheims, and the bishop had crowned him and her victory had been simple.

The voices were simple. Her friends came and spoke with her: Margaret and Katherine and Michael. They told her what to do and, if it seemed good to her, she did it.

Even at her trial it had been simple.

The inquisitor had asked, 'Did St Michael appear to you naked?'

And she answered simply, 'Think you that my master had not the wherewith to clothe him?' There had been a suppressed smile, a grudging admiration, but she, dangerously without irony, had not understood that: the inquisitor had asked a simple question and she had simply answered it. The voices told her what to say sometimes and sometimes, using the old skills of little girls teased by naughty neighbour boys on village greens, she knew what to say all by herself. She was not, after all, a foolish sheep girl, but a spinster, skilful as a spider.

The inquisitor had asked, 'Do you submit to the judgement of the Church?'

She had answered clearly, 'I submit to Our Lord, who sent me on my mission; to our Lady, to all the blessed saints and the holy ones of paradise.'

The inquisitor had asked, 'Then you do not submit to the Church?'

She did not understand why he was pretending to be so stupid; he knew the answer as well as the priest at home who had taught it to her. She had answered, 'As I see it, Our Lord and His Church are one, so there will be no difficulty there.'

And she had believed it, quite simply.

Now, however, the time of simplicity was over. There was a difficulty there. She wanted to hear Holy Mass and receive communion. Wanted. Needed. Desired. The Church, which is Our Lord and Our Lord who is His Church, said — or did they? — they said but did they mean to say did she say did she mean to say she wanted to hear Mass the voices say St Margaret said the inquisitor who was the voice of the Church which is Our Lord said that Margaret and Katherine did not say but she said they did say they said that she should not receive communion no yes they said but who was saying? or she thought they

Elizabeth Stuart in *Spitting at Dragons* describes Joan as 'the incarnation of inversion' (p. 60).

Joan always called herself Jean La Pucelle, Joan the Maid. There is a long tradition of female transvestism within hagiography (e.g. Eustochia or the Papess Joan), but Joan transforms this tradition. She wore men's clothes throughout her 'mission' but never pretended to be a man. She would never explain what meaning this had for her, saying only that her Voices commanded it. But it was obviously of great importance, intricately and intimately connected to her understanding of her calling – it was her decision to resume male clothing four days after her recantation (possibly because she hoped to be re-admitted to Mass and communion) that led directly to her execution.

Joan's dilemma is a classic one. If the Church *is* the Body of Christ then its authority is identical with Christ's. On the other hand Joan's self-authorization was underpinned by her absolute conviction that her voices were those of three specific saints, who were after all also 'the Church' – triumphant and in heaven. These voices had been 'authenticated', moreover, by her own bishop, and by the theologians of Poitiers who had subjected her to a three-week investigation before Charles had dared 'employ' her. The whole issue of self-authorization (supported by whatever means), self-authentication, has been a particular maze for *women* in Christianity: 'While men wrestle with the devil, women wrestle with men' (Elizabeth Stuart, p. 137). The dilemma has been least pressing, or most successfully managed in some ways, in those phases of Christian history, or within those theological sections of Christianity, where the free movement of the Holy Spirit (**Maximilla, Perpetua** perhaps) or interior consciousness (**Mary Fisher,** contemporary feminism) are highly valued, and during periods of more general social instability when anti-clericalism is usually strong and precise gender roles are reconfiguring.

In more stable times, like Joan's, the situation for women is much harder – particularly for those like her who did have a very strong sense of conservatism and love of order. Women have used various (not necessarily conscious) strategies. Stubbornness has proved effective (e.g. **Clare**); and so has life within women-based communities. **Teresa of Avila**'s highly skilled adoption of a specifically 'feminine' rhetoric is examined elsewhere: however, she was a remarkably intelligent and self-conscious woman (so was **Josephine Butler**, another, slightly different, utilizer of 'feminine' mythologies) – this strategy is hard to play. The most common alternative is to call

said if she dressed like a woman which was right because she was a woman they said. And they tricked her but was it the voices that tricked her the Church said the voices tricked her but the voices said the churchmen tricked her and the voices were of God when they said because if they were not of God then she could not have taken Orléans and the arrow in her heart was that a trick or was the fact that she lived a trick and the voices were of God but so were the Churchmen and they said and they said and she said and then she did not say. It was not simple.

In the end it was not saying, it was dressing. She, who was not and had never tried to be a man, dressed as a man. The voices told her to, even though she thought this was stupid and unimportant, but she liked to please her friends and it was, somehow, and she did not know how, somehow it was very important. But now the voices of the Church told her to dress as a woman, and that seemed sensible so she did, but that meant that she did not believe the voices came from the saints of God, but she did not not believe it. She knew they were voices from God, but so was the voice of the Church from God. It was not simple.

So she put on a dress and that pleased the voices of the Church and she went back to her prison for ever and ever, and in the silence the voices of her friends told her that they were angry. That she had betrayed her mission, and that God's honour was offended

Communion, sweet Jesus; communion in and with the Church and with her sweet Jesus. But this also was communion, communion of the saints, and communication.

And Margaret's dragon snapped at her, and Katherine's wheel tore her and the flaming sword that keeps Eve from her own garden, the sword of the archangels which Michael had used to throw down Lucifer himself, brands her brain with brightness until she does not know anything except that she is about to sick again and even that is not simple.

If Our Lord and His Church were one, then the voices were demonic and she was a witch and she had not saved France and the King was not the King. But if the King was the King, and France was saved, and the voices of her heavenly friends were as real and as sweet as the church bells pealing in the morning and the evening across the meadows of Champagne, then Our Lord and His Church were not

on a 'higher' power, for example, that of class, or – better still – that of the miraculous direct intervention by God, or the angels and saints. A miracle, vision or other direct supernatural summons *cannot* be automatically repudiated by the churches. Joan's deployment (God's deployment in Joan) of this last strategy was remarkably successful in enabling her to do something that is more or less unique – not just woman as warrior, but peasant as military general. The complex political situation which she found herself embroiled in, however, finally defeated even her extraordinary degree of authority.

Additionally, Warner suggests that Joan's authority was derived in part from a 'folk' religious tradition which had prepared the French for the coming of a 'Virgin Saviour'; a contemporary visionary, Marie d'Avignon, had prophesied that an armed woman would save the Kingdom and intellectuals like Christine de Pisan (a proto-feminist writer) were convinced that Merlin, the Sibyl and the Venerable Bede had all foretold her appearance. In a completely different context (that of the Zimbabwean Independence War) David Lan, in *Guns and Rain*, has demonstrated the authority that apparently 'outsider' groups can gain by becoming linked in popular consciousness with mythic or folkloric expectations.

The whole issue of 'Voices-Hearers' – and in particular of personal friendship and communication between women located in history and their friends in heaven – is problematic. Mainstream contemporary psychiatry sees voice-hearing as a necessarily pathological (probably psychotic, and often schizoid) symptom – regardless of the content or the affectual experience of the hearer. Treatment is usually by drug intervention. (This has been challenged recently – especially in Holland – on the basis of a research finding that 60 per cent of voice-hearers had manifested no psychiatric disturbance whatsoever; some current treatments aim to help 'hearers' find strategies for accommodation and management.) However, 'obeying' voices is still regarded as dangerous, even if hearing them is not.

The medieval world took an entirely different position. The possibility of being spoken to by independent external forces was taken for granted: the job of confessor, theologian, community – or in this case, judge – was to discern whether the particular voices were holy or demonic. If the former, they should most certainly be obeyed, but if the latter, then paying any attention to them was sinful. Some of the techniques for discernment were clearly wise and sensitive: did the voices encourage prayer and good works,

one, and her desire to hear the Mass was foolish and she was about to be sick again.

All alone, like that, for four days and four nights. But also not alone, unless the voices were delusions, because they spoke to her.

She was tired. The voices were stern. She was tired. Her voices were stern.

She was sick all the time, her stomach retching. And either the voices of the saints were right, or the voices of the Church were right. Either. Or. One or the other. One. Not the other.

She was just a simple country girl, how could she know which?

She was just the arm of the Lord at the gate of Orléans and none of this was her business.

She was stomach-sick and heart-sick.

Then the wimple that she wore was so heavy, heavy, heavy on her head. Pressed at her ears so that she could not hear *anything* properly any more. Scratched at her chin. She ran to the bucket, and tripped on the skirts; and the gaolers laughed as they had never laughed when she was The Maid, the woman on the loose who was no loose woman. Then men had been companionable and respectful; then she had been strong and pure – not with wimple askew and vomit on her breast, where before she had carried the wound of Christ, pressed into her flesh by the arrow outside Orléans.

And, with her guts writhing and seizing, as though she had swallowed a dragon, the blood of Eve came out of her, whence before only the milk of Mary had flowed.

For four days. She lay in her womanish disguise, curled on the floor of her prison; or drifted, half alive, in memories of church bells, and garlands – dancing – singing – round the fresh gold green of the beech tree in the wood. The beech tree, tree of childhood, tree of fairies, greener than the standards of the knights who rode behind her boldly in the sortie from Compiegne. She lay down in stupor and rose in agony.

Joan was a woman, always, who did things not in her head but in her body; for her there was no division, and so, in the end, there was no decision.

After four days, there was a May morning and early, before cockcrow even, before sunrise and still grey, cool, half dark, and the moon, as transparent as heaven, dipped towards setting. In the

or prevent them? were they teaching the Christian faith (as interpreted by the examiner)? were they distressing or consoling to the hearer? and so on. Unfortunately, the devil was frequently believed to be immensely cunning and deceptive, so that even a good life and sound theology did not prove a divine origin. This was especially so for women, who were, of course, more easily deceived. Many people (including **Teresa of Avila**) also thought that – quite apart from the devil's interventions – there was also the strong possibility of self-delusion, an over-excited imagination, mental instability. A large part of Joan's trial was therefore directed to the task of discerning the source of her voices. Unfortunately for her she was being tried by her enemies, who had more than a theological interest in finding that the source of her authority was not divine. It is important to realize that Joan was judged by an ecclesial court, on charges of witchcraft and heresy. The issue of authority in relation to women's ministry is a continual thorn in the side of the churches.

Joan, inevitably, made the situation still more complicated for a modern interpreter. She claimed her voices were those of Michael the Archangel and two very specific women saints – **Katherine** and **Margaret**. (More commonly, voice-hearing saints like **Teresa of Avila** and **Catherine of Siena** heard the direct voice of God the Father, or of Christ, or simply 'received locutions': these are less obviously empirically testable.) The ecclesial court decided that these voices were not delusionary but demonic – they had to, in order to execute her. By 1456 (only twenty-five years later) after a campaign led by her mother, a papal commission quashed the verdict and declared her innocent. At her beatification in 1907 the Church went further and declared her voices authentic. However, the reforms of the calendar of saints during the Second Vatican Council decided that neither Margaret nor Katherine had any historical reality. Who then spoke authentically to Joan? Warner argues that Joan gave names to her voices only under pressure to make clearer her sense of their actual aural presence, and her namings should not be taken too literally. This does not feel entirely satisfactory.

Joan was tried and convicted as a witch. Some of the evidence used against her was a rural ritual from Domrémy which involved garlanding and dancing and singing round a beech tree in an oak wood called 'the Fairy wood'. Although Joan always denied that she had heard her voices under this tree, the idea was widely held at the time (and is replicated in many of the pictures of her as a child in children's hagiographic material). Joan has been claimed by many different groups – from lesbian feminists to

apricot-coloured east the Lady Star shone cool, bright, distant, beautiful; heralding the birth of the sun. She did not wake for she had not slept, but she got up and put back on the doublet and hose. She noticed, with a sad knowing what would come of it, that in the night she had chosen the voices, the voices of the saints, her friends.

She was not sick any more.

But she was burned: heretic, apostate and witch.

right-wing nationalists. Not surprisingly, she has also been claimed by those thinkers who see witchcraft as a real surviving phenomenon from a women-centred, pre-Christian religion. Most famously, Margaret Murray in *The Witch-Cult of Western Europe* and *The God of the Witches* claimed Joan was a member of a secret coven. While there are clearly aspects of Joan which fit easily into the witch model, one is left with her own passionate commitment to Christian orthodoxy, which emerges in the trial documents – if she was a coven member, she was both a cowardly one and a highly skilled liar. The fear of being thought a witch was an additional burden for all self-authenticating women in this period, as is made clear in the lives of various other saints, while today the danger is more likely to be 'charges' of psychiatric disorder.

St Gobnet

The book says
She was a fifth-century virgin
born in County Clare
She fled a family feud
to the Aran Islands
She built a church there

A vision instructed her
This was not to be
the place of her resurrection
In another place there she would find
nine white deer grazing

In another place
she searched and gave her name
Kilgobnet near Dungarvan
Long enough to leave her name
How many years make up
a nameplace

Scraps of cloth of legend to
trim the trees
ribbons, lace or medals
dancing over the wellmouth
How many years make settlement
the place of resurrection

Gobnet: 5th century
Beekeeper and founder, born County Clare
Founded churches in the Aran Islands,
Kilgobnet, near Dungarvan, and a nunnery at Ballyvourney
Feast: 11 February

Like many of the early Celtic saints, little is known about Gobnet, but her cult is still alive in parts of Ireland. Amongst the early churches, people were declared saints locally, solely by popular devotion. Canonization was not a legal procedure but a 'fact' of life.

The procedure began to change in the Western Church during the eleventh and twelfth centuries until, under Innocent III, canonization was reserved to the pope. The saints already recognized were regarded as *de facto* saints, but proposed new saints were submitted to rigorous juridical procedures. (In the Eastern Church the older system has remained the basis for recognizing saints.) From time to time the Roman Catholic Church has instituted purges of those it considers unfit to be saints – demoting some to local level, and expunging those it considers no longer to have any credible basis. Far more of these are women than men – but the system is in itself utterly erratic and discreditable – saints of a flagrantly legendary character such as George, **Wilgefortis** and Ursula remain in the canon, while others of great antiquity and popularity such as **Margaret of Antioch**, Barbara and **Katherine of Alexandria** (all beloved in East Anglia) have been purged.

The status of the early Celtic saints, deriving as they do from the pre-canonization period, is at once both more surely rooted in local devotion and more ambiguous within the Roman Church as a whole, exemplifying again something of the tension between the institution (the Roman Ecclesia) and the expression of spontaneous, indigenous and locally centred spirituality (the Celtic practice), between the centre and the periphery.

In another place she persisted
a hundred miles westward, beyond Cork
below the Mullaghanish mountains
At Baile Bhuirne,
Balleyvourney, here she found
the white deer of her vision grazing

Here she settled, here she built
her nunnery, here she learned her
skill with bees, instructed
by St Abban, here she perfected
her solitude and her throw,
scared off intruders with a timely stone
lobbed across the glen

Here now her peace
belongs to all the dead who lie
about the ruined church
invoking her aid. On their thoughtful round
the living faithful
keep her careful memory

Here now nearly four hundred years
pilgrimage has come
disposing its tattered hopes
and rags of prayers
blessed by Clement's indulgence
trickles of the once busy stream
still strewn beneath high summer's
pendulous hawthorn trees

The book says
'It survives now,
as visits to some buildings
and a holy well of
uncertain date.'

The books say. The gravestones
bear her name. The people
make their pilgrimage.

St Gobnet pray for us.

SOURCES

David H. Farmer (ed.), *The Oxford Dictionary of Saints*, 3rd edn (Oxford University Press, Oxford, 1992).

Daphne Pochin Mould, *The Saints of Ireland* (Dublin, 1964).

The material for the poem comes mainly from the latter. The pilgrimage was approved by indulgences issued by Clement VIII in 1601.

Pilgrimage

❦

Encounters on the road in the way of no particular place far from anywhere.

Following the route of an empty grey wet day, chilled to the bone, Cork to Kerry, suddening upon, half-buried in hedge-hawthorn, a rusting sign, 'Temphaill na Gobnaitt'.

Wrench the car round. Rattle up a wet stony lane. Halt by the cemetery wall. Reconnoitre under thick laurels beneath a wrought-iron arch crowned with a hart, spelling in Gaelic and English, 'Holy Well'. Follow the railed path punctuated with glass globe lights. Somewhere below a hidden stream rushes.

The path opens out into a dark clearing before an old railed tree. Surely a tinkers' encampment. Laces ribbons jam-jars sacred-hearts novena-cards gewgaws mugs old buckets festoon the tree, litter the steep slimy steps down to the well.

No presence here except the chewing clanking cow-sounds from the farmyard behind. No life except one naked light bulb swinging in the half-derelict farmhouse, shutters banging, rich manured hock-deep earth freshly churned.

The cow tracks rise through soft buttercupped cowpat-embossed meadows to the graveyard.

The disused church is locked.

Here it is not this day's liturgy that speaks but yesterday's stones. Everywhere thanks and prayers to Gobnet.

The ancient altar stone of Gobnet, worn smooth, labelled, flowers to bless it. Dedications to her on almost every gravestone. Instructions for the stations of the cross at intervals. It is all told clearly. Follow the signs, and make the round.

Up to her grave and the old circular stone. To the small enclosed worn turf, to her statue, overlooking the whole populace of the faithful departed, crammed sociably in death and life.

The statue was proudly cut some forty years ago, its base wreathed in careful, rampant bees. Dedication in Gaelic. The civic pride of Ballyvourney paid the artist, freshly plants and tends the flowers.

Lunchtime.

We sit and watch. People come. Carefully read the instructions. Compare, advise and check. Unhurried make the round.

Return to their cars and leave. Matter of fact.

Outside we two finish our stale rolls and continue our way.

Pilgrimage is not legendary nor remote. You fit it into every day. Between household and office tasks. You take time out.

Give reverence. And the real saint protects you.

When you die in Ballyvourney your gravestone records Gobnet's care of you in life through death to life.

Mary from Magdala

❦

It takes a surprisingly long time to die from crucifixion. Mary is shaken by how long it takes, and there is nothing to do except watch. It takes longer than passionate grief can last. She catches herself wishing that she had begun prostrate because it would be an easier position. And now, having begun standing she cannot lie down, because he, raised up there, is unable to move and for her to do so would be a betrayal. He has, she feels, been betrayed enough. There is nothing she can do except stand there.

Later she thinks of something else. So she takes off her veil and pulls the long pins out. Her hair, that extraordinary red-gold hair, tumbles down like a bright wave in the hot sunlight and lies over her shoulders, curling below her waist, announcing to all the world that she is a whore. She does it partly to share his humiliation, but more because she knows that if he can still see, it will remind him of sweet breezes across corn fields, of the glory of the lilies and of long evenings of wine, singing and happiness. It is an old joke between them. The first time she had meant it as a joke. Giggling she had let down her hair, then as now. She had spent the last of her savings on the extravagant ointment. She had bound a scarlet ribbon under her breasts. She had meant only to tease him, to shake for one moment his impeccable composure. It would be a good joke. She had waited until the dinner was well under way, until she was sure he would be bored by their prim and conceited manners.

When she came in he had turned and smiled at her. He had been leaning on the table talking, as usual; but he had glanced up, sensing her arrival, and seeing her outfit grinned hugely, at her and at the undercurrent of nervousness that flickered around the room – because of course she had known some of the civic dignitaries there, known them too well for their liking. He and she had known their

Mary Magdalene: 1st century
Disciple, Gnostic apostle,
witness to the Resurrection, penitent
Feast: 22 July

❦

The synoptic Gospels (Matthew, Mark, Luke) describe Mary of Magdala as one of the women from Galilee who were companions of Jesus and an intimate part of his 'inner circle' during the years of his ministry. She accompanied him to Jerusalem and was present at the crucifixion, after the male disciples (with the exception of John) had fled, and at his burial. With Mary the mother of James and Joses, and with Salome (whom some traditions saw as the midwife who had delivered Mary in Bethlehem, and had been converted then and there; other traditions make her the mother of James and John — who were called the Sons of Thunder), she went to the tomb at daybreak on the first day of the week to anoint his corpse. An angel announced the resurrection to them, and they fled terrified (Mark 16:1–8).

John's Gospel develops the story (John 20:11–18). In this version Mary goes to the tomb alone. When she finds the tomb empty she goes to fetch Peter and John. They confirm her story and then go home, but she remains to mourn. Here Jesus himself appears to her — although mysteriously she does not recognize him, 'mistaking him for the gardener', until he uses her name. He specifically instructs her not to touch him, but to go and tell the brethren that he has risen. She goes and says, 'I have seen the Lord', but they do not believe her.

Although there is no biblical evidence for the identification, from the earliest times the Church in the West conflated Mary of Magdala with the unnamed 'sinner' (prostitute) in Luke 7:36–50, who washed Jesus' feet with her tears, anointed them with ointment, kissed them and wiped them with her hair, while he was eating with some Pharisees. This led to the episode in which Jesus rebuked Simon the Pharisee, and affirmed that 'her sins, which are many, are forgiven because she loves much.'

A similar identification was made between Mary of Magdala and Mary of Bethany, the sister of **Martha** and Lazarus, who also anointed Jesus' feet with costly ointment, so that the whole 'house was filled with the fragrance'

fear and laughed together and they had hated him for that.

And here, here now, on this hot hilltop, she knows that it is her joke, among other things, that has brought him here. They pushed their luck too far in the hill towns of Judaea, just as they pushed it in the temple this week; they had touched too many people's fears and pride in their own joyful freedom. She, as much as any soldier or Pharisee or fickle bystander, she has brought him here. And she also knows that he would still have grinned hugely, still have turned loyally, still have condemned them as the hypocrites they were, even if he had already heard the sound of the nails hammering through the bones of his wrists.

The first time she had meant it as a joke. But when she bent over his dusty feet she had begun to cry. She had lowered her head so that no one would see. She had tried to wipe the tears away with her hair. He had saved her. He had called her a loving woman, because of her profession. The first time he had said this she had been irritated by such naïve stupidity. But she had learned that it was not that: simply, he knew her better than she knew herself. He knew her to be loving even if whoring was the only way she knew to love and live. Give it up, he had said, and come with me, just as he would have said it if she had sold something else in the market-place. Her tears fell over his feet.

He had liked her. He had introduced her to his other friends and they had become her friends. He had introduced her to his mother. He found her beautiful, wise and funny. He found her loving. And in his finding she found herself all these things and grew into them.

When the dust had been washed from his feet by her tears, she had massaged her ointment between his cracked toes. She liked him too. She liked his world, she felt at home there among his mixed bag of friends. To like him, to be with him, all you had to do was accept that friendship, to accept and be accepted. It was not easy, it was hard. All of them were broken and sad and lost somewhere, all of them defended themselves against each other. But he didn't, he didn't defend himself. With him she no longer needed to defend herself either. He accepted, and so she could accept that she had talents and worth hard bought from her own past.

Eventually someone at the dinner had protested, protested that he should even let her touch him. She had felt his fingers come down

(John 12:3–8). Mark adds an episode to this story, which has proved immensely significant to contemporary feminist theologians. Jesus concludes his criticism of the disciples' criticism of her with the words, 'wherever the gospel is preached in the whole world, what she has done will be told in memory of her', which not only provided Schüssler Fiorenza with the title to the authoritative book on feminist hermeneutics *In Memory of Her*, but has also inspired the feminist worship-rite of washing feet (or, for practical reasons, more often hands!).

Although modern biblical scholarship repudiates these identifications, they are still replete with meaning. That the woman who anoints Jesus in life should be the one to try to do so in death allows a prophetic reading of Mark 14:6 and 8 and gives the resurrection reunion a depth of poetic feeling. The narrators of the early period knew what they were up to; and later the visual artists added to the interpretation – Mary of Magdala is nearly always shown with her head uncovered, her hair loose and long. This iconography came originally from the idea of the 'loose woman' with the loose hair; but after she becomes a saint it sets her outside and beyond the Pauline injunction, free from his rules as he had wished Christians to be from the Judaic law. This picks up so strongly from the Lucan version, where the Pharisee is rebuked for putting the law above love, that it seems sad to lose it to a biblical reductionism – there is nothing in the gospel accounts which denies the identification between the 'sinner' and Mary of Magdala. (With Mary of Bethany there are real narrative problems and it is probably more straightforward to treat them as separate persons.)

'She has done a beautiful thing for me', says Jesus (Mark 7:6); and it is precisely this 'beautiful thing' that he then does for his disciples at the last supper (John 13:4–9). This suggestion of Jesus learning from Mary is one of the instances of the physical tenderness and intimacy between them which is marked in the Gospels.

Because of her role in proclaiming the resurrection and because of the friendship between them, Mary of Magdala was used by the Gnostics in a defence of women's ministry (see **Maximilla**), and some traditions went further, explicitly suggesting that Mary and Jesus were lovers. This tradition has been given a modern, feminist interpretation in Michèle Roberts's novel *The Wild Girl* – an example of the continuing imaginative power of women saints.

firmly on her head, soothing her against a pain she was immune to. He said 'Her sins are forgiven because she loves much.' It was that simple. In his pride in her she had been able to leave with dignity. She had walked tall across the room with her hair flowing down her back and her alabaster pot held high.

So now at last she moves. She moves still nearer to the cross, as near as the soldiers will let her. For the next three hours she will stand there, her glorious hair cascading in the sunshine, so that, long after he needs the knowledge, he will know that someone remembers, that someone is proud of him. Just by being there she will tell him her whole truth. She will tell him that she will never wear a veil again. That she, because of him, is proud of her hair which is long enough, beautiful·enough to wipe his feet with and which, this evening, will be long enough, beautiful enough to cover his wounds so that his mother will not have to touch them. That she who anointed him in his life will be there to anoint him in his death. That, thanks to him, she is now proud of a past which has made her tough enough not to be ashamed of this horrible, drawn-out, shameful dying.

She is a whore and he loves her. There is nothing to be ashamed of. When she recognizes him in the garden it will be a meeting of friends.

More orthodox legendry added detail to these confused and brief biblical references to her. In the traditions of the Eastern Churches she was said to have gone to Ephesus with Mary, Jesus' mother, and John the evangelist. She lived and died there, and her tomb was shown to pilgrims in the eighth century. A still later narrative made her the fiancée of John, the beloved disciple, whom he had given up when he was called to be an apostle. The West was more committed to the identification between her and Mary of Bethany (which is why, since Mary of Bethany chose 'the better part which shall not be taken away from her' of sitting at Jesus' feet and listening to his teachings, in preference to serving his supper with her sister **Martha**, she has become the patron saint of contemplative nuns) and preferred the tradition in which she, with Martha and Lazarus, travelled to southern Gaul where they evangelized Provence. Later Mary retired to a hermitage in the Maritime Alps and finally died at Saint Maximin. Vézelay, in southern France, claimed her relics during the eleventh century.

The intimacy between Jesus and Mary of Magdala was apparently more often understood as a special friendship than as a sexual relationship. This (along with the penance element in her story) may be the reason why so many later saints felt such a close bond with her. (This experience of close friendships between living persons and saints is common.) The most extreme version of this friendship is perhaps **Catherine of Siena**: her close friendship with Mary of Magdala led, Catherine reported, to Christ and his mother inviting Mary of Magdala to 'adopt' Catherine as her daughter and intimate; after this visionary experience, Catherine could always call upon Mary for advice and support.

After the Blessed Virgin, Mary Magdalene has proved one of the most popular and enduring saints in Christendom. She can be identified in pictures by her hair. The belief that she was a sinner – of the worst kind – and emphatically *not* a virgin, who was also the dear friend of Jesus and the witness of the resurrection, obviously provided a strongly needed means of hope for many Christians.

Miracles of Hild

Silence for the bird sang
the bird sang so
often the bird sang
sealing your ears
in the skybound heights

space is if
silence is as if

Give me she asked   quick response
what I seek may I have
mine I give that I receive
miracle of the mantle

On a deep dark day
in the lightless thicket of winter
up the steps

fear trapped her/e/in I
don't hear or
touch
anybody's glory

intellect stuttered
or stone spoke
of the life you cannot choose

Hild: 614–680
Abbess of Whitby, scholar and teacher
Feast: 17 November

She spent her first thirty-three years very nobly in the secular habit . . . [She was] of noble birth . . . the daughter of Hereric, King Edwin's nephew . . . she received the faith and mysteries of Christ through the teaching of Paulinus of blessed memory . . . she withdrew to the kingdom of the East Angles . . . [where] she continued a whole year . . . then Bishop Aidan called her home and she received a hide of land on the north side of the river Wear where for another year she lived the monastic life with a small band of companions.

After this she was made abbess in the monastery called Heruteu [Hartlepool] . . . soon after . . . she was appointed to rule the monastery [probably at Tadcaster]. . . . Bishop Aidan and other devout men who knew her visited her frequently, instructed her assiduously, and loved her heartily for her innate wisdom and her devotion to the service of God.

. . . Establishing a Rule of Life there . . . [after] some years . . . she undertook either to found or to set in order a monastery at a place called Streanaeshalch [Whitby] . . . which she carried out with great industry. She established the same Rule of Life . . . teaching them to observe strictly the virtues of justice, devotion and chastity . . . above all things to continue in peace and charity. After the example of the primitive church, no one was rich, no one was in any need, for they had all things in common and none had any private property. So great was her prudence that not only ordinary people but also kings and princes sometimes sought and received her counsel when in difficulties.

. . . All who knew Hild, the handmaiden of Christ and abbess, used to call her mother because of her outstanding devotion and grace.

After she had presided over the monastery for many years . . . She was attacked by a fever . . . for six years the sickness afflicted her continually; yet . . . she never ceased giving thanks to her Maker and to instruct the flock committed to her charge both in public and private.

. . . In the seventh year of her illness . . . her last day came. About cock-crow she received the viaticum of the most holy communion and, summoning the handmaidens of Christ . . . she urged them to preserve the gospel peace among themselves and towards

but seek
the seeker said you should know
it through making
believe life

But stone spoke
I belong
sang whose pride or reason

Is owning owned
and longing broken?

the roofless arches
skychurches
democratic stones dedicate

go on air with aching
the gift in the note

is *this*
you came for *this*
  and hear that wintry bird bawl out
air-piercing defiance

climb the two hundred and one
stone steps
on St Stephen's day
for only *this*
is it nothing
nada who pass
by incarnation
cancel the event expect
no second
coming

all others; even while she was still exhorting them, she joyfully saw death approach . . .
she 'passed from death into life'.

Bede, Ecclesiastical History of the English People

Hild's cult was established within a century, for there is an entry for her in the eighth-century Calendar of St Willibrord. After the sacking of Whitby in the ninth century by the Danes, Hild's relics were supposedly removed to Glastonbury, although they were also claimed by Gloucester.

Legends tell that the wild geese on their way to and from the Arctic came to pay homage to Hild on the wide marshy estuary below Whitby Abbey – 'pleased with the company of so pious a mistress, and allured by the prospect of an eternal throne'. The wild goose is an emblem of the Spirit, and is widely used in both Franciscan and Celtic spirituality.

Another legend refers to the ammonites and other fossils frequently found along the cliff:

The cliff was greatly infested with serpents, that lurked in the shrogs and bushes about, to the great terror of the abbess and her nuns; upon which she prayed to God that He would cause them to crawl down the cliff and be converted into those stones found on this coast, called to this day by the country people for this supposed miracle, St Hilda's stones.

Sabine Baring-Gould, Lives of the Northumbrian Saints

Before Hild was born her mother had a vision in which she happened to pull aside her gown, and discovered beneath it a jewel – 'of such marvellous lustre that it diffused its brilliancy over the entire island'.

By 657 Hild, already Abbess of Hartlepool, was recognized as 'one of the greatest ornaments of Northumbria, famed all over the island of Britain, not only for her extraordinary knowledge, but also for her charity, meekness and humility'. Under Hild the abbey became a great school of learning. Many who studied there later became scholars, preachers and teachers, and at least five became bishops. The abbey was a double community of men and women who lived apart in separate houses, under the strict rule of St Columba of Iona, one abbess or abbot governing both sexes.

Her zeal for education was not confined to building up libraries and instructing clerics in Latin language and literature. Under her rule the Anglo-Saxon cowherd and poet Caedmon was encouraged to produce his vernacular devotional poetry.

Liturgy of St Hild

❧

Take me often from the tumult of things into Thy presence.
There show me what I am and what Thou hast purposed me
to be. Then hide me from Thy tears.

The joy I feel today, my Lord, is only a shadow of your joys for
me, when we meet face to face.

You are the keeper of the treasure we seek so blindly.

You alone know what my soul truly desires, and you alone can
satisfy those desires.

My soul's desire is to see the face of God
and to rest in His house
My soul's desire is to study the scriptures
and to learn the ways of God
My soul's desire is to be freed from all fear and sadness
and to share Christ's risen life

Often I strain and climb
and struggle to lay hold
of everything I'm certain
You have planned for me.
And nothing happens:
there comes no answer.
Only You reach down to me
just where I am.

Commit your way to the Lord
Be still before the Lord and wait patiently for Him

I trust in thee O Lord
I say, thou art my God
My times are in thy hand
My times are in thy hand.

The most important event in the annals of Whitby was the synod held in 663/4 to settle the disputes between the Roman and British churches; it was a measure of the high regard in which Hild was held that so critical an event should take place at her abbey. Ostensibly relating to issues such as the time for the celebration of Easter and the form of monastic tonsure, the synod in fact became the battleground between the Roman and Celtic Christian churches and its outcome was to influence the course of Christianity in Britain thereafter. Hild supported the Celtic church, but when the decision went in favour of the Roman church, she accepted it.

In her old age Hild frequently retreated to the daughter house at Hackness, set in a wooded valley enclosed by hills, for meditation and prayer, to escape the constant demands on her time from visitors who came to her for advice.

When Hild died, her young friend, Bega, a nun at Hackness, later foundress of the abbey at St Bees in Cumberland, had a vision on the night just before Hild's death:

> . . . she seemed to hear the death-bell of the abbey ring out the summons for the sisters to assemble and pray for a passing soul; and immediately the ceiling of her room appeared to open and reveal the starry sky. Presently [she saw] the abbess ascending to Heaven, escorted by a convoy of angels, who sang in ravishing strains anthems of praise as they winged their way upwards, when the vision was lost in the depth of space, and the ceiling resumed its ordinary appearance.

S. Baring-Gould and J. Fisher, *The Lives of the British Saints*

THE CELTIC AND THE ROMAN (CF. **GOBNET**)

Large areas of Scotland, North Wales and Ireland were never conquered by the Romans. As a consequence, the Christianization of the fringes of the British Isles and Ireland was to a large extent unshaped by the fortunes of Christianity under its Roman guises during the decline and fall of the Roman Empire in Britain. (Some Celtic areas, such as South Wales, which endured strong Roman legionary presence, show a more complicated pattern.) As a consequence, the Celtic church that grew under the leadership of such saints as Patrick, Bridget, Columba (Colmcille) and Aidan, developed quite differently from its Roman counterpart.

The Homily of St Hild

❧

Trade with the gifts God has given you
Bend
your minds to holy learning you
may escape the fretting moth
of littleness of mind
that would wear out
your souls.
Brace your wills to action
that they may not be
the spoils of weak desires.
Train your hearts and lips to song
gives courage to the soul.
Being buffeted by trials, learn to laugh.
Being reproved, give thanks.
Having failed, determine to succeed.

Hild's abbey at Whitby followed the Celtic rites and the Celtic model, which was more eremitical, ascetic and penitential, devoted to personal holiness and poverty. Individual monasteries followed particular rules and there was no cohesive centre of doctrine. The evangelizing, wandering quality of Celtic spirituality meant that bishops did not reside in dioceses and administer, but were far more likely to be 'on the road'. The Celtic church is in some senses a contradiction in terms, but the shared values of scholarship, creativity, devotion to the evangelical call, extreme poverty and asceticism characterize the spirituality of these monasteries and abbeys.

The clash between the Roman and the Celtic was bound to come to a head. Although it was symbolized by the apparently trivial matters of the tonsure and the date of Easter — actually not so trivial at a time when Lent was kept very strictly and when different members of the same royal family followed the two different churches — the Synod of Whitby was the crucible in which the fate of the Catholic Church was settled. Had Rome not won the day there would be a very different Catholic Church today. However, it is clear that support for Rome was very convincing among some bishops, such as the key figure Wilfred, who identified so strongly with the European system that he went to France to be ordained as bishop.

From Whitby on the organization and centralization of the Church grew, typified by the removal of the major Northern diocese's centre from Holy Island (Lindisfarne, beloved of the Celtic saints, Aidan and Cuthbert) to the thriving commercial and political centre of York. While Hild supported the Celtic church, when the decision went in favour of the Roman church, her example in accepting the majority decision is held to have influenced the rapid growth of unity around the new system.

SOURCES

Sabine Baring-Gould, *Lives of the Northumbrian Saints* (reprint: Llanerch Enterprises, Llanerch, 1990).

S. Baring-Gould and J. Fisher, *The Lives of the British Saints*, 4 vols (Hon. Soc. Cymmodorion, London, 1907).

Bede, *Ecclesiastical History of the English People*, ed. B. Colgrave and R. A. B. Mynors (Clarendon Press, Oxford, 1991).

Sylvia Mundahl-Harris, *St Hilda and Her Times* (Abbey Press, Whitby, 1985).

The Northumbria Community, *Liturgy of St Hild*, reprinted in *Celtic Night Prayer from the Northumbria Community* (HarperCollins, London, 1996).

F. Ross, *Ruined Abbeys of Britain* (n.d.).

Rose of Lima

❀

Heart of darkness.

*She engraved on her emaciated body, by her discipline, the wounds of the Son of God
. . . she gave herself such blows that her blood sprinkled the walls . . . her confessor
having ordered her to use an ordinary discipline and leave off her iron chain, she made
it into three rows and wore it round her body . . . the chain soon took the skin off and
entered so deeply into her flesh that it was no longer visible . . . in her ardent desire
for suffering she made herself a silver circlet in which she fixed three rows of sharp
points in honour of the thirty-three years that the Son of God lived upon earth . . .
she wore it underneath her veil to make it the more painful . . . so that with the least
agitation these iron thorns tore her flesh in ninety-nine places . . . to keep herself from
sleep she suspended herself ingeniously upon the large cross which hung in her room
. . . and should this fail she attached her hair [the one strand at the front which she
had not shaved off] to the nail in the feet of her Christ so the least relaxation would
inflict terrible suffering upon her . . . Rose represented forcibly the necessity she felt of
suffering this continual martyrdom in order to be more conformable to her divine
spouse.*

Was it the Indians? She cannot say so later, she cannot even remember perhaps. As a child in the high country where her father managed
the silver mines and each evening, their backs bleeding, the Indians
came up from the pit of hell where they dug out the silver ore for
Spaniards' profit and were marched past her house and she saw their
beauty, their brutality and their brokenness and their dark eyes in
their golden faces looked at the child with contempt. Beautiful and
broken. Desirable and defeated.

She watched them awed, and she found them beautiful. Can this

Rose of Lima: 1586–1617
Virgin, first Roman Catholic saint born in the New World
Patroness of South America and the Philippines
Feast: 30 August

⚜

F. W. Faber, *The Saints and Servants of God* (London, 1847), pp. 27–45 (oh, yes, there's *lots* more). Faber's work is a translation and abridgement of J. B. Feuillet. It is frankly a perverse text: Faber is apparently unable to distinguish between historical biography and his own speculations on Rose's state of mind — and he is morbidly fascinated by her physical self-abuse, viewing it almost ecstatically. None of the modern writers who speculate on her psychopathology, however, seem remotely interested in the psychological state of the male (nineteenth-century) writers who popularized her in Britain and presented her constantly as a child saint suitable for small girls. Rose's extraordinary physical courage is reduced to a frighteningly passive response to God's work in her.

Although modern hagiography has endeavoured to stress Rose's works of charity — 'social work', teaching and so forth — the truth is that she was canonized originally because of (i) the growing desire for an American-born saint in the seventeenth century; (ii) the extraordinarily strong and enthusiastic local cult that developed during and, very powerfully, immediately after her death; and (iii) the truly remarkable (horrific) nature of her penitential life.

During part of her childhood, Rose's father was employed as an overseer in a silver mine. The degradation of the Peruvian Indians, and their effective enslavement, shocked harder hearts than a small child's. Rose certainly believed that her sufferings were undertaken for the conversion and salvation of this damned people. There has been some speculation that Rose was in fact part native Indian herself; whether or not this was the case, she grew up very close to a defeated and humiliated people. The bloodthirsty rituals of Inca religion *may* also have had some influence on her.

be the core of a passion for suffering, a passion for justice – and a desire to give with nothing to give except her own flesh, her own desire? Her own sexuality.

The Indians. The loving. The desire. The fear. The fear of the desire. The desire. Were they as Christ to her, golden and suffering? Defeated but still contemptuous. She must not desire the Indians, but she may desire Christ. She cannot love the Indians, unless she will suffer for them because suffering is all she has to give.

For freedom consists in voices that have been broken and blood that has been spilled. Freedom tastes of pain.

The Indians. The blood on their backs, the exhaustion in their eyes, all that beauty broken and brutalized. The terror and the glamour of their wildness. The defeat of their drunkenness. Their beauty, brutality and brokenness.

Heart of darkness.

The brutal and defeated Indians cried out to heaven for vengeance, but in their eyes was contempt because she was Spanish and female.

Jesus, her fierce Indian, demands her love, but in his eyes is contempt, for she is lustful and female.

She is not worthy but she must not disobey. When she wanted to marry him, be his entirely and forever, she fell into paroxysms at her own presumption. But it was these convulsions, this humility, that captivated the heart of the Son of God.

Heart of darkness.

Did he love her grovelling?

Her unworthiness seduced him.

So she lived, despite her mother's worries, despite her confessor's orders, despite the inquisitive investigations of the Inquisition, in a hut in the garden where she carried out her extraordinary penitential

Peru had been savagely conquered by the Pizarros only forty years before her death: the duping, deceiving and destruction of the Incas by supposedly Christian 'heroes' might well inspire an extreme personality like Rose to penance.

This quotation (unsourced) was used as an Amnesty International advertising slogan in the 1980s. It was not perceived then as psychopathological – perhaps we do not take this idea seriously enough.

The idea that one could offer up suffering on behalf of others, if one was so virtuous that one did not 'need' it to get into heaven oneself, was a dangerous invitation to generosity. Thérèse of Lisieux, in the nineteenth century, was one of the first to challenge the theory – preferring to see herself as a 'victim of love' rather than a 'victim for justice'.

The idea of the mystical marriage had been popularized by **Catherine of Siena**. Rose used Catherine's experience in various ways – not just in desiring this wedding experience, but more importantly in becoming a Dominican tertiary (that is to say someone living according to Dominic's rule, but outside the normal conventual setting). Being a tertiary provided a special space for individual women – under the protection of an international order, but free from the domestic obedience the standard religious life required. Other women tertiaries have included Elizabeth of Hungary and Elizabeth of Portugal in the thirteenth century and Angela Merici in the sixteenth.

Interestingly Rose's mother was one of the few people who seemed seriously concerned about Rose's activities, and made affectionate efforts to restrain her teenage ecstatic. For this she has been treated (by Faber *et al.*) as a

life, and received consolations untasted by lesser mortals. And died aged thirty-one, and they could not bury her because the local populace did not want to be parted from that battered, broken, abused, beloved, ecstatic body.

Such saints pose delicate questions of religion and psychology
— especially for women, for women today.
   Perhaps her life is best understood as an attempt to make reparation for the widespread sin and corruption in contemporary society.

Perhaps. I struggle for it and am lost. It is frightening; very frightening. I cannot understand her will so set, so focused in its desire, so turned to the dark, to her own inner darkness. So desiring. So perverse.
   I do not know the heart of darkness — the huge dark God who gives her this dark joy. I do not know. I do not want to know. I do not dare to know. And in the darkness, I desire to know.

'worldly woman'. This part of the narrative is one that gets left out of children's 'Books of Saints' – their writers do not wish to encourage female teenage rebellion.

The quotations here are from Donald Attwater (*Penguin Dictionary of Saints*) and David Farmer (*The Oxford Dictionary of Saints*), neither of whom seems to know quite what to do with Rose.

After her death, Rose lay in semi-state in the cathedral. Attempts to remove her for burial led to widespread rioting. Her local popularity was enormous, and exerted great pressure on the authorities to canonize her. There was also a European desire to see an American saint – true fruit of the missionary endeavour. This combination of ambitions may explain the canonization of someone who had been investigated (though cleared) by the Inquisition, and who was openly manipulative of and disobedient to her confessor.

The seventeenth-century Mariana da Flores (note the flowery name and remember that 'Rose' was not a baptismal but a chosen name) is another example of a South American woman saint whose penitential life falls outside the usually acceptable norms – although such activities are not, of course, confined to South America. (See F. Parkinson Keynes, *The Lily and the Rose.*)

There is a darkness and a violence in all interiority. Rose of Lima, I believe, incarnated this in a strange and difficult way, born of her time, but breaking out of it into all the complicated masochism with which women must engage if they are to worship and love an exclusively male God. See Sara Maitland, 'Passionate prayer: masochistic images in women's experience', in L. Hurcombe (ed.), *Sex and God* (Routledge and Kegan Paul, 1988).

Jean Donovan and the El Salvador sisters
Sisters and workers with the poor of El Salvador
Murdered by the military 2 December 1980
Carla Piette, drowned August 1980

UNCONDITIONAL LOVE: A PALIMPSEST

*It's a great thing to be on a journey into the unknown, particularly when you trust
the cabbie . . .*

Carla Piette

*I almost could [leave El Salvador] . . . except for the children, the poor bruised
victims of this insanity. Who would care for them?*
   *Whose heart could be so staunch as to favour the reasonable thing in a sea of their
tears and loneliness? Not mine, dear friend, not mine.*

Jean Donovan, letter to a friend, two weeks before she died

small flames of love, impossible to extinguish
who followed Christ into El Salvador:

JEAN ITA MAURA DOROTHY
AND CARLA

December is high summer in El Salvador –
   hardly a shower disturbs the certain repetition
   of baking days and warm clear nights.
      subversives
      they gave up their lives
      to serve the poor
      to minister to the oppressed
      to relieve the sick
      to feed the hungry

> to the military they were a
> legitimate target
> in the back of the white mission van
> Jean   Ita   Maura   Dorothy
> abused   raped   shot
> 2 December 1980

In El Salvador 'it is not a crime for a soldier to kill a civilian'. In America the Reagan administration declared the Maryknoll sisters 'political activists', not nuns. 'From the perspective of the staunch Conservative traditional middle-class Catholic of Latin America, the ideas and beliefs of the liberation theologians are anathema . . . the American missionaries . . . as personified by the Maryknollers and the Cleveland mission team . . . represented a threat.'

> So they laid her out
> She was the first one
> She was so disfigured
> her face was so disfigured
> the bullet collapsed the bone structure of her face
> you couldn't really be sure it was Jean
> Then they pulled the next body out
> I think it was Maura
> They pulled her over to the side
> some of the people came over
> and broke branches off the trees
> and covered the two bodies
> I remember the stench was terrible.
> They pulled up Dorothy.
> She was dressed in jeans
> but the jeans were on backwards.
> The campesinos found them without their jeans on
> They put the jeans back on
> And then they brought up Ita
> It was like bringing up a child
> Her body was crumpled and broken
> Then they laid them all out there
> and the people covered the bodies with branches.

Evidence given by Patricia Lansbury, American Consul

❧

The van, the white van, yes. And what he remembers is the music. Dance music, loud and clear filling the night air . . . That was what woke him . . . And here it came — a white van swaying from side to side down the rough road as it raced down the hill towards him, with all the windows open and the radio blaring and all the lights on bright. Inside? The lights were on inside the van. Oh yes they were drinking. The old man raises an imaginary bottle and tilts his head back. Like this. Four, maybe five of them, in civilian clothes. Yes, yes, that he is convinced of, because he remembers thinking how strange they should be having such a party after curfew. No, no women. Just the men. Drinking and playing music.

Antonio Ramos, migrant cotton picker, giving evidence at
the inquiry into the sisters' deaths, two years later

❧

Carla Piette's Prayer

Waters of mountains — waters of God
cleanse us, renew us, so shabbily shod
   Rios de Chile, streams of burnt snow
melt us, tow us, beyond friend or foe
    Currents so fast, pools deep and clear
    tune us, quiet our hearts still to hear
Lord of the river, God of the stream
    teach us your song, our dryness redeem

❧

UNCONDITIONAL LOVE

JEAN

Something more was calling her.

Jean Donovan was working on the outskirts of La Libertad, a small, dusty port of 15,000 inhabitants on the Pacific coast fifteen miles west of San Salvador. Despite her feelings of inadequacy, she had charge of five rural parishes, with a total of 140,000 people. Her tasks involved training local leaders to administer health programmes and to distribute food; basic health; instructing catechists, without the aid of a priest. As the task was so gargantuan the missioners knew they could only touch on things.

One project involved distributing the Caritas food aid for six thousand harvest workers in a shanty town near the airport with no electricity, running water or sanitation.

She delivered supplies by motorbike. At night, when the workers returned from the fields, she held celebrations of the Word.

If the people were lucky there would be a priest to celebrate Mass once a month, otherwise one of the sisters would conduct the celebration in the small wooden shack that served as a community church.

Jean's letters record that she would read a passage from the Bible, after which the parishioners would repeat it. Then everybody would discuss the meaning of what had been said.

In the last months of 1980, after Carla's death on a night-time and, as always, dangerous mission of mercy, Jean and Dorothy, with the white Toyota van, formed the Rescue squad, the backup team, which went out taking the food and supplies to the beleaguered peasant communities in Chalatenango, ferrying priests and rescuing refugees.

I'm never sure if I've got enough to share with people and then I realize that I do, it's God that helps us, he sort of carries us, because I couldn't do this by myself.

Jean

Ita Ford and Carla Piette, and after Carla's death, Maura Clarke, were working in Chalatenango, one of the poorest mountainous rural areas, bordering Honduras and Guatemala.

In the battles between the guerrillas and the security forces, the people's choices amounted to — join one and be killed by the other, or leave the country.

The church's mission was to set up refugee centres and to supply food and medicines. Every day, counts of the dead bodies faced the sisters – part of their work was to reassemble the bodies and bury them in defiance of the security forces.

In the first five months of 1980 over two thousand ordinary Salvadoreans had been killed.

I don't think we could have dreamed up this job before we came – but we came to help and this is what we are being asked to do.

Letter from Ita Ford to her sister Rene

If you choose to enter into other people's suffering or to love others you at least have to consent in some way to the possible consequences.

Ibid.

The whole Gospel of John is about love, the whole reason for living is love, and if we can just breathe a little bit of love, a little bit of warmth and a little bit of concern . . . extend this to this people here.

Dorothy Kazel

If someone [Jean] knew was picked up . . . she would march into the barracks and demand from the officer in charge the immediate release of the prisoner, threatening to bring the entire US embassy down on his head unless she got her way. She got away with it . . . but she left behind her a dangerously humiliated enemy.

Gwen Vindley, administrator of the Maryknoll Lay Mission programme

Before they killed them, all six guardsmen abused the women sexually. When it was all over Sub-Sergeant Colindres Aleman said he had done it this way because the women were subversives. The soldiers were paid hundreds of dollars. The regional commander, Colonel Edgardo Casanova, ordered the nuns killed.

The Maryknoll Order ran the only existing programme for lay volunteers in Third World missions. It was founded in the 1920s exclusively as an order of missionaries, with its headquarters at Ossining, New York.

The background to the situation in Latin America just prior to 1980 was that at the 1968 Conference of all the Latin American bishops at Medellin in Colombia it was recognized that there existed a situation of injustice that was tantamount to institutional violence requiring far-reaching and urgent change. This was the beginnings of the theology of liberation when, redefining the Church as the Church of the poor, priests went to live alongside the peasants and the Christian Federation of Salvadorean peasants was formed. Immediately the government targeted the new union, and within a few years the priests themselves became the target of the death squads.

The task the priests undertook to initiate reform was to introduce basic literacy through the development of basic Christian communities, educating the peasants in democracy through the setting up of people's councils. The Bible and civic action went hand in hand.

In the late 1970s the violence escalated – a current slogan was 'Be a patriot – kill a priest' – and foreign priests in particular were targeted.

The mission teams in El Salvador in 1980 included a scattered number of largely North American lay missioners and nuns who were attempting to look after the parishes abandoned by their own priests who had fled the death squads.

The Maryknoll team constantly asked themselves why they were there and what kept them.

So many of the priests had left — what happened if they left too? As Americans they still had contacts and could sometimes rescue parishioners.

It was on the way from the airport in the dark that the van was hijacked and driven off. The last sight of the four of them alive was at the terminal building around 7 o'clock.

In keeping with the Maryknoll tradition, Ita and Maura as nuns were buried among the people for whom they worked and died in Chalatenango:

In the small overcrowded country cemetery at the bottom of the hill leading into the town, their bodies were laid to rest beside Carla Piette's on Saturday, December the sixth.

On Friday December the fifth there had been a joint funeral mass for all four in the capital, San Salvador. A wake was held throughout the night in the parish church in La Libertad and a second mass at 4.30 a.m. there. In the crowded church, the caskets containing the bodies of Jean Donovan and Dorothy Kazel were handed from person to person to the waiting car; outside the square was packed.

In the square beyond the church along the street outside the windows of Jean's apartment and down the narrow streets of the port, the people of La Libertad and Zaragoza, of Santa Cruz and the surrounding communities lined the route out of town to the airport road . . . The small cavalcade of vehicles started out along the final stretch of their Salvadorean journey, moving slowly through the dense lines of defiant triumphant applause.

God can and will bring good out of evil, even out of the greatest evil.

Dietrich Bonhoeffer

If you stand with the poor, identify with them, feel their insecurity, their rejection . . . you begin to understand the world in a new way.

Father Michael Crowley

I'm afraid to be dependent, even on God.

Jean Donovan

It was not the catastrophe she found astonishing — it was the possibility that she herself might actually be able in some way to help alleviate it that seemed to fill her constantly with amazement and joy.

Timothy Allman on Jean Donovan in 'Rising to rebellion', *Harper's Bazaar* (March 1981)

A contemporary definition of sainthood?
To be filled with joy that you might be able to help
to lighten the effect of evil in people's lives?

SOURCES

Main source: Ana Carrigan, *Salvador Witness: The Life and Calling of Jean Donovan* (Ballantine Books, New York, 1984). In some cases the words have been adapted and rearranged.
Sheila Cassidy, *Good Friday People* (Darton, Longman & Todd, London, 1991)

Wilgefortis

In Mendocino in northern California, an anonymous sculptor carved from a redwood trunk a remarkable work of folk art, representing a variation on the theme of Death and the Maiden. Father Time does not seize the modest young woman to rape her, or otherwise snatch her away, in the style of Hans Baldung Grien or Holbein, but instead stands calmly behind her, braiding her hair, like a good father sending his young daughter off to school.

Wild hair. Long hair, loose. Childlike, free. Or wanton, like a magdalen. Hair is for the heroine, the lovely princess, loose, flowing, wind-blown. Lots of hair, very long hair, golden or dark as ebony – extreme hair, essence of femininity, of youth, of sexuality. But on the top of your head the stories meant, princess.

Does not nature itself teach you that for a man to wear long hair is degrading to him, but if a woman has long hair it is her pride?

But on the top of your head the apostle meant, woman.

AD 1212: night-time in Umbria. Clare removes her hood, kneels at Francis's feet, her head on his lap, and feels the harsh thin hands, which are ungentle but loving, cut off her soft, still childlike curls. They catch the candle-light and gleam, but Francis does not notice their extraordinary blondness – a colour that makes them still touching in their little box nearly eight hundred years later. He has cut off her pride and made her chaste, made her virtuous, manly, pure and hard.

Wilgefortis (also known as Uncumber or Liberata): no date
Virgin and martyr
Feast: 20 July

Marina Warner, *From the Blond to the Beast*, p. 347. Warner's chapter on hair and its meanings in fairy-stories is particularly illuminating.

Paul, in I Corinthians 11:14, 15.

When **Clare** ran away from home to make her submission to Francis, he signed his reception of her by cutting off her hair: the unusually blond curls were kept as relics and can be seen in Assisi.

AD 1429: high noon in high summer in Rheims. The trumpets blare, the crowds gather, awed, delighted. The Dauphin is crowned Charles VII, King of France. Beside him, in full armour, her standard in one hand and her helm in the crook of her elbow, stands his Knight Champion, her hair cut short still, as she had cut it first in her homeland in Champagne only a year ago. She has cut off her pride and made herself chaste, virtuous, manly, pure and hard.

AD 1591: morning in Lima. Two little children are playing in the garden. The girl is just five years old and her little brother is four. He throws mud at her hair and she starts to cry. He says (or her hagiographers say he says), 'My dear sister, do not be angry at this accident, for the curled ringlets of girls are hellish cords which bind the hearts of men and draw them into the eternal flames.' She goes into the house and cuts all her hair off with her mother's scissors. She has cut off her pride and made herself chaste, virtuous, manly, pure and hard.

The princess has long hair, free in the wind.

The saint has cropped hair, like a boy, though never quite like a man.

All this hair is important. Long or short, it marks womanliness, the good woman or the lovely woman. But hair has its place, as women should, and its place is on your head; on the top of your head, not on your chin.

Wilgefortis was one of the seven children of the King of Portugal. *A promising start for a fairy story, and no doubt her hair was long and wind-blown, because it is certainly recorded that she was very beautiful.* She was so beautiful that the King of Sicily wanted to marry her. *The plot is shaping up well now.* But she had secretly become a Christian and taken a vow of virginity and she did not want to marry him, because apart from the vow, he was a pagan, like her father. *Ah, wrong genre. This is not a princess folk-story, but a saint folk-story; nonetheless it is a good starting-point for that too.* Her father was (*they always are*) inexorable. He insisted, threatening her with violence. The wedding, he announced, would be in the morning. In the privacy of her chamber she prayed to God, to do something that would get her out of this terrible mess. *Now she will run away in the night, she will cut off her hair and disguise herself as a man; she will go to a*

Joan of Arc.

Rose of Lima. This anecdote is recorded in F. W. Faber, *The Saints and Servants of God*. It seems rather unlikely language for a four-year-old to use, but Faber expresses his gratitude to the nasty child for thus inspiring his sister.

Standard hagiography tends to become somewhat embarrassed by too obviously folkloric tropes, although in fact many of the legends of the saints share patterns and even imagery with both pre-Christian myths and European folk-stories. This seems both natural and inevitable: most commentators have little difficulty with, for example, the way that *The Dream of the Rood* poet presents his Christ as Anglo-Saxon war hero, going gladly to the fight (even to the extent of altering the biblical account and having Jesus eagerly strip himself for the battle to come). Cultural adaptation of this sort does not seem to carry the danger-signals that stories like that of Wilgefortis do. Yet large parts of the hagiographic legends were told and maintained within illiterate or sub-literate communities and therefore had to be adapted to the oral traditions and ways of 'telling'. I suspect that some of the difficulty is related to the fact that stories and cults treated in this way slip out entirely from the control of theologians (clerics) and can no longer be managed. What is more interesting to me than the way these stories do fit into ancient patterns is the ways that they do not: the legend of Wilgefortis is both redolent with folk-tale and also different from it. The emphasis remains a religious one, rather than a recreational one.

convent, or seek the protection of an ancient hermit; she will cease to be a princess and become a saint.

That is what always happens. In the morning when her maids came to dress her in her wedding gown, and drew back the curtain from her bed, they stepped back appalled, they threw their hands in the air, some of them screamed, one – though she was notorious for her excessive sensibility – even fainted.

Wilgefortis, Princess of Portugal, had grown a beard. *Oh come on.*

Not a few hairs, not the kind you can pluck out and hope for the best, not the entrancing peach bloom of extreme youth, nor the whiskery mole-trim of extreme age, but a full curly beard and luxuriant moustaches. *No. No. This is not how the story is meant to go. This is disgusting and horrible. Yuck. Neither princesses nor saints have hair on their chins. Only freaks and circus ladies.* They hoped they might cover it up – under the wedding veil and a disciplined silence. But it was too late, and the screamers too loud. The rumour went scuttling down the corridors, blown on a miraculous breeze, until it came to the ears of the King of Sicily. *Who ought, of course, to be faithful and brave, like Galahad, and thus free the poor bewitched princess from this horrible enchantment, but the story is out of control now, not behaving properly at all.* Not surprisingly he withdrew at once from the contract and went back home. The King of Portugal was so angry that, without further ado, he had his daughter crucified. *Wrong again, what about torture, demands for recantation, miraculous interventions, heroic resistance, and the conversion of thousands?* On the cross she prayed that everyone who remembered her sufferings should be liberated from all encumbrances and troubles.

This is a very silly story. Thomas More, that sane and affectionate saint, thought so. He sneered at her popular cult, at the way foolish country women would leave little piles of oats at the feet of her statues:

> *whereof I cannot perceive the reason, unless it be because she should provide a horse for an evil husband to ride to the devil upon, for that is the thing she is so sought for, as they say. Insomuch that women have therefore changed her name and instead of Saint Wilgeforte call her Saint Uncumber, because they reckon that for a peck of oats she will not fail to uncumber them of their husbands.*

The way of dealing with such legends (of which this is only a rather extreme example) has tended to be to dismiss them. Liberal theologians complain of superstition, and conservative clerics of secularization; but neither address the question of why these stories sprang up and how they nourished faith, which they certainly did.

Cross-dressing and transgendering is a persistent theme in iconic legends of saints. There are countless traditions, starting with **Thekla**, of women who in one way or another took on maleness. Marina Warner's chapter on this in her *St Joan* is illuminating. The reasons why these mythical or semi-mythical women so disguise their gender are diverse: disguise, either from a desire to expand their own choices or to escape from limitations imposed on them from outside, is common.

It is also a theme in the historical reality and certainly the imagination of saints, even quite unexpected ones. **Catherine of Siena** took Euphrosyne as a patron saint – precisely because she had disguised herself as a man and lived within a monastery. Thérèse of Lisieux wrote of her desire and her childhood plans to change sex so that she could become a mission priest. **Perpetua of Carthage** assumed maleness in her ecstatic dreams in order to fight with Satan. At the imaginative level this seems to have been acceptable, in a way that males taking on female identity even in the imagination does not appear to have been.

It was also important that the legends did not go too far: the legend of Pope Joan, which takes this theme to its natural conclusion, was firmly stamped on – she has the dubious distinction of being *both* anathematized *and* declared never to have existed.

If part of the performance of sanctity is to press against the confines of material reality, this is not surprising. The confines of female lives press hard on the aspiring, but it remains sad that maleness has been seen as both authority and protection for so long. This remains a problem for the Church to address.

Thomas More (spelling modernized).

Contemporary demythologizers do not even bother to laugh at Wilgefortis' devotees – they rationalize them away, with a simple certainty that is almost touching:

This curious legend . . . is not the survival within Christianity of a hermaphrodite cult, but simply an erroneous explanation of the crucifixes of the 12th century and earlier which depicted Christ fully clothed and shod wearing a beard. The most famous example was at Lucca . . . to explain this type of image, wrongly believed to be that of a woman, presumably in an age which had become accustomed to the unclothed type of crucifix figure, the legend arose.

This does not seem a much more satisfactory story actually. In fact it seems very nearly as silly. Sillier.

And does nothing at all to explain her popularity.

It is about hair really, hair and what it signifies for women – who must grow it long *and* cut it off; who must keep it beautiful *and* keep it covered; who must strive to be both princess *and* saint; and who must always, always and forever, put up with evil husbands, because, as the apostle says,

I want you to understand that the head of every man is Christ, the head of a woman is her husband, and the head of Christ is God. Any man who prays or prophesies with his head covered dishonours his head, but any woman who prays or prophesies with her head unveiled dishonours her head – it is the same as if her head were shaven . . . For a man ought not to cover his head, since he is the image and glory of God; but woman is the glory of man. (For man was not made from woman, but woman from man. Neither was man created for woman, but woman for man.) . . . Does not nature itself teach you that for a man to wear long hair is degrading to him, but if a woman has long hair, it is her pride? For her hair is given to her for a covering . . . we recognize no other practice, nor do the churches of God.

Obedience to a evil husband is a wearisome duty – there are not many stories to help one meet that dreary obligation. One knows one is neither princess nor saint. A peck of oats, a silly story, a gossip with one's women friends, a giggle, the hope of a saint who will understand. A little, necessary consolation.

D. H. Farmer, *The Oxford Dictionary of Saints*, p. 404. Farmer gives a surprising (interesting) amount of space to this non-existent saint and, in his opinion, foolish cult.

Paul: I Corinthians 11: 3–16.

Although Wilgefortis is mentioned in a number of Continental martyrologies, she did not figure in the English ones. Nonetheless, there a hymn and a collect to her in the Salisbury *Enchiridion*, and a statue of her can be seen in the Henry VII Chapel at Westminster Abbey. There were also images of her in Worstead, Norwich and Boxford (all in Norfolk) – this localization is perhaps not surprising since her cult seems to have originated in fourteenth-century Flanders, with which East Anglia had close trading connections. These images were wrecked by Edward VI's commissioners who valued her clothes (the dressing of statues of saints, like dolls, was a common practice) from two of the shrines at 16d. and 14d. Apparently she was not a saint much patronized, at least in Norfolk, by the rich and successful.

From the Katherine Passion

❧

... neither prosperity nor riches nor any worldly honour nor any suffering or torture can turn me from the love of my lover in whom I believe. He has married my maidenhood with a ring of true faith and I have committed myself to him truly. We are so fastened and tied as one, and the knot so knitted between us two, that no desire, or mere strength either, of any living man, will loosen or undo it. He is my life and my love; he is the one who gladdens me, my true bliss above me, my prosperity and my joy, and I want nothing else: my sweet life, so sweetly he tastes and smells to me ...

(Katherine's speech describing her marriage to Christ, before the Emperor Maxentius)

... That all those who think of my pain and my passion for your love, Lord, and call to me when they must endure the pain of death ... in need or in trouble ... you will quickly hear them, heavenly Saviour. Drive off all evil from them, war and woe and untimely weather, hunger and every hatred that harms and oppresses them ...

(Katherine's prayer, before her execution)

Come my dear lover, come now my spouse, dearest of women! See, the gate of eternal life waits for you all open ... all those who in their inmost hearts remember you and your passion, how you endured death — every time they call to you with love and true belief, I promise them speedy help from the heavenly kingdom.

(Christ's reply to Katherine)

Katherine of Alexandria: c. 4th century
Martyr, philosopher, bride of Christ
Cult suppressed 1969
Feast: 25 November

The *Katherine Passion* was part of a tradition of materials provided for the use of solitaries by those following another kind of Christian life. They were written for women who could read neither Latin nor French, that is, for simple Christians, not coenobitical nuns. Not only were the first solitaries not necessarily monks nor even particularly 'churchy' people, they were often both inarticulate and uneducated.

Katherine represents the most heroic possible model of femininity, while also being credited with a compassionate concern for the suffering and the dying. She was much loved by medieval women mystics, for whom, in her mystic marriage, she formed a remarkable role model. Many medieval paintings feature her marriage to the Christ Child, a recurrent theme. She appears with **Catherine of Siena** many times, sometimes with **St Clare**, and, in the mural in Winchester Cathedral, surprisingly, with Margery Kempe, never a candidate for sainthood.

Part of her popularity may be attributed to her versatility in patronage — she is patron of youth, students and scholars, because of her victory over the pagan philosophers, as well as nurses and craftsmen — the latter presumably because of the wheel made to torture and kill her, which burst into fragments, killing thousands of spectators. The wheel is the symbol by which she is nearly always represented, but she also carries the ring of her marriage to Christ and the pen.

Katherine is one of the most significant female saints in the medieval imagination, certainly in the British Isles, after the Blessed Virgin Mary. She ranks second only to **Margaret of Antioch** and **Mary Magdalene** in the number of her dedications and representations, but is foremost in the number of narratives devoted to her. Her protection was esteemed to be particularly powerful.

Mystic Marriage (Parmigianino)

before the mirror
he holds your ringed finger
   the blue stone
is it the Christ child this cherub
   the mirror shows
holding your fourth finger
the ring with its blue stone at the
centre of the painting
we see you close your arms spread wide
from ring to wheel open
– your hair swept up, your left hand resting
on its massy rim –
your young face, your breasts, keen, pointed
   the mirror shows
the mystic marriage of your dream
to another, perhaps His mother
who sees herself

The model of femininity held up by the virgin martyr saints like Katherine was definitely not self-effacing: they were 'saintly viragos', filled with boldness, quite capable of slaying or taming dragons and companies of knights, of converting Roman empresses and outwitting packs of philosophers. The model for pious readers offered in the lives and legends of the saints did not match the cultural norms and assumptions of pre-scribed femininity, but the heroines' feisty character must have struck a chord with ordinary women when their Passions were enacted on feast days.

Margery Kempe, a valuable source of information on the trends of medieval spirituality, refers to both **Margaret** and Katherine as her supporters. Interestingly, for her the most important saint, after Mary, Anne and Elizabeth, was **Bridget of Sweden**, who died in 1373. (See *The Book of Margery Kempe*, trans. and ed. B. A. Windeatt.)

The significance of the women saints as examples to follow is clear from the essay on the horrors of marriage, *Holy Maidenhood*, composed in the thirteenth century for the use of anchoresses:

> *Be honest now! Is it not all, or at least partly, for this, to cool your lust with the filth of your body, to have delight of your fleshly will by having sex with a man? . . . What will your coupling together in bed be like? . . . She must put up with his desire . . . often in great pain . . . she has to put up with all his crudities and indecent fooling, however filthy they turn out to be.*

To dissuade women from wanting children, a graphic description of the horrors of childbirth follows:

> *. . . inside in your belly a swelling in the womb which distends you like a water-bag; pain in your bowels and stitches in your side and your loins will ache very painfully . . . the burden of your breasts with your two nipples and the streams of milk which run out . . . your mouth is bitter and everything you chew is nauseating.*

All this to persuade well-born young girls to dedicate themselves as brides of Christ, following the blessed example of Mary and of

> *St Katherine, of St Margaret, St Agnes, St Juliana, St Lucy and St Cecilia and of the other holy maidens in heaven, [who] . . . not only gave up the sons of kings and noble-men, with all worldly wealth and earthly happiness, but suffered severe pains rather than accept them, and cruel death in the end. Think how good it is for them now, and how they give thanks for it now in God's arms, queens of heaven.*

A. Savage and N. Watson (intro. and trans.), *Anchoritic Spirituality*

Bergognone's Catherines with the
Virgin and Child

❧

She is young
very young.
He stands
a solid toddler
on her knee.
He looks to you
your hands praying
your eyes cast down
long rippled hair falling
down your back.
She holds your sister saint's right hand
who holds the shining lily her eyes
like yours like hers
cast down
to the decorous wheel beneath your feet

Katherine's protection in England extended to all kinds of situations, the weather included. Her chapels and shrines were to be found frequently on hilltops, like that at Abbotsbury in Dorset, as beacons or watchtowers to sailors and travellers, and as the patron saint of young girls she was invoked, through her special status as a bride of Christ, by young women anxious to secure a husband:

> *Sweet Katherine, a husband*
> *sweet Katherine, rich*
> *sweet Katherine, handsome*
> *soon sweet Katherine, soon.*

The poems on pages 132, 134 and 136 are based on three paintings in the National Gallery, London:

Parmigianino, *The Mystic Marriage of St Catherine, c.* 1527, Bologna;

Ambrogio Bergognone, *The Virgin and Child with St Catherine of Alexandria and St Catherine of Siena*, 1490, Certosa di Pavia; and

Moretto da Brescia, *The Madonna and Child with Saint Bernadino and Other Saints* (altarpiece), *c.* 1550. This painting also shows St Clare on the Virgin's right hand.

A NOTE ON THE CULTURE OF CRUELTY

The tortures so closely and lovingly described in medieval passions, of both men and women, at one level do operate as entertainment value. However, besides the explicit motives of legend-tellers to instruct and to entertain, dwelling upon physical pain and the processes of disintegration of the human body served another purpose. It brought the remote life of the saint up into close focus, through the common kinship of the flesh, and given the general experience of physical illness, hardship and cruelty, the bodily processes of the expropriation of fluids, the eruption of inner organs through the bodily envelope, the mutilation and dismemberment of the whole body into fragments (see the same process in relics) provided a route into *intimacy of connection* with the saint. It served, at one level, paradoxically, to stress the *humanity* of the saint – as indeed did the parallel medieval cult of Christ's face, or indeed of his foreskin – while at the same time stressing their exemplary character because of their sufferings.

Fragmentation, as Caroline Walker Bynum has shown (*Fragmentation and Redemption*), is a key metaphor in understanding medieval spirituality.

Saints Triumphant *(Moretto da Brescia)*

Saints triumphant strike their poses
demonstrate stigmata books and croziers
here below, clear-edged, determined
the virile founders of your church,

above their heads billowed draperies
announce a heavenly female world
where aloft the rumpled clouds
support you with your infant groom

follow closely tender converse
securely held on Mary's knee

THE *KATHERINE PASSION* AND THE MEDIEVAL LIVES OF THE SAINTS

In Cambridge University Library there is a late-fifteenth-century manuscript of a devotional book, one of many produced at this time, which is a compilation of 'popular romances which are pious, lively and full of incidents and marvels ... suited to the edification and entertainment of ... devout readers of modest intellectual accomplishments' (McSparren and Robinson, Introduction to facsimile edition (Aldershot, 1979), MS Ff 2 38), together with three saints' lives: **Mary Magdalene**, Thomas and **Margaret of Antioch**.

Like that compilation, Books of Hours were in common use amongst the laity at this time. Among the nine specially effective intercessory saints celebrated in another manuscript with prayers in verse, **Margaret** features again, together with Katherine of Alexandria, Barbara and **Martha**, sister of Lazarus.

These lives would be familiar to literate and non-literate alike, from being the subject of sermons on the saints' feast days every year or read in place of sermons. Amongst the most frequent were retellings of the lives of the New Testament women, such as **Mary Magdalene** and **Martha**, and of the early women martyrs, such as **Margaret**, the dragon-slayer, Juliana, or Katherine herself.

Before 1200, the lives of the saints were nearly always written in Latin and were the property of the clergy and the monastic communities – the earliest of them date back to the seventh century. In the eighth and ninth centuries the appetite for the lives increased significantly, but it was not until the twelfth century that they began to appear in the vernacular. By the 1200s, collections of saints' lives such as Jacob de Voragine's famous *Legenda Aurea* (*The Golden Legend*), most widely known through Caxton's fifteenth-century translation, were widely diffused across Europe.

Brought to the West by pilgrims, Crusaders and traders, the adventurous lives, full of fantastical happenings and marvellous occurrences, quickly became popularized. By the 1300s many versions of the saints' lives had been translated.

The most striking characteristic of the narratives featuring women saints was the heroines' passionate and defiant defence of their virginity as well as their faith in the face of appalling torture and execution. Besides Katherine of Alexandria, and **Margaret of Antioch**, Dorothy, Barbara, Juliana, Cecilia, Agnes and Ursula feature frequently.

A pilgrimage to the late-thirteenth-century church of
St Lawrence, Little Wenham, Suffolk

❧

On a grey May day, a dead day, we took the car into the silences, the unkempt, already green and white sweet-smelling thickets of southern Suffolk. It is Cup Final afternoon, Manchester United versus Liverpool. The world outdoors is empty.

Having collected the heavy old key, incongruously from a neat 1960s Span house, we set off to find the disused church. Several attempts and conversations later, the castellated towerhouse of Little Wenham rises up tantalizingly, shrouded in woods. We pass the swingeing new Suffolk County Council footpath and bridleway signs, and find ourselves trapped in a marshy rendering of the Bermuda Triangle. We abandon the car.

Everything sleeps. Huge barns newly roofed. Empty houses, the lath and plaster gaping. Notices saying 'Private. Keep out'. My head thuds dully, emptied of expectation.

One coot alarms the moat.

Suddenly, above us on a knoll, we see it.

There is a pretty fragile wooden porch. Inside all is bare. A huge stooped ochre figure of St Christopher carrying the Christ child on his back like the Old Man of the Sea looms up out of the disintegrating plaster facing the door and disappears from the waist downwards like a wraith in the mist, back into the stream of time. To the right of the plain-glazed east window, which floods the white-washed interior with light, the three delicately delineated figures of the saints, their robes a pale wash of faded ultramarine, their expressions serene, their headdresses, their hems barely discernible, held in dissolution.

They are quite unlike anything I have ever seen. Closest to the window, **Margaret of Antioch**, her long spear barely visible, the dragon at her feet indiscernible. I nod to her in recognition: I have pursued her for months in windows, on screens and pew-ends across the county and into Norfolk – in England her especial home. The

Little Wenham, a short way south of Ipswich in Suffolk, is famed for the excellence of its thirteenth-century wall-paintings, most notably of Katherine, **Margaret of Antioch** and, depending on the viewer, Barbara or **Mary Magdalene**. (The 'pot' in the saint's left hand, interpreted by Pevsner and others as Mary's emblem, could be the tower of Barbara, another very popular East Anglian virgin martyr.) E. Duffy, in *Holy Maydens, Holy Wyfes*, lists Barbara, along with Agnes, Dorothy and Edmund, as first in popularity on East Anglian church screens of this period. Katherine appears third, with Mary Magdalene, after John the Baptist and Etheldreda.

Edification and entertainment were the twin goals of the writers of the popular saints' lives, as they were of the painters of legends and embellishers of screens and windows. What had its roots in hagiography designed to instruct and edify the religious – nuns, monks, anchorites and anchoresses, priests – by the late fifteenth and early sixteenth centuries had become a genre of popular narrative.

Such narratives relished the 'bizarre and . . . lurid . . . the supernatural . . . the weird, the wonderful and the slightly salacious . . .' . They were stories in which the themes that recur over and over again are those of 'sexual purity and bloody defilement, chastity and lust, physical and spiritual beauty threatened by bestial cruelty' (Duffy, *Holy Maydens, Holy Wyfes*).

The *Katherine Passion* tallies precisely with this description. When Katherine refuses to worship the Roman gods, the narrative plunges with relish into a detailed description of the hideous instrument of torture

next figure is unmistakably Katherine.

Like a child postponing the orange Smartie I pass over her quickly to take in the third figure, **Mary Magdalene** – or is it Barbara? – hemmed in by the overweening pride of the seventeenth-century passion for funeral monuments. I acknowledge her; she and I have shared secrets. I sit in her church in one of our own parishes, and watch her golden hair light up the east window. But today it is Katherine, pride of artists, queen of bells, heroine of legends, whose form arrests me.

Her head is held to one side, an expression of ambiguous sweetness, bearing in her left hand her wheel aloft like a toy ball, and, is it smugness – teasing – or pride in her smile? I watch her. She is demure, graceful, gracious; she is quite unlike my ardent young philosopher from the Vulgate *Passion*, unlike the heroic image occasioned by all those hilltop chapels in remote places dedicated to her. What has she to do with suffering, with knowledge, with passionate sacrifice?

My spirits slump; disappointed I sit apathetically while my husband carefully sets up photographs.

And then I see it. Strangest of all impressions: the colours. The dresses' green and ochre have all the elegance, the freshness and subtlety of a twentieth-century painting, a Duncan Grant, the decorativeness of Angelica Bell – but the faces and hands are black. Through happenstance I have been given a glimpse into another world – a world where saints are black.

Time's revenge on the work and the church's emptiness obliterates the intricacy of the curves of the saints' poses, the loops and frets of the intricate Gothic arcades with which the painter has framed them. It blurs the folds of gowns, smudges the delicate shoes, disperses the headdresses as if in the slight stirrings of a late breeze come to rescue the stagnant day. Staring out strongly now from the plane of the wall as I read her, Katherine challenges me in this strange alchemy to ignore the dress and comportment of courtly romance or medieval tapestry, to disregard the flowing gowns, the pointed shoes, the characteristic ogee curves of early English fourteenth-century art and to wrench myself away from the world of the Très Riches Heures, the devotional manuscripts and their richly illumined pages – all the seductions of academic curiosity. My mind drifts away to buried images of the Black Madonna.

designed to break her spirit and subdue her into compliance with the Emperor's will:

> *Command four wheels to be made over three days; let the spokes and rims be pierced through with iron spikes, so that the points and the iron nails pierce through very sharply and strongly, and stick out far on the other side, so that all the wheels are spitted through with spikes keener than any knife, row on row.*

Katherine, who has already defeated fifty philosophers in argument, though she is only eighteen, far from being intimidated by the torturers' machine, prays to God to shatter all four of the wheels to splinters. Immediately an angel swoops down from heaven,

> *straight down into [the wheel] like a thunder-clap and hurled such a blow at it that it all started to clatter and split apart, to burst and break into pieces like brittle glass, both the wood and the iron . . . [so] that fully 4,000 of that wicked people were killed.*

In case that is not enough violent excitement, the Empress, converted by this display of the power of Katherine's God, is tortured by being dragged outside the city gates, her breasts torn 'up . . . to the bare bones with iron awls' and then her head is 'swept off . . . with a sword'.

Katherine herself survives to utter her last prayer before her head too is swept off. Whereupon the angels return to bear her body away to Mount Sinai, 'twenty or even more days' journey from where she died'.

NOTE ON THE EARLY MANUSCRIPTS OF THE *KATHERINE PASSION*

A small group of MSS have survived from the thirteenth century. The one quoted from is one of a group of six copied *c.* 1225–50. The editors describe it as:

> *small, between 5 and 9 inches high, compact enough to be easily held in the hand. Written neatly and clearly . . . on good parchment . . . which is still exceptionally clean . . . quite plain . . . usual blue and red paragraph markers, capital letters and headings . . . copied somewhere in West Midlands not far from the Welsh border — possibly Wigmore Abbey — dedicated to St James, a few miles South West of Ludlow.*

Quoted in Savage and Watson, *Anchoritic Spirituality*

A remote, 'redundant' (the technical term) country church, and the black-faced saint. Time left and gone, time not yet taken up. The saints' time, God's time, our time.

I thought it trickery at first, fortuitous that she should be there smiling down at me, if that is a smile upon her face, and then I thought of the Crusader routes by which the cults of these Eastern saints arrived in England and further West; and I thought how right that the technique of secco has apparently allowed the flesh tints to blacken, while the other colours maintain their tincture, thus underlining perfectly the saints' exotic origin. These most-loved saints of the popular imagination, nowhere more reverenced than in East Anglia, are not the medieval saints who —

gazed benignly out from the screens and tabernacles of late medieval England . . . country people themselves, like St James the Great at Westhall . . . with his sensible shoes, hat and staff, or St Anthony on the same screen with his friendly pig, or St Sitha, alias Zita of Lucca, at Barton Turf or Litcham All Saints or North Elmham, dressed in kerchief and apron, clutching her shopping-bag, keys, and rosary, like any hard-working English housewife (to whom she was well-known for her help in recovering lost property, especially the household keys).

Eamon Duffy, *Holy Maydens, Holy Wyfes*

They are not homely figures. In the dream of errancy set up by our inept wanderings circling the lost building, I confront the *otherness* of the Saint.

For what, after all, are the saints if not those who present to us the Other, the beyond of known, mapped life?

. . . the communion of saints is never an abstract or ethereal thing . . . it is rooted in this earth, in places where people have lived and loved, and seen the glory of God shining out in the common light of every day.

A. M. Allchin, *Celtic Christianity: Fact or Fantasy*

This life, this 'every day' is transfigured by our constantly losing ourselves. Of which our ineptitude this particular day is paradigmatic, my misreadings and stupidity the means of a gift of grace.

Tired after all the ill-humoured meanderings through impenetrable paths of dull undergrowth I came to your building with a card-file mind, full of references and 'attitude' and stumbled upon what I was given to see here.

The translations from the Latin into Middle English were partly for public performance on feast days of the saint, but especially for the anchoresses who would have no Latin.

The earliest example of a miracle play, in Dunstable, c. 1110, is one on Katherine's life.

IMAGES AND MEANINGS

Paradoxically the gruesome and fanciful details of the lives that 'edified and entertained' an emergent popular readership were often in church images condensed into a language of sweetly smiling faces and bland emblems – the wheel of St Katherine, the tower in which Barbara was confined by her father, the lamb of St Agnes, St Dorothy's basket of flowers and, more gruesomely, St Agatha's breasts. (She was tortured by rods, rack and fire, and lastly her breasts were cut off – she had dedicated herself as a virgin to Christ.)

Agnes was another marriage-refuser – in this case a thirteen-year-old killed by a sword-thrust through her throat, who is quite often represented by this image. (She was the only saint to whom **Clare** made reference.) Dorothy too was executed for refusing to marry or to worship idols. The two positions are intertwined in these narratives: to refuse marriage with a non-Christian, tyrannical male, backed by the power of the state, *and* to refuse to give up one's beliefs, constituted a message of defiance against the *status quo* that 'heretics' such as **Marguerite Porete** and **Joan of Arc**, and those who did not fit in, such as Margery Kempe, could learn self-authentication from.

Saints, by the late Middle Ages, were seen as

> familiar and helping figures, to whom [the people] were connected by affective ties, based on actual/assumed membership of the same community – place, profession, social group. . . . [By the] late Middle Ages the cult of the saints had become so profoundly integrated into the life of society that it had become an essential part of life . . . overlapping [the] sacred and the profane.
>
> A. Vauchez, 'The saint'

As late as the 1530s the saints' images were being painted on the newly installed and often lavishly decorated rood-screens – their names, emblems and statues part of the refurbishing of the parish churches that reflected the prosperity of the period (see Eamon Duffy, *The Stripping of the Altars*).

Your silence and your strangeness submerge me.
It is good to be overwhelmed.
To be without words.
I leave to start again.

We close the door and walk back down the knoll, out into the marshy scrubland along the public footpath skirting the moat. Distantly, through the chestnut trees, for a few seconds, the fairy-tale crenellations of Wenham Castle tower rise up, then sink again into the obscuring green.

Questions continue to nudge me. Why does our Near-Eastern derived faith offer no images of dark-skinned saints? And how did it feel to be a peasant summoned to worship in a church emblazoned with such courtly images? We have a fair idea who provided them — but how were they read? Was this their model of the saints, of Mary, and of Jesus? Was for them the Almighty a *grand seigneur*? What kind of heavenly love reached them?

My mind goes back to **Julian of Norwich** and her 'even' Christians; to her vision of the world as the nut held in the palm of her hand; the homeliness of her metaphors; and then to the Beguines (see pp. 167–71), the women who pioneered lay spirituality eight hundred years ago; and I wonder about the meanings of religion, not to the lettered and articulate, the theologians and bishops, the men who have made the Church, but to the people whose Church it is, the ordinary women, children, and men.

In France or Spain or Italy, where **Rita of Cascia**, the patron of desperate causes, is still prayed to after six hundred years by women whose husbands are abusive, unfaithful, violent, unsupportive of their families — she is in some parts of Italy more popular than any other saint apart from the Blessed Virgin Mary — it is easier to grasp a little of popular conceptions. Attending a feria, one can lift a corner of the dusty curtain of Enlightenment prejudice and catch a glimpse of the heart of devotion still beating in the procession before which the whole town stops still, some dusty hot afternoon while the saint is carried shoulder-high and garlanded through the streets.

But in England or Wales, over the long centuries of Protestantism, in the stripped walls, the empty window niches, the smashed screens and decapitated images of the churches, it can be hard to quicken that heart.

SOURCES

The Vulgate version of the *Katherine Passion* (Cotton Titus D. xviii (BL)) *c.* 1200–1220, reproduced in A. Savage and N. Watson (trans. and intro), *Anchoritic Spirituality*. The legend dates from the ninth century, probably fuelled by the establishment of St Katherine's monastery at Petra with its associated legend of Katherine's body being borne there by angels. The *Katherine Passion* provides an exemplary account of the life and death of a saint – her courage, wisdom, discretion, the intimacy of her union with Christ, her imitation of Christ's suffering and death, all provide a model for medieval readers in whatever form of religious life, lay or clerical.

Main source: A. Savage and N. Watson (trans. and intro.), *Anchoritic Spirituality: Ancrene Wisse and Associated Works* (Paulist Press, New York, 1991).

A. M. Allchin, *Celtic Christianity: Fact or Fantasy* (Inaugural Lecture, University College of North Wales, Bangor, 1993).

Caroline Walker Bynum, *Fragmentation and Redemption: Essays on Gender and the Human Body in Medieval Religion* (Zone Books, New York, 1992).

E. J. Dobson, *The Origins of Ancrene Wisse* (Oxford University Press, Oxford, 1976).

Eamon Duffy, *Holy Maydens, Holy Wyfes: The Cult of Women Saints in Fifteenth and Sixteenth Century England* (Oxford University Press, Oxford, 1990).

Eamon Duffy, *The Stripping of the Altars: Traditional Religion in England 1400–1580* (Yale University Press, New Haven, 1992).

Jacques Le Goff (ed.), *The Medieval World*, trans. Lydia Cochrane (Collins & Brown, London, 1990).

A. Vauchez, 'The saint', in Jacques Le Goff (ed.), *The Medieval World*, trans. Lydia Cochrane (Collins & Brown, London, 1990).

Jacob de Voragine, *Legenda Aurea* [*The Golden Legend*], trans. William Caxton (London, 1878).

Pilgrimage: Tobar na Molt, Ardfert, Co. Kerry

❧

'Between the mystery and the absurdity lies the numinous.'

Guarding the shrine is a duty she undertakes, shrugging – yes, she whitewashed the hut, keeps the turf, did we fasten the gate, the cattle get through. A cosmopolitan Irishwoman, perhaps seventy, active and upright in bearing. No big deal, she could have said, forty years in London, no aura of the insider, the keeper of the mysteries. She dismisses payment of 50 pence. Are you Catholic?

I want to say yes. Too complicated. Deliver the short untruthful answer that obeys the categories. No, we're Protestant.

Wanting to say, we're Catholic, Anglican not Roman.

'The major festivals of the shrine are the Saturday before St John's day – the Saturday before Michaelmas – the Saturday before May 1st. The round is paid in the following way. Oh, next month we have a nun, a Protestant from America. She rang up. She is bringing a party and the MP from Dublin. She is Protestant but she wants to come, bringing a big party.'

We nod. 'Thank you.'

Continue our way.

The lanes criss-crossed. The shrine was not signposted. Across the fields exactly as the young man had described. If you did not know you could not find it. Hidden, arcane knowledge.

The ground falls away from the lane, the rich Kerry fields drop down into marsh spattered with stumpy blades of young flag irises.

In the oval enclosure the turf is short-cropped, a briar bush with one red ribbon caught in it blows bent in the wind. Sweet pungent hawthorns deck it. Beside a scummy, stagnant pool – a small freshly whitewashed stone hut. Dried swabs of the whitewash garland the hedgerow.

Ita (Ide): died c.570
Teacher, 'foster-mother of the saints of Ireland'
Feast: 15 January

IDE'S WISH

'I will take nothing from my Lord . . . unless He gives me His Son from Heaven in the form of a baby to be nursed by me.'

So Christ came to her in the form of a baby, and she said then:

Little Jesus, Who is nursed by me in my little hermitage, even a priest with store of wealth, all is false but little Jesus . . .. Sons of princes, sons of kings, though they come to my land, not from them do I expect any good, I prefer little Jesus.

Sing a chorus, maidens, to the One Who has a right to your little tribute; He is in His place on high, though as little Jesus He is on my breast.

Author Irish, anon. (?ninth century), in K. H. Jackson, *A Celtic Miscellany*

The devotion to the Christ-child was a feature of many medieval women mystics. (See also **Clare.**)

Apart from **Brigit of Kildare**, Ita is probably the most famous woman saint of Ireland. She is said to have been of royal origin, born near Waterford, and was originally called Deirdre. She moved to Killeedy (Limerick) where she founded a small nunnery and lived for the rest of her life. Her spiritual life was like that of other Irish ascetics, much devoted to prayer and fasting.

An Irish lullaby for the Infant Jesus is attributed to her. As with many of the saints, her *Life* was written some centuries after her death. She is also mentioned in Alcuin's poem on the Irish saints. Her cult is still alive today in the localities associated with her, like many other Celtic saints. (See **Gobnet.**)

Wind and birds. Words and stone. Text and cross. Three small crudely carved figures of the Irish holy family of saints, their features squashed by the elements through thirteen centuries and more. Erc the bishop as father, Brendan the navigator as child, Ide/Ita the teacher as mother. Families long before priests must be celibate.

Beyond, neat modern figures of the holy family, gaudy in their glass-fronted niches like souvenirs of Blackpool, Knock or Lourdes. Further on a low mound on which rests a white-painted board – gloss this time – in childish lettering – 'St Ita's Grave'.

Whose words are recollected through the fame of those she taught.
Like Hild. As women's are.
The door of the hut stands open. We read the texts propped on benches, stuck to the walls.

'Exiled while all the while the door stood open.'

To take part I am bidden.
Why. I've no idea.
The water in the well is scummy, unappealing. A few coins dot its bottom.
And yet I cross myself. Watch myself cross myself.
And yet I prostrate myself before the old stone altar.
Watch myself prostrate myself.
It is not my culture and I walk the round.
As I can, I do, remember.

Hail Mary, Queen of Heaven, blessed art thou among women. Jesus Christ, son of the living God, nursling of the most holy Saint Brigit, of Ide and of Clare. Have mercy upon me a sinner.

Words learned, words rehearsed, words lodged somewhere below consciousness. Occupy the mind like rhyme, like rhythm.
Beneath, something budges. A small heaviness. A micro-shift.
Whose weight exhausts.
Drains the body.

For the rest of the journey out of the county I sleep fitfully, cradled by the car's jolting over the potholes.

When he was two . . . Brendan was removed to Killeedy, where St Ita took him in charge. She herself had founded the nunnery, and it is told of her that she had, besides her high measure of sanctity, a fair knowledge of the world's backsliders through girls who made renunciation a passing phase.

Brendan . . . learned from Ita . . . the things that were most displeasing to God — hating others, embracing evil, and trusting riches; and those which found his favour — steadfast belief in him, the simple life, and generous charity. He absorbed self-control by example; Ita kept an enormous stag-beetle on her body as perpetual chastening.

Brendan Lehane, *Early Celtic Christianity*

The amount that we do know about Ita contrasts with the virtual absence of information about many other early Celtic women saints such as **Gobnet,** and even **Melangell.** This is a direct result of her having fostered and schooled Brendan, who is a major saint in Ireland. Similarly, in the early Christian period, saints such as Paula are known through their connection with Jerome.

It would be interesting to calculate the number of women saints whose name and approximate date/location only are known. It happened, of course, to many of the male saints too, for in the early centuries before the processes of sanctification were settled, under the reforms of Alexander III and Innocent III following on from those of Pope Gregory, minor saints tended to have a very local attachment. Unless the legend was taken up and promoted by the Church, as happened with St Brigit, the lesser saints' stories were lost.

Descriptions of Ita, as of **Brigit,** recall those of the Virgin Mary, and the old altar at Tobar na Molt is said to depict the three Irish saints as a Holy Family triptych.

Dreaming to connect.

Maybe the losses. Maybe the fogs the confusions the clarities the dumbness the tears. Maybe a tumbling hope?

Is this too pilgrimage?

In the dark. Waiting.

It was in sequel to the abandonment of the twenty-foot fishing boat.

Earlier, in twelve-foot seas we went to make our real pilgrimage, out in the Atlantic to reach the earliest Celtic monastery with intact oratories and cells, on the two-hundred-foot pinnacle of rock, seven miles out. The boat in its rocking waves bobbing like a child's toy, the engine stuttering, grinding on past the guillemots, into the narrow rock-bound cove of Sceilig Michael, beating against the narrow jetty. Up the wind-battered cliff-hung two thousand three hundred vertiginous steps to the plateau on which they chose to live and praise God.

A pilgrimage I never wish to make again, bruising my faith in boats, tipped me headlong into sickened prayer cast out in Jonah's ocean.

> *Fanatics have their dreams.*
> Those monks.
> Their unreasonable, unswerving conviction.
> Trapped, and tossed me briefly in its tempest.
> Their conviction mirrored in their whorled walnut-
>   whip stone cell forms still tightly coiled against
>   rain and storm, unshaken after 1,300 years.
>
> Dear God no.
> Leave me safely on the dry land by grass and stream
>   and copse and hill.
> Do not ever ask me to hurl myself again against
>   your monstrous sea.
> Teach me off course to wait.
> And let the next of the steps carved out of nothing,
>   through your mercy, St Ide, not be hung between
>   sea and sky.
> Your beauty and your summons, Lord.
> Water may be my sign, but I am earth.
> Leave me to earth . . .

✤ Ita ✤

SOURCES

Mary Condren, *The Serpent and the Goddess: Women, Religion and Power in Celtic Ireland* (Harper & Row, San Francisco, 1989).

K. H. Jackson (sel. and trans.), *A Celtic Miscellany: Translations from the Celtic Literatures* (Penguin, 1971).

Brendan Lehane, *Early Celtic Christianity*, 2nd edn (Constable, London, 1994).

Seeking perpetual felicity

❧

In the late nineteenth and early twentieth centuries a quantum leap occurred that shattered the comfortable assurances of Newtonian 'truth'. It was the amazing synthesis of previously separate areas of thought/investigation. The sciences of electricity and magnetism merged: chemistry was engulfed by atomic physics. Biologists uncovered electro-chemical processes within living matter. The previously independent 'powers of nature' were seen to be convertible into one another. They were simply different forms of energy. Soon matter went the same way: the building blocks themselves became nothing but particles of compressed energy . . . .

The objective observer was added to the list of post-nuclear fatalities. The presence of the observer and the instruments of investigation actually affect the behaviour of some particles. Space expands in a strong gravitational field. Time slows down in a strong gravitational field. The basic ingredients of the material universe refuse bondage with the traditional either/or boundaries of dichotomous thought.

The contemporary scientific revolution has effected the dissolution of one of the most extensive superstitious myths of the age: the materialistic, clockwork universe.

But perhaps all this need not be considered on the old true/false scale of dichotomies and polarities. Perhaps it can be used merely to suspend our disbeliefs temporarily.

❧

Vibia Perpetua is twenty-two years old. She is nursing her first baby. When he cries her breasts respond, magically, which is both satisfying and embarrassing. He feeds on her body, and he helps her understand. When she is away from him for more than a few hours her

152

Perpetua of Carthage: d. 203
Martyr
Feast: 7 March

The title opposite comes from a sermon of Augustine of Hippo (354–430) on the Feast Day of Perpetua and Felicity, which, in one of his less attractive rhetorical (and sexist) flourishes, he concluded: 'The weakness of women more marvellously did vanquish the ancient enemy, and the strength of men [their companions] contended to win a perpetual felicity.'

Perpetua was martyred in AD 203 in Carthage, under the persecution of Diocletian, with Felicity, a slave, and four male companions. Augustine preached on her feast and Tertullian mentioned her visions. Felicity and she were inserted into the canon of the Roman Catholic Mass from very early times. Not much more was known about her for several centuries, but in 1688 her *Passio* was discovered among some other manuscripts originating from Monte Cassino. This *Passio*, whose authenticity is not challenged, is the earliest writing by a Christian woman still extant (cf. *The Martyrdom of Perpetua*, trans. W. H. Shewring). It is a remarkable and moving document, covering both the chronology of martyrdom and some prophetic dreams that Perpetua received while in prison. All *facts* recorded in the story, unless otherwise mentioned, are drawn from the *Passio.*

The implications for feminist theology of modern scientific understandings – both as metaphor and as material record of the works of creation – are profound. This opening page is a paraphrase from an essay by Nancy Passmore in *The Politics of Women's Spirituality*. See also Sara Maitland, *A Big-Enough God.*

Vibia, here, is a family name (Roman society put patronyms first). Only high-class Roman and provincial citizens used these names; it is one of the clues we have to Perpetua's social status. Others emerge in the text, e.g. on p. 20 (all page numbers are from the Shewring edition: see above) she is

breasts grow heavy and hard, painful. He needs her and she, therefore, needs him. She loves her son, ignores her husband, respects her mother and hates her father. She is beautiful, nobly born, highly articulate and very well educated. She is used to being admired and getting her own way; but despite this she is often frightened. When she is frightened she becomes even more articulate, protecting her fear, which she despises, with a bright certainty which others find convincing. If you like her you say she has natural leadership potential, or what a pity she wasn't a boy. If you don't like her you say she is a bossy show-off. When she knows that the stage is set for her own martyrdom she thinks, rightly, that she is very young to die, but also, rightly, that she will look fabulous in the arena.

Vibia Perpetua keeps a journal. It is not altogether honest. She knows it will not be read until after her death, until she has become a martyr. It will be a testament of her passion; it will be read by the congregations along the Mediterranean coast and up in Greece and the islands. Perhaps even in Jerusalem or Rome. She knows this so clearly that, although she means to be honest, she cannot avoid a certain self-consciousness, a certain reconstruction of herself so that she looks like a saint and martyr of the Church. She knows, for instance, that she did not speak to her father with quite the bold certainty, the high-bred impertinence, the elegant wit, that she records. She knows that when they took her child away her breasts ached and dripped and spoiled her tunic. She does not know if the child, like her, wept and whimpered through the night. But somehow whimpers and damp soggy patches down her front do not shape the narrative in an appropriate direction. She wants there to be some point to her sad demise and the point will be the edification of Christians throughout the Empire who will not really be too edified by the inconveniences of sudden weaning.

Felicity is different. Felicity is silent. Obstinate. There comes a point, she has come to believe, where only sullenness will work. There comes a point when you just have to hunker down in grim sullenness, not answer back, not respond, just lurk in the deep cave of your own silence, and endure. It will be enough, just; and it will be everything.

Felicity is pregnant with a child she does not want. She has stepped outside the condition of her own slavery to assert her right to believe in a god in whom there is neither slave nor free. It is an enormous effort laying claim to such a new

described as 'nobly born, liberally educated and honorably married'. Her father is permitted to visit her in prison, to try and persuade her to make the necessary sacrifices. (Apart from the phrase above, her husband is never once mentioned.)

Perpetua records two splendid encounters with her father (pp. 20 and 23–4), the latter during her formal trial. Her child was taken away from her when she was arrested; returned for a while when 'the prison was made a palace for me' (p. 21). Her father took the baby away after the formal conviction and would not allow her to have him back. She passes over this last occasion rather briskly, recording only some slightly flimsy-sounding thanksgivings.

Passions, like epistles, were used liturgically. One still extant and earlier than Perpetua's makes this clear. *The Passion of Polycarp* (c. 69–155), written by his congregation, is in the form of an epistle directed to fellow churches. There were probably others. The introductions to both Passions make it clear that the compilers intend and expect them to be read aloud.

Perpetua is, inevitably, the central character not only of the journal but also of the introduction and conclusion which were edited on to her own text, at much the same time. The feast, however, commemorated both women; and we do learn something about the other companions. Felicity (the only other woman) and Revocatus were both slaves. Perpetua, these two, Saturninus and Secundulus were arrested together: they were all catechumens (trainee Christians) and not yet baptized. They were later joined voluntarily by Saturus, who seems to have been their Deacon, or instructor. He baptized them in prison and they received communion – the 'love feast' (rather neatly contrasted to the 'free feast' usually granted to prisoners on their last night (p. 31) – the night before they died). Felicity was pregnant.

There is nothing overt in the *Passio* to suggest the tensions in the relationship between Perpetua and Felicity that I have developed. However, Perpetua does omit all mention of Felicity's childbirth – which is described by the editor as 'grace' on equal terms with Perpetua's visions. In fact, although Perpetua mentions all the other companions by name at least once, she does not mention Felicity at all.

possibility. She has to burrow into the inside of her own silence and hug herself there. There is nothing else.

She also leaves things out when she cannot quite understand them. She did not agree with the others when they decided to pray for Felicity's premature labour. She cannot but feel that Felicity does not have the right to risk the life of her child just in order to get martyred. Despite her boldness, she is a daughter of the ruling élite, she believes the children of slaves are precious. And secretly she is rather proud that 'her' Empire is too civilized to send pregnant women to the arena. Even more secretly she would rather like to be the only woman in the expedition.

Moreover she finds the whole thing rather vulgar. Noisy prayer and a certain amount of oil, wine and emetic, followed by a screamingly painful labour supported by the companions offering advice that can have been acquired only in brothels. She senses that Felicity does not like her, that Felicity sees through her and may even be laughing at her. So none of this gets recorded in the journal, though she knows it should be.

About the dreams, though, Perpetua is honest. She knows that dreams do not belong to the dreamer but to God. She records them with care.

For three weeks they are in prison. Perpetua and Felicity kneel back to back in the darkness and everything is taken away from them. Their babies are taken away: Perpetua's by her doting family; Felicity's by the unloving guards. The one thing Perpetua truly loved, the one thing Felicity truly hated. There is nothing in this new space except the dark. There is nothing except their resistance to each other. No, no, they will not give up their dislike. They will not move towards each other. It is their last stand, their last claim, their last privilege. They refuse. Perpetua dreams her dreams and declares her visions. Felicity clings to her own secret silence.

They cling to their hatred and neither will comfort the other.

The night before they die, something changes. The change begins, rightly, with a joke. Saturus, suddenly shamefaced as a child, admits that he is shit scared of bears. He is horrified, terrified, appalled, rendered senseless and pathetic, by bears. He knows absolutely that he cannot die bravely if he is obliged to be killed by a bear. What can he

Imperial law in this period protected pregnant women from the arena (only for the duration of their pregnancy). Apart from an attempt to preserve certain humane standards, this may have been affected by a worrying fall in the Empire's population: children (especially those of citizens) were highly valued, by both individuals and the State.

Worried that she would be left to suffer alone later, the companions decided to pray for a premature labour for Felicity. This was successful. She then gave birth, harrowingly, in a public gaol, mocked by the wardens, to a daughter who was raised by her sister (pp. 29–30).

The dreams: very nearly half of Perpetua's own text describes the dream-visions that she was receiving throughout this time. They were clearly expected and anticipated by her friends. Her brother (who seems also to have been a catechumen) asks her to ask God for a dream before the trial, so they can know whether they will have 'a deliverance or a passion' (p. 21). The whole community are satisfied that her dream response will be authorized. Perpetua's dreams are very vivid. In the one in answer to her brother's question she walks across the body of a dragon in order to get access to a ladder (which itself was festooned with wonderfully Freudian phallic symbols – sword, spears, hooks, etc.). She successfully climbs the ladder, arrives in a garden and is given a chunk of sheep's milk curd to eat by a welcoming white-headed shepherd (which she received 'with cupped hands' – practically the only direct Christian symbolism in any of her dreams, if indeed it is reference to the eucharistic celebration and reception).

Even more fascinating is her last dream, 'the day before we fought' (p. 26): she entered an arena and was commanded to fight with a 'giant Egyptian'. She was aided by some 'beautiful young men' who stripped and oiled her, and she '*became a man*' (cf. **Joan of Arc**, *et al.*: it is sometimes depressing how necessary it was to women, throughout the Church's history, to assume maleness in order to act with physical courage). She wrestled with the giant and ended victoriously dancing on his head. They are wonderful, and very authentic-feeling, dream reports. Marie-Louise von Franz has submitted them to a highly provocative Jungian analysis (*The Passion of Perpetua*, Jungian Classic Series).

Equally interesting, historically, is the way they are used by the presenter/editor: see his introduction (*Passio*, p. 19), and most particularly his conclusion, p. 35 – where he deliberately equates this witness and the

do? They pray for a leopard for him. They pray not simply for a not-bear, but quite specifically for a leopard. For his peace of mind and for their honour they ask the enormous and unnameable God, for whom they will die in the morning, to let Saturus be killed by a spotty cat. It makes them laugh.

Somewhere in the laughter, in the silliness and the sadness of it all, Perpetua and Felicity find each other. Because nothing matters any more. Or because everything does. Or both.

So next morning they march into the arena as friends, holding hands, united in love. They are singing and their songs are the songs of freedom and of friendship. 'We came here willingly,' says Perpetua for both of them, and she has been practising this speech for three weeks, 'willingly, so that our freedom may not be obscured.' We are free, she declares, while their post-partum, dripping women's bodies cause an unwelcome disturbance to the ogling crowd. 'For this cause, for freedom, we have dedicated our lives.'

We have come here willingly, so that our freedom may not be obscured.

Freedom, Felicity knows, but does not say, freedom consists of voices that have been broken and blood that has been spilled. Freedom tastes of pain.

There is the crowd. The soldiers. Bears and wild cats and boars. And a leopard – oh yes. A mad cow tosses the women, but holding hands they help each other to their feet. They sing, they are still singing. They are led to the place of execution. They exchange a kiss. It is called the kiss of peace, but for both of them now it is a kiss of love and anticipation.

Their throats are cut.

Felicity, stubborn to the last, consents to die.

Perpetua, flamboyant to the last, insists on assisting her incompetent and pain-inflicting executioner with his job. She points with her elegant finger to the precise point on her neck where the axe-man should direct his blow. At the very final moment she knows she cannot look at Felicity's still-twitching decapitated trunk, so she has to talk. It is painful for the poor young executioner and she recognizes this though without too much guilt. Her last wish is that she were brave enough not to need to score points off a conscripted youth's social shame, brave enough not to have to show off. It is too late even for that.

visions with those of the biblical canon and regards them as coming directly from the Holy Spirit, with such enthusiasm that it has led many people to suspect that he – and possibly the martyrs themselves, whose names are enshrined in the centre of 'orthodoxy', the Canon of the Mass – may in fact have been heretics – Montanists (cf. **Maximilla** for an explanation of Montanism and its significance for women). However, it should be noted that dreams were given prophetic standing in the Acts of the Apostles also.

Passio, p. 32. Perpetua was arguing that she and the rest could not be asked to wear, for mockery, the costumes of the priestesses of Ceres, goddess of fertility (or in the men's case the priests of Saturn), since it was for the freedom to deny such gods' existence that they were there in the first place. 'Injustice acknowledged justice' and they were stripped. This disturbed the crowd because Felicity was so obviously post-partum. They were finally supplied with 'loose robes'.

Amnesty International poster (1982).

Saturus was indeed dispatched by a leopard. The bear they meant to set on him lurked in its den and refused to come out (p. 33)! I do not understand quite why a mad cow was so particularly insulting to women, but the text makes clear that this was the devil's work, deliberately to 'mock their sex' (p. 33). By custom, if the wild animals proved inefficient and the victims survived enough mauling, they would eventually be executed in the arena itself, so the crowd could watch to the end. In the interval they were allowed to be comforted by their friends at what were called the 'gates of life'.

It may be the fact that Felicity died first which gives her priority in the eucharistic Canon. ('Felicity and Perpetua' it reads. Other experts think that it may in fact refer to a different Felicity. I hope not.)

Passio, p. 35: 'Perchance so great a woman could not else have been slain (being feared of the unclean spirit) had she not herself so willed it.'

As she travels out, goes away, returns home, dies, I want to call to her:

Sweet sisters, I want to call out, sweet sisters, what is this clarity? What is this eager embrace? Give me your strong knowledge, your strong embrace of death. Give it to me, I beg them, but there is no answer. They have gone to a new place. They live and love and do and be as human people in a social world that is charged and changed, transformed, remembered, reinvented by the promise of resurrection and the recognition of presence. They are pierced to the heart and made alive with the consciousness of God, the love of Christ, and the power of choice. In the moment of their turning, in the moment of their turning to each other, in the darkness, when everything else had been taken away. Then, there, at that moment, in that space, they became free women. I want what they have, and it is so strong and sweet that death has no more dominion but becomes one more thing to be embraced . . . ah, sweet lover, when no other love remains, the ecstasy of love, the horns of the cow, an easy way, perhaps, from there, once you are there, an easy route to hypostatic union and simple sisterhood.

They bleed to death on the hot sand of the arena.

They are singing, rejoicing, praising. They have gone to a place where I want to be; where I want to be and yet which I mistrust, which I fear. I want them to tell me, to embrace me, to enfold me, to take me there, there to the gates of heaven and hell, where the martyrs sing the victory songs. So sweet, so easy, so tuneful, graceful, final. Ecstasy. Oh the sweet draining and the high spout of blood as the jugular is severed and fear is drowned in the red fountain, washed white in the blood of the lamb.

> It was a long, long time ago. But remember, time is relative and slows down, relatively, in a strong gravitational field.

> They were just two obscure women, in a small provincial town in north Africa. But remember, space is relative, and expands, relatively, in a strong gravitational field.

The *Passio* concludes, as it commenced, with a sort of hymn in praise of martyrdom.

O most valiant and blessed martyrs! O truly called and elected into the glory of Our Lord Jesus Christ! Anyone who magnifies, honours and adores this glory ought to read these witnesses likewise, as being no less than the old, unto the Church's edification; that these new wonders may also testify that one and the same Holy Spirit works ever until now, and with Him God the Father Almighty, and His son Jesus Christ Our Lord, to Whom is glory and power unending for ever and ever. Amen.

Passio, p. 35

So have I. But I am not easy with celebrating the suffering of women – the contexts of masochism. On the one hand, to be prepared to 'go the distance'; to recognize the personal cost, the damage to oneself of lying, or denying love – which is always offered as one of the central reasons for 'coming out' sexually, for instance – remains a 'requirement' of courage; though, on the whole, we do not get tossed by savage cows and then executed – or indeed physically tortured in any direct way. Would we expect this of each other's commitment to honesty? Should women's martyrdom for their own sense of truth be seen, admiringly, as one extreme end of a continuum of courageous honesty? On the other hand, a good deal too much hagiography has been littered by ecstatic rapture in the suffering itself, and particularly in a sort of salacious detailing of the physical agonies of women – including by the women themselves. The genre is littered with individuals (of both sexes, though predominantly women) who seem to have organized their whole lives around a greed for violence and death – and the Church has rewarded them with sanctity, canonization. Hagiography is also littered, it should be said, by individuals who pursued bold and joyous courses through life and met death merrily on their way to do something else; and with high-principled people, whose understanding of the destruction of selfhood that comes about through not telling the truth caused them to look death straight in its mean eyes and find it preferable to capitulation. There remains, however, a strain of ecstatic lust for martyrdom which could well be described as masochistic, and a determination in many hagiographers to emphasize this element in the lives of women (cf., e.g., **Rose of Lima, Katherine of Alexandria**). One reason why the *Passio* seems important is because it is a woman's own explanation of what she is up to – and clearly Perpetua at least has no manic enthusiasm

Their love and their life-blood have created a field
strong enough.

It is finished. It is beginning.
They bleed to death on the hot dry sand of the arena. They
rejoice. The Church rejoices. Am I rejoicing?

for torture – it is just an unfortunate consequence of faith. This whole issue of martyrdom and masochism raises crucial questions for women: how would it be, for instance, if God was not male and therefore did not, imaginatively, claim women as heterosexual brides, in patriarchal marriages? (Cf. Sara Maitland, 'Passionate prayer: masochistic images in women's experience', in Linda Hurcombe (ed.), *Sex and God*.) How should we 'rejoice' over the courageous death of women?

Loing-Près

'and who hath God hath al
this soule hath God in hir bi divine grace.'

We do not know the date of your birth
We only know the date of your death.
We know you were called Beguina,
from Hainault, or Hainaut,
We do not know the details of your life
All we know is the date of your death.

Can a book kill a woman?
In winter when small birds hop
disparaging the ice
just this side of survival
these are lean times
for radicals

The woman writer holds a mirror
revolutionary courage
to stare out the glass
what no one wants to be shown
you hold on to your stubborn thought

You pledged your life
wagered silence to trudge for
Great Church's eternity
watching
they wept for you, your
intransigent vision

Marguerite Porete / Margarita de Hannonia (d. 1310)
Mystic, writer, martyr, declared heretic for her teachings in
Le Mirouer des Simples Ames (The Mirror of Simple Souls)
and burned at the stake

'Loing-Près', Far-Near, is Porete's paradoxical term for God. The quotation is from the medieval version of *Le Mirouer*, in Peter Dronke, *Women Writers of the Middle Ages*, and the poem 'Love, what do you wish of me?' is from the same source, adapted by Wendy Mulford.

Margarita de Hannonia came from Hainaut, in southern Flanders. The only known biographical fact is that she was burned as a relapsed heretic at the stake in Paris in 1310 for her writings and teachings.

Her judges referred to her as a 'beguine'.

Some time between 1296 and 1306 her work *Le Mirouer des Simples Ames* (*The Mirror of Simple Souls*) was declared heretical and publicly burned; Marguerite was forbidden to write and spread her doctrines. She appeared before the papal authorities in 1306/7 accused of heresy, and was imprisoned for eighteen months in Paris. She refused to recant. Her main heresy lay in refusing the Church's ultimate authority.

Marguerite was an educated woman. She taught that the soul could be so united with God that it was annihilated – which was unacceptable to the Church as it rendered its intervention unnecessary. Once so united, she taught that the soul was sinless and had no need for penance. Her treatise, she said, was dictated to her by Love, who in the dialogue is questioned by Reason. It is Love that teaches the soul its way to perfect union. Theologians and other clerics, she says,

> *Will not have any understanding of it,*
> *So learnèd are your minds,*
> *If you do not proceed humbly*
> *And Love and Faith together,*
> *The mistresses of the house,*
> *Do not cause you to surmount Reason.*

wedded to a Love they dare not risk
tough, recalcitrant,
political in your hope
like those who in this century sang
their lives away to tattered flesh
in Chile, in South Africa,
in Burma, El Salvador,
scorched and raped, fought and sang

We do not know the date of your birth.
We know you were a Beguine from Hainaut.
The date we know is the date of your death.

It was not the manner of your life
your organizing amongst the workers
your message of liberation
to an oppressed people
that killed you
you were not a Rosa Luxemburg
a Ruth First,
your cutting vision came
from Love transformed

Mystic, apostle, you spread your message
throughout North Europe after
your death anonymously
in secret the religious
studied your teachings

'Little holy church' cancelled your life
for a book, a mystical treatise,
a debate
between Lady Love, Lady Reason,
and the Free Soul

A debate lit the faggots for the bonfire of your life
Your silence and your courage released your words

THE BEGUINES

The beguines appear to have originated in Belgium, and while their name came to be synonymous with heresy they were in fact both popular and influential in their time. Many affinities have been noted between the spirituality and life-styles of the beguines, the Humiliati in Italy, and other lay women who settled in groups apart to lead a religious life at the turn of the twelfth and thirteenth centuries, during the time of great spiritual revival which also saw the birth of the new mendicant orders of the Dominican and Franciscan friars. Beguine lives were communal, giving up their own households, dedicated to prayer and to the service of others, particularly in nursing the sick and in teaching. They also supported themselves through weaving, bleaching, carding, spinning, lace-work, embroidery and other occupations.

Beguines could be single, married or widowed and made only informal temporary vows, including usually one of celibacy, while they remained in the beguinage, which they might leave at any time. The movement arose because of the unwillingness of established convents to take in the large number of widowed and unmarried women, and the high price of their dowries. While there were a number of beghards, or men who followed the beguine life, their numbers were never so significant, and all the major communities were of women.

Contemporary reactions such as that of the priest, later cardinal and member of the curia, Jacques de Vitry, biographer of Mary of Oignies, one of the most notable beguines for her sanctity and her visions, were almost universally favourable. The beguines were praised as being 'in the midst of worldly people . . . spiritual, in the midst of pleasure seekers . . . pure and in the midst of noise and confusion they led a serene eremitical life' (Fiona Bowie and Oliver Davies (eds), *Beguine Spirituality*).

By the mid-thirteenth century women who called themselves beguines were to be found right across Europe from Spain to the Low Countries and from France to Hungary. They attracted powerful support from some of the nobility and from Louis XI of France, as well as many bishops and clergy, and Jacques de Vitry succeeded in winning the verbal approval of Pope Honorius III in 1216.

Inevitably, before long their success bred suspicion, since the beguine communities were examples not only of *uncontrolled* women, but also of

We do not know the date of your birth
We do not know the facts of your life
We think you were a beguine from Hainaut
We only know the date of your death
The first of June in the year of Our Lord
Thirteen hundred and ten

❧

Love, what do you wish of me?

❧

L ove, what do you wish of me?
   I contain all that was and all that will be
Everything fulfils itself in me
Take of me whatever you wish
Whatever you desire I will not refuse

Love tell me what is it you wish of me?
I am Love in which everything is fulfilled
The thing that you long for
We long for too. Love
Tell us your naked desire

women who must have seemed to many of those connected with the religious life to be both having their cake and eating it, and thriving while they did so. Clerical opposition was fuelled too by often outspoken criticism of the Church from amongst the beguines; this was the major strand in the Church's determination to silence Marguerite Porete – her disregard of the human institution, Holy Church, which she renamed 'Little Church', in contrast to the 'Great Church' which was God's own Church, freely available to everyone. Soon, as in Marguerite's case, beguines were accused of holding the heresy of the 'Free Spirit' – that it was possible through inward grace to attain perfection without the aid of the Church. The more threats to its authority the Church perceived, the more the accusations (and quickly the persecutions) grew. At the Council of Vienne in 1313 the beguines were condemned by the Pope, barely one hundred years after Honorius granted his approval of them.

This was the context in which Marguerite Porete was declared a heretic and burned at the stake three years before the Council.

The character of the beguine initiative which makes them of particular interest today to women who are drawn to a religious life with other women but who do not wish to enter a religious institution is that there was no set pattern to their life. The patterns of the beguine communities evolved, free from the restrictions of monastic enclosure, according to the local conditions wherever the groups sprang up. There was no hierarchy, and each community developed its own rules to meet its own needs, so that for example the balance between study, prayer and contemplation and charitable activity varied between each community.

Beguine communities were often granted land to build on, or bequeathed land themselves in their wills for that purpose. By the beginning of the fourteenth century there were a number of settled beguine convents, still maintaining the balance between service, manual work and contemplation, but the pattern of life varied widely, especially between countries.

The beguines also took in other women, widows and unmarried women, who paid rent, as well as their own female relatives, so that the community could become a quite extensive network of women. Houses might be built by families or patrons for women who wanted to join the beguinage, and the young women who came brought their own household possessions. Vows of poverty were not taken, since beguines did not see poverty as an end in itself, the main virtues they promulgated being charity, humility and companionship. Their dedication was a simple one, in effect to serve the Lord Jesus Christ, as a beguine, and to live religiously. Gradually a form of novitiate developed in some countries, whereby an older beguine would train the young aspiring one for a year or two, and some form of habit evolved, although the main emphasis remained on living simply and without ostentation.

Beguines had their own spiritual directors and chaplains, often Dominicans or Cistercians; they attended mass daily and had a regular schedule of divine office, prayers, readings, lectures, confession, penance and the observance of feasts.

In the quality of their independence and the breadth of their differing experiments in communal living the beguines can well be seen as forerunners of the women's movement. They refused easy classification, as nuns, wives or mothers, and in the conduct of their women-only communities ran counter to the assumptions of their times. That they were not easily assimilated is shown by the fact that they experienced a renascence in the seventeenth century, at least in Belgium.

They offered a cultural context, albeit a diffuse one, in which the spirituality of women as diverse as Mary of Oignies, Mechthild of Magdeburg and Ida of Nivelles could develop. The writings that came from this background provide a rich source of insights into the forms of medieval women's intense spirituality.

SOURCES

Fiona Bowie and Oliver Davies (eds), *Beguine Spirituality* (SPCK, London, 1990).

Peter Dronke, *Women Writers of the Middle Ages* (Cambridge University Press, Cambridge, 1984).

E. W. McDonnell, *The Beguines and Beghards in Medieval Culture* (New Brunswick, NY, 1954).

Amy Oden (ed.), *In Her Words: Women's Writings in the History of Christian Thought* (SPCK, London, 1995).

Katherine Wilson (ed.), *Medieval Women Writers* (Manchester University Press, Manchester, 1984).

A letter to Dorothy Day

❧

~~Salve Beata,~~
~~Dearest Dorothy,~~
~~Dear Dorothy Day,~~
Dear Ms Day,

You were to be one of the treats of writing this book: I was giving myself – among other things – a chance to get to know you better.

I thought you would be a teacher for me. I thought you would explain how to renounce the bourgeois self, how to identify with the poor, how to be a Catholic and a socialist pacifist, how to enter into a life of prayer which was grounded in radical socialist politics and genuine love. I had been inspired – haven't so many of us? – by your work.

For those who are sitting on park benches in the warm spring sunlight. For those who are huddling in shelters trying to escape the rain. For those who are walking the streets in the all but futile search for work. For those who think there is no hope for the future, no recognition of their plight – this little paper is addressed. It is printed to call their attention to the fact that the Catholic Church has a social program – to let them know that there are men of God who are working not only for their spiritual, but for their material welfare.

You will probably laugh at me, but I thought we might even be friends. I thought, given the things we share, that we might end up one night, after I had opened my tawdry soul to you and you had lovingly exposed my own triviality to me and explained and inspired and moved me (recognizing, of course, that underneath, I was really one of those people you said you wanted to meet, 'who really felt that God was a devouring fire, and that they were ready to cast themselves into the flames in seach of him'), we might end up giggling and I would ask you whether it was really true that you had attended a

Dorothy Day: 1897–1980
Founder of the Catholic Worker Movement

'Greetings, Holy Woman'. 'Beata' was the term used by her friends and disciples to describe **Catherine of Siena** during her lifetime.

After a period of being a communist journalist and a bohemian, Day converted to Roman Catholicism in 1927. In 1933 she (with Peter Maurin) founded a monthly newspaper in New York dedicated to fighting communism with a positive Catholic programme of social reconstruction: the *Catholic Worker*. Day described the paper at different times as personalist, anarchist, pacifist, communitarian or radical. The quotation is from the first editorial (*Catholic Worker* I, May 1933). From the paper a movement developed, which unquestionably influenced the whole development of US Catholicism and immigrant identity. It urged total identification with the poor, as Christs. Although 'the whole enterprise was riddled with contradiction. An enormously strong-willed woman, Day came to espouse one of the most abject brands of self-abnegation in American religious history' (J. T. Fisher, *The Catholic Counter Culture in America 1933–1962*, pp. 1–2). Day has become something of a heroine to socialist Christians; and although her canonization by the Catholic Church would not seem to have a snowball's chance, she is one of the women adopted by feminists as a Cause. In some ways this is a little strange, since – in ecclesial terms – she was neither liberal nor radical.

Rather improbably the work and ideas of Huysman were very influential in relation to Day's thought, or at least its atmosphere. He was a leading decadent writer (*À Rebours* (1884) remains the exemplary art-for-art's-sake novel). At the same time he had an obsession with spirituality in the

Black Mass with Huysman in Paris in the early 1920s? and why, for God's sake, you called your daughter Tamar? It is a pretty enough name, of course, but were you thinking of the young widow who pretended to be a prostitute and seduced her father-in-law, or of the raped princess?

Now, quite frankly, I feel conned.

You are just one more medieval saint, born in a wrong time, a leper-kisser, a quietist, a life-hating death-lover, a decadent romantic with a radical vocabulary, an adorer of masochistic suffering as the root of the loss of self and the mystical dissolution into the crucified Christ.

Damn.

Listen to yourself:

Half the children in juvenile courts are Catholic. Yet the population is only one-third Catholic. You will say, 'Catholics are poor.' But Catholics should be helped by poverty. They should love poverty. It is a privilege. It should be easier for them because they have less of the world. But they want more world, more money, to gain recognition, power, the esteem of the world.

Sickness, calumny, injury. Lives of saints filled with it. Our enemies are the galley slaves that row us into heaven. Say a rosary for them. Love your enemies. They make us into saints . . . We should be grateful for what we are — a bundle of original sin. Dirt.

A mother's children cause her terrible suffering of mind and body. One may say her husband, good though he may be, causes her suffering. Yet would she be without it? She looks at her body, deprived of beauty, her flesh sagging, her hair, her skin, losing its color and she is delighted to be so used, by love, by life. There may be occasional regrets, but casual ones. In general she will be happy to have fulfilled the job she was put here for.

'aesthetic Catholic' tradition and after his re-conversion in 1891 ('I have just published a Satanic book (*Là Bas*). I want to write a white book, but for that I must be white myself. Have you anything that will bleach my soul?') wrote *En Route*, *The Oblate* and *The Cathedral*, all of which Day read, 'and it was those books which made me feel I too could be at home in the catholic Church' (Day, *The Long Loneliness*, p. 107). There has been consistent gossip that in the early 1920s Day indulged in pagan rituals either in Paris or in New York.

Day's daughter was named Tamar Teresa. There are two Tamars in the Old Testament. See Genesis 38:6–30 for the mother of Perez and Zerah, who were the children of Judah, her father-in-law; and 2 Samuel 13:1–9, and 1 Chronicles 3:9 for the daughter of King David, who was raped by her half-brother.

Day, *All Is Grace*, p. 41 (unpublished MS, Catholic Worker papers, New York). *All Is Grace* mainly consists of Day's notes from the Catholic Worker retreats which were started in 1941. Their principal message was that salvation was dependent on an assent to the suffering and folly of the cross. S. Vishnewski, a deeply loyal and committed Catholic Worker, described them as having 'a sort of coldness . . . where the best world would be . . . where a baby was baptized and put to death right away, instead of living through it all'. At the same time, despite or because of their implicit Jansenism, they enabled many Catholic Workers to develop a passionate affectual faith, and courage.

Day, *All Is Grace*, p. 191.

Day, *All Is Grace*, p. 97. The family was highly sanctified within the Catholic Worker Movement, which was also passionately anti-contraception. When her daughter, married at eighteen, was wrestling with a sick and unstable husband, acute poverty, and nine children, Day walked out of her own house rather than engage in conversation with her sister, Della, who suggested to Day 'not to urge, as a Catholic, Tamar to have so many children'.

I would like to bring out the fact that by this act of the hierarchy they (worker priests) are being providentially pushed still lower in the social scale . . . [I]f the priests can not belong to [the unions] they will be the ragpickers, or dishwashers, or hospital attendants (who are recruited so often among the drunks who are brought in to the hospitals). They will become the casual laborers, the migrants, the ones without respect or status, or sense of strength that union and unity gives. They will be truly the suffering.

In the end you go too far. Too far. You glorify insanity.

We must say it again because of its tremendous significance. It reveals more than anything else his utter selflessness, his giving of himself. He has given everything, even his mind. He has nothing left, he is in utter and absolute poverty. The one thing he really enjoyed, exulted in, was his ability to think. When he said sadly 'I cannot think', it was because that had been taken from him literally. His mind would no longer work. He sits in the porch, a huge old hulk. His shoulders were always broad and bowed. He looks gnomelike, as though he came from under the earth.

What sort of God wants this sort of self-giving? You go too far.
I think I sort of feel betrayed. I did so want to like you.
I like it when I read of your wild youth and your wicked ways and the intensity of your conversion.
I like the thought of a saint who has had an illegitimate baby; who has been a 1920s Paris Bohemian; whose disciples can record, slightly shocked and slightly awed:

Dorothy startled me over coffee one morning when I mentioned one of my then favourite poets, Hart Crane. 'Oh that Hart,' she said. 'I used to have breakfast with him all the time when I was pregnant with Tamar.'

I like the idea of a saint who can give a lecture on a radical interpretation of the doctrine of the Mystical Body, wearing a beret, with a cigarette hanging out of the corner of her mouth throughout.

I like it when you participate in strikes and rallies, and clamber through windows and behave like a proper socialist heroine — and then go on off on retreat and make it look seamless.

Day, MS letter, undated (?1954), to the editor of *Faith Today*. This was in response to the hierarchy's edict in 1953 forbidding French worker priests to belong to trade unions – thus ending a bold attempt to re-involve the Church with the French working class. This sort of remark in the end meant that the Church could tolerate her. It 'had nothing to fear from Day as long as she viewed authority as another sign of contradiction lighting the path to self-abnegation' (Fisher, *op. cit.*). It was probably the fact that Cardinal Spellman believed her when she said that if he 'ordered us to close down tomorrow, we would' which prevented him from doing just that.

Day, *On Pilgrimage* (Catholic Worker Press, 1948), p. 84. Peter Maurin, a French priest, was Day's inspiration, and his philosophy, as interpreted by her, was the foundation of the Catholic Worker Movement. They were originally joint editors of the journal. Maurin was, in wordly terms, extremely eccentric, to the point where even Day could say, 'I was sure that he was a great saint and a great teacher – although to be honest I wondered if I really liked Peter sometimes ... he had a one-track mind, he did not like music, he did not read Dickens or Dostoievski, and he did not bathe' (*Loaves and Fishes*, Harper and Row, 1963, p. 93). Towards the end of his life he went completely insane, which Day is here celebrating.

Michael Harrington, *Fragments of the Century* (Dutton, 1973), p. 20.

Nothing in this 'letter' should detract from the real and heroic commitment that Day did show to social engagement. I am, here, interested in the underlying themes of psychology, motive and location of the ego; but this only has meaning in relation to the dialectic that it forms with her consistent actions.

I like it when you say things like:

I first became a Catholic because I felt the Catholic Church was the church of the poor and I still think it is the church of the poor . . . I think it is the church of all immigrant populations that came over or were brought over for prosperous, Puritan, money-making developers of this country, ravishers of it, you might say . . . I had never heard of the encyclicals.

I felt that the church was the church of the poor, that St Patrick's had been built from the pennies of servant girls, that it cared for the emigrant.

I just don't like it when you say things like: 'It is only by denying satisfaction of the flesh that we strengthen the spirit.'

I don't like it because I'm afraid it might be true.

You are a sign of contradiction and who wants that from her friend?

Anyway you are not going to be my friend. You go too far, and it is not any fun. You force different questions, which cannot be the questions between friends.

Like: can you go too far in the right direction?

Like: does motive, does psychological narrative, matter, in the end, if the poor are fed?

Like: what is the strength of the self that can give itself away? Is a self without the boundaries of autonomy, that self that seeks and achieves dissolution into Christ, into the mass of the oppressed, into insanity, a self at all? Out of what resources can the ego destroy itself?

Like: are those who love life and creation and the world and sex and joy, necessarily lukewarm about heaven, and therefore about justice? Will they (will I) like the Laodiceans necessarily be spewed out?

I feel convicted by you, and I don't like it. And I don't like it partly because I really don't know whether I am innocent or guilty; I don't know if you are.

Day, from a transcript of the radio programme 'Still a Rebel', in *Bill Moyers' Journal*, WNET, 1973 (Catholic Worker papers).

Day, *The Long Loneliness*, p. 150. In her autobiography Day relates this second half of the quote as her answer to a priest who inquired about the influence of Catholic social thought on her conversion. I think it need not be taken quite literally, but as a determined self-presentation of one moved by compassion and identification with the poor, rather than as a theological 'theorist', a position she avoided and rejected throughout her life.

There has been a reductionist endeavour in recent years to reduce all marks of holiness to pathology, and all struggles with faith, with interiority and with Otherness to psychological manifestations. The difficulty is how to reply to this, 'Yes but' not being entirely adequate to deal with such scientism. I do not really think that psychological explanations are not true – but they continually leave me feeling 'so what?' or 'then what?' If holiness is a liminal state (as we are arguing throughout this book), then it is inherently an unstable one: it is not surprising that many of its manifestations are, or are very similar to, psychopathological conditions. Does this matter? Are heroic lives less interesting, less noble, if lived by the neurotic? Is mystery more explicable?

The people of Laodicea were evangelized very early in the Church's history, probably by an Ephesian called Epaphras, a convert of Paul's. However, the writer of Revelation warns his readers against their 'lukewarmness' and announces that since they were 'neither hot nor cold' God would 'spew them out' (Rev. 3:14–17).

You wanted, you said, 'to die in order to live; to put off the old man and put on Christ. I loved in other words, and like all women in love, I wanted to be united to my love.'

I don't want that.

I wanted a catholic heroine and I got a saint.

I wanted a saint and I got a romantic decadent.

I wanted a romantic Catholicism and I got a judgement.

I wanted judgement and I got a whole set of doubts.

I wanted doubt and I got your certainties.

I wanted certainty and I got a whole lot of unanswerable questions.

I still want to know how you did it? And was it worth it?

Yours sincerely.

PS: I am reminded of a silly story about the other Miss Day (Doris, the singing-and-dancing one). Her biographer asked an old friend of hers about her youth and he replied, 'Don't ask me – I knew her before she was a virgin.' Why does this seem relevant?

Day, *The Long Loneliness*, p. 149.

I still am not sure I am being fair. A different way of looking at it might be: 'She was also the most significant, interesting and influential person in the history of American Catholicism' (David O'Brien, 'The Pilgrimage of Dorothy Day', *Commonweal*, 107 (1980), p. 711).

'Without holiness, no [wo]man shall see the Lord'

Extracts from the Preface and beginning of Amanda Berry Smith's Autobiography

'You ought to write out an account of your life, and let it be known how God has led you out into His work.'

I began to think of it . . . seriously and prayed much over it . . . Asking thus for light and guidance, I opened my Bible while in prayer and my eye lighted on these words: 'Now, therefore, perform the doing of it, and as there was a readiness to will, so there may be a performance also out of that which ye have.' (2 Cor. 8: 11)

. . . My friends who know me best will make allowances for all defects in this autobiographical sketch . . . Three months of schooling was all I ever had. That was at a school for whites . . . a few colored children were permitted to attend. To this school my brother and I walked five and a half miles each day in going and returning and the attention we received while there was only such as the teacher could give after the requirements of the more favored pupils had been met.

I was born at Long Green, Maryland, Jan 23rd 1837. My father's name was Samuel Berry. My mother's name, Mariam. Matthews was her maiden name.

My father's master's name was Darby Insor. My mother's master's name, Shadrach Green.

. . . I first taught myself to read by cutting out large letters from the newspapers my father would bring home . . . [at the school] many a day I would get but one lesson and that would be while the other scholars were taking down their dinner kettles and putting their wraps on.

My old Mistress . . . was very kind to me, and I was a good deal spoiled, for a little darkey.

They were getting me ready for market . . . so they spoiled me.

Amanda Berry Smith: 1837–1915
Evangelist, missionary

✥

Born into a family of slaves in Maryland, Amanda's father secured the family's freedom and most of them settled in Pennsylvania.

The *Autobiography* describes her conversion at nineteen, two difficult marriages, and the turning point in her life when, at the age of thirty-one, she received the 'blessing of entire sanctification'.

From that time on she lived and worked as a preacher and an evangelist. Her fame spread through America and Britain, to India and West Africa, where she attracted thousands to her meetings.

She founded the Amanda Smith Home for Colored Children in Chicago in 1895 and spent the last part of her life working on behalf of African American children.

After the death of Mariam's young mistress from typhoid fever, Samuel Berry was allowed to purchase his wife and thirteen children, by the instructions of her will. Otherwise the family would have been split up, each of the children going as dowry to the young girls getting married.

Once free, they moved north to Pennsylvania, beyond the jurisdiction of slavery, for in the South masters were known still to capture valuable slaves and disregard their purchased freedom.

Settled in Pennsylvania, Samuel Berry quietly continued in the work he had begun in Maryland of assisting his oppressed brothers; the Berry household became a sanctuary for runaway slaves en route to freedom.

One of Amanda's sisters was still in bondage; trusting in the Lord, she says, she paid the $50 to free her – a sum she had no chance of earning. The Lord provided: Amanda happened to find $300 dropped by a certain gentleman who, impressed with her honesty when she returned it, gave her $50 reward.

Amanda Berry worked as a washerwoman. She was first married in 1854; it was not a happy marriage. She had two children and her husband died in the Civil War.

Father worked every hour to buy his freedom.

[He] had proposed buying us some time before, but could not be very urgent. He had to ask, and then wait a long interval before he could ask again.

Somehow I always had a fear of white people . . . a kind of fear because they were white, and were there, and I was black and was here! . . . [but I] heard the words from Galatians clearly:

There is neither Jew nor Greek, there is neither bond nor free, there is neither male nor female, for ye are all one in Christ Jesus.

. . . [The preacher said] . . . There are a great many persons who are troubled about the blessing of sanctification; how they can keep it if they can get it.'

'Oh' I said, 'he means me, for that is just what I have said. With my trials and peculiar temperament and all that I have to contend with, if I could get the blessing how could I keep it? Now someone has told him, for he is looking right at me and I know he means me.' And I tried to hide behind the post, and he seemed to look around there. . . .

He used this illustration: 'When you work hard all day and are very tired,' – 'Yes', I said, and in a moment my mind went through my washing and ironing all night, 'When you go to bed at night you don't fix any way for yourself to breathe,' – 'No', I said, 'I never think about it', – 'You go to bed, you breathe all night, you have nothing to do with your breathing, you awake in the morning, you had nothing to do with it.'

'Yes, yes, I see it.' . . . 'You don't need to fix any way for God to live in you; get God in you in all His fullness and He will live Himself.'

'Oh!' I said, 'I see it.' And somehow I seemed to sink down out of sight of myself, and then rise; it was all in a moment. I seemed to go two ways at once, down and up. Just then such a wave came over me, and such a welling up in my heart, and these words rang through me like a bell: 'God in you, God in you,' and I thought doing what?

Ruling every ambition and desire, and bringing every thought unto captivity and obedience to his will. How I have lived through it I cannot tell, but the blessedness of the love and the peace and power I can never describe. O, what glory filled my soul! The great vacuum in my

She met her second husband, James Smith, a local preacher, in Philadelphia; by him she had one daughter, Mazie. When Mazie was thirteen, Amanda sought 'sanctification'.

Amanda's down-to-earth good sense shows through in this passage about healing:

> *My neighbour prays and is wonderfully healed; she is a Christian and so am I; we have both been blessed of God; I pray and am not healed; someone tells me it is lack of faith on my part, or there is something wrong in my consecration, or there is something wrong in me somewhere, and that is the reason I am not healed. Now comes the question: 'How do you know that? Who told you so?' So that I must either stand judged, or else I must judge, and where do I get my authority for so doing? The Lord help me Amen.*

She describes her day's work — for one dollar twenty-five cents to two dollars a day, ironing, getting breakfast, washing windows, scrubbing — until in 1870, 'I left my home at God's command and began my evangelistic work. . . . Oh! how I was troubled. I did not know what to do, for I had spent all my money; father did not have much means and . . . I generally provided . . . for all the family.'

Her vision of Jesus, standing 'about six feet high; loose flowing purple robe; His hair and beard as white as wool . . . His face indescribably lovely', like her racial views, belongs to a particular circumscribed tradition of thought and imagery; yet throughout the *Autobiography* the reality of the courage, warmth and good sense of the writer shines through. Her first forays into preaching, in Salem in 1870, caused her much trepidation:

> *Brother Cooper made the announcement: 'Mrs Smith is from New York; she says the Lord sent her', with a kind of toss of the head, which indicated that he did not much believe it. . . . There was a large congregation. The gallery was full and every part of the house was packed. I stood up trembling. The cold chills ran over me. My heart seemed to stand still. Oh, it was a night. But the Lord gave me great liberty in speaking. The holy Ghost fell on the people and we had a wonderful time.*

Eight years later she was invited to England:

> *Go to England! Amanda Smith, the colored washwoman, go to England. . . . I have to ask the Lord for so many things that I really need, that I am not going to bother*

soul began to fill up; it was like a pleasant draught of cool water, and I felt it. I wanted to shout Glory to Jesus! but Satan said, 'Now, if you make a noise they will put you out.'

I was the only colored person there and I had a very keen sense of propriety; I had been taught so, and Satan knew it. I wonder how he ever did know all these little points in me, but in spite of all my Jesus came out best.

. . . Hallelujah! Hallelujah! Amen.

I did not shout, and by-and-by Brother Inskip came to another illustration . . . .

'If God in the twinkling of an eye can change these vile bodies of ours and make them look like his own most glorious body, how long will it take God to sanctify a soul?'

'God can do it,' I said, 'in the twinkling of an eye,' and as quick as the spark from smitten steel I felt the touch of God from the crown of my head to the soles of my feet, and the welling up came, and I felt I must shout: but Satan still resisted me like he did Joshua . . . .

[Later] . . . when they sang those words, 'Whose blood now cleanseth', O what a wave of glory swept over my soul! I shouted Glory to Jesus. Brother Inskip answered, 'Amen, Glory to God.' O, what a triumph for our King Emmanuel. I don't know just how I looked, but I felt so wonderfully strange, yet I felt glorious . . . .

Many times since then my faith has been tried sorely, and I have had much to contend with, and the fiery darts of Satan at times have been sore, but he has never, from that day, had the impudence to tell me that God had not done this blessed work. Hallelujah! What a Saviour!

Him with what I don't need — to go to England. It does well enough for swell people to go, not for me.

Having decided to turn down the invitation she had no peace of mind —

I wept bitterly and prayed . . . I prostrated myself full length on the floor, and wept and prayed as never before. I said, Lord, I must know what is the matter with me . . . after a few moments' stillness it was as though some one stood at my right side and said distinctly:

You are going about telling people to trust the Lord in the dark, to trust him when they can't see him.

Yes Lord I have done so.

Well you tell other people to do what you are not willing to do yourself.

O Lord, I said, 'that is mean and by thy grace I will not tell anybody to do what I am not willing to do myself . . .' And clear and distinct came these words 'You are afraid to trust the Lord and go to England, you are afraid of the ocean.'

My! it took my breath, but I said, 'Lord that is the truth, the real truth.'

Amanda Berry Smith stayed in England twelve years, leaving her daughter behind, and became a popular and respected preacher across Britain. In characteristic fashion she summed up her experiences there:

I met with many strange things in different places in England, strange views of all sorts. I don't know whether it is worse than here, but the isms and cisms and fanatics — dear me, where are they not? They are like the flies and frogs of Egypt, all over.

Another incident she recounts reveals her humorous self-possession in the face of these isms. A certain London curate, wishing to convince her of the doctrine of transubstantiation, cornered her and talked at great length. Despite her tiredness and her conviction that what he said was 'bosh' she heard him out, then when he had finished she said:

'Oh that is the way you understand it . . . . Well there is only one thing about it that is hard for me to do.'

'Now what is that Mrs Smith?' with such an air of complacency as though he could soon clear that away.

'Why, it has always been such a hard thing for me to believe what I know is not true.'

Leaving England behind she went to India and then settled for eight years in Monrovia in Liberia (Africa), where she adopted a young African boy and brought him up. Suffering from increasing ill-health after all her

work to improve schooling and health in Liberia, she retired to Chicago where during the last part of her life she worked to improve conditions for black American children, founding the Amanda Smith Home for Colored Children.

Something of the impact she made upon the Church of her time is evidenced in the letters with which she concludes the *Autobiography*, for example, this from Bishop William Taylor in 1889 to a former President of Liberia:

> *... Sister Amanda is one of the most remarkable evangelists of these eventful days in which we live ... everywhere owned of God in America, England and India as a marvellous, soul-saving worker for the Lord Jesus.*

The words with which she closes the *Autobiography* could be her epitaph: 'Without holiness, no man shall see the Lord.'

She fully expected the younger women 'who have talents, and who have had better opportunities than I have ever had' to take up her work in the battle for Christ, to 'take up the standard and bear it on', and to do more than she was able.

It is hard to imagine that any evangelist in the pre-media era could have reached more people than Amanda. She worked hard for justice – for education, health and care for the children of Liberia, even though her views were constrained by both colour and colonial prejudice. (She identifies herself as an American, against her African colleagues and her 'flock'.)

Her passion for real relationship with God, her pursuit of holiness and integrity, inform all her writing. In her self-awareness, her conviction, courage and humour, Amanda Berry Smith is an authentic person and a role model who could be a peculiarly nineteenth-century Protestant saint.

SOURCES

Main source: Amanda Berry Smith, *An Autobiography: The Story of the Lord's Dealings with Mrs. Amanda Smith, the Colored Evangelist* (Garland Publishing, New York, 1987) (first published 1893).

Amy Oden (ed.), *In Her Words: Women's Writings in the History of Christian Thought* (SPCK, London, 1995).

Lydia

The Roman empire of the first century is a huge restless place. Rome itself is the reliquary of a bold republic, now led by a series of distinctly peculiar Emperors. Political stability is fragile. The long straight roads out of Rome head off across more than half of what we now call Europe and a good deal of western Asia too and they resound to the tramp of the legions. Political stability is so fragile that it is dependent on these marching feet, the feet of power, the great conquering army which is still expanding the limits of empire. Within these limits there are continuous comings and goings, especially across the Mediterranean, the sea at the centre of the world: traders, officials, messengers, gossips, vagrants. It is a restless society.

Philippi, the city named in honour of his father by Alexander the Great four hundred years before, is as restless as anywhere. The great Via Egnatia, which links the Aegean to the Adriatic, runs through the centre of the town, and is always noisy. Along it the troops march by day and the equerries gallop through in the dark watches. Philippi is a military communications centre, a supply depot, a strategic pivot and an inevitable night stop for the east–west traveller, a hurly-burly place, where there are rich pickings for the sensible and sad endings for the foolish.

Lydia, a dealer in the purple dye-trade, is a listening woman. That is how she comes to be rich and successful. That is why she is respected by her colleagues; loved, feared and obeyed by her extensive household; held in affectionate esteem by her neighbours, who enjoy her hospitality and give her plenty of chatter to listen to. She has had that ability – to listen and learn while still being free to act – right from her youth. That hearing of the undertow of truth and then following it with ears and mind first, and then with decisive actions. That was,

Lydia: 1st century
Founder of the Church in Europe

Acts 16:11–15. At the opening of Chapter 16 Paul has been 'forbidden by the Spirit' to preach any longer in Asia. He travelled down to Troas, where he received the vision of the man from Macedonia saying 'Come over to Macedonia and help us.'

In response to this vision Paul (probably now joined by Luke, since the narrative for the first time shifts from the third to the first person plural) sailed from Troas to Samothrace, then Neapolis, and finally Philippi, where they landed.

The narrative here follows Acts closely.

Lydia is only mentioned once more in the Bible, in Acts 16:40. When Paul and his companions were released from prison in Philippi they 'went out of the prison and visited Lydia'. Here they found the new Christians gathered so 'they exorted them and departed'. The suggestion that the new Christian community met as church in Lydia's home is strong: and the claim that she is the founder of the Church in Europe is not frivolous.

It is to textual evidence of this kind that Elisabeth Schüssler Fiorenza sensitized us in *In Memory of Her*, when she recommends 'reading the silences' attentively to see how integral women are to the early history of the Christian Church.

Roger Brownrigg, in *Who's Who in the New Testament*, states Lydia was 'a pagan, and only loosely attached to the little Jewish community' in Philippi, but he does not source this information. Acts 16:14 says that 'she was a worshipper of God'.

She unquestionably was a woman of independence and authority. Luke says (16:15) that her whole household was baptized with her; and she was free to insist that Paul and his companions stay with her at her house. If Acts is a genuine first-person narrative, then Luke's final slightly exhausted

for example, how she had known the right moment to come down to the coast from Thyatira, her home town, and set up a trading house in Philippi itself.

Lydia listens.

She talks too, a big woman, bold and forward; she cannot afford to be shy, or girlish, not in her business. Her friends laugh at her, affectionately, because she is big and bold and bossy. But before she talks, she listens.

She listens to everything; because although she is rich and successful and happy she is still puzzled about something. She is not sure exactly what. It annoys her. It is something about the gods. They do not seem to her to be quite up to their job. There are the thuggish Roman gods who rape and call it seduction and have manners and morals for which she would dismiss any messenger boy or kitchen slave; there are the chilly Greek ideas that the men call gods but any sensible woman can see that they have very little to do with her; and there are the strange exclusive gods whose cults come from the east and who seem bizarre, messy, gruesome and keep an honest woman up at night.

Nonetheless ... but ... at the same time ... she is certain that there is something, some way of it. She listens because, as usual, she wants to learn. She wants to learn so that she can act sensibly.

There is no shortage of things to listen to, it should be said. Philippi, there on the Via Egnatia, seethes with high philosophy and crazy prophetesses, and divine messages and hopeful omens and silly superstitions. But it does not feel solid to her; she likes to weigh and measure things, carefully, as though they were the purple dyestuffs in which she deals so successfully. The gods the Romans inherited from the Greeks may have become risible, but there are many alternatives — cults, societies, deities, rituals, mythologies, superstitions, religions: too many and all lacking solidity. She does notice, though, that among the most stable and worthwhile of these religions is Judaism: it is ancient, respectable, dignified and beautiful. She associates herself with the Jewish women of Philippi, who are her friends. There are not many Jewish women in Philippi, they do not even have a synagogue. But on the Sabbath they gather down on the banks of the little River Ganga; they pray the old prayers, sing the songs, and chatter, women's talk as women do, and Lydia listens. This is her holiday.

'And she prevailed upon us' is a convincing human detail and I have drawn on that in my characterization of her.

Thyatira was in Asia Minor, about 100 miles north of Ephesus.

The Roman Empire was extremely tolerant of religious opinion. This tends to be forgotten because of the heroic cult of martyrdom that grew up within Christianity; Christians proved unassimilable within the Roman dispensation. (See **Perpetua** for some explanation of this.) By the middle of the first century dissatisfaction with classical gods and with the cult of the Emperor resulted in a wave of religious cults, many of them originating from the eastern provinces of the Empire. The cults of Isis and Mithras are both well known.

Judaism occupied a special place in this historical movement: it was respected for its ethical standards and for its ancient roots. Proselytes (would-be converts) were common; Paul's insistence that you could be a Christian and share these Jewish roots without being bound to its laws, particularly circumcision, was one of the more attractive elements of his message. Proselytes were a significant group in the early Church. As a 'worshipper of God' (probably a proselyte) Lydia was thus particularly well placed to form the nucleus of the new church.

One day when she leaves her house and goes down to the river there is a little group of men there. There is a man called Paul: a rather small man, bald, bow-legged, whose eyebrows meet in the middle, and who has a laughable nose — a large, red, hooked nose. He talks. He talks. Dear God, how much he talks. And Lydia listens.

He talks about a friend of his. He talks about God. He talks about both at once, as though almost they were the same. A high mysterious God, the God of the Jewish women, and Paul's friend, a carpenter, a village boy — as though they were the same. A friend of his, he tells her, and of his companions, of hers if she wants. This is interesting.

His companions talk too. One of them, Doctor Luke, talks about this friend as a man who liked meals. Lydia smiles — she has not heard before of a God who likes good cooking, long meals, with stories and singing, jokes and warmth and friendship.

Then they say He died and rose again. They say He died and rose again. They say He died and rose again and now lives for ever.

When he talks the power of the ugly little man is unveiled. Suddenly she sees that he is strongly built, and graceful, full of grace so that at times he looks like a man; at other times, though, at moments while he talks, he looks like an angel. If she were not a listening woman she would see only that he is ugly, but she doesn't. She sees that he is an angel, a messenger, a bringer of good news.

And her bossy, noisy, busy heart opens. It is not just her ears that hear, but her whole self. Perhaps this is Paul's secret — it is always these prosperous, bossy, busy, listening women whose hearts are open to his words. Lydia is exactly the bossy, busy, brave woman that a new, struggling, arrogant, eminently persecutable Church needs now.

Now is not the time for ecstatics, for virgins, for radicals, for lunatics, for ascetics, thaumaturges, penitents, anchoresses, intellectuals, poets. Now is the time for Lydia, the rich merchant in the purple-dye trade.

Her heart opens when Paul talks; and in its opening all Europe is opened to his mission. Because Lydia immediately invites them home, insists on feeding them, insists on them baptizing her, her household, her friends. It is a sunny Sabbath evening and she insists they come to her house for supper. This supper is a little, busy moment in which history is made, a moment for Christianity and therefore the whole

This is how the second-century writer Onesiphorus describes Paul in the apocryphal *Acts of Paul and Thecla*.

The evidence for a single writer, and one personally acquainted with events, is strong for Luke's Gospel, and was believed by Justin Martyr before the middle of the second century. Since Luke's Gospel focuses so strongly on the universal message of the Incarnation – and therefore on the human character of Jesus – it reflects a personal warmth towards women. It is particularly the Gospel for feminists, because it is experiential, artful and personal. This does not, of course, mean that it is not patriarchal: it is a text of its own time, but it does give us creative material to build on. If Luke truly travelled on the missionary journeys, his sensitivity to women's concerns in his narrative makes a pleasing sense in the context of so many converts being the sort of woman that Lydia seems to have been.

Onesiphorus (*op. cit.*) continues his description: 'Strongly built, he was full of grace, for at times he looked like a man, at times like an angel.'

The early Church did in fact find room for ecstatics, for radicals, lunatics, thaumaturges, penitents, intellectuals, and even poets. The ecstatics, at least, caused Paul considerable concern, as his letters to the church in Corinth make clear. But the stress on holding goods in common, feeding the poor, acting lovingly and bearing up under persecution – in both the Gospels and the epistles – does suggest that a sober, domestic leadership was as important to the establishment of the faith.

shaping of Europe. It is a moment made by Lydia, because she is a woman who listens and then acts.

There is something else too, something in her warm capable love for him that draws from Paul a tenderness – that draws from his restless mind the happiness, gratitude, affection and reassurance of the letter to her Church that he will later write from prison:

I thank my God in all my remembrance of you, always in every prayer of mine for you all, making my prayer with joy, thankful for your partnership in the gospel from the first day until now. And I am sure that he who began a good work in you will bring it to completion at the day of Jesus Christ.

The letter is flooded with his joy. Joy and rejoice. She will, because she listens to the letter's heart, suggest they count. Themselves under persecution, they will count eagerly, they will count and learn that he uses the words 'joy' and 'rejoice' no less than fourteen times in his brief letter. They too will be filled with his hope and joy, will be of such good cheer. Lydia gives Paul such joy, there in Philippi, there in her well-run and joyful house-church, that he can give that joy back to the whole world.

When she hears his joy, Lydia will send him a food parcel, and this will make them both happy.

And . . . perhaps . . . it must be so, perhaps . . . over supper, those first suppers, Luke – Luke who is travelling with Paul when they arrive in Philippi from Troas, Doctor Luke whose gentleness and love of the human self glows in his every word – Luke will start to tell stories about Martha, about Martha and Mary, about the busy bossy household in Bethany. Stories about his friend's mother, and the brave wayward troublesome child growing up in a busy Nazarene household, growing in wisdom and truth, finding favour with God, because his mother works and manages and sings the songs of freedom. Luke had forgotten, in the bright excitement of the Spirit, in the stark shining of the new world, had forgotten the comfort of the Bethany household and how happy their Friend had been with such women. He had forgotten, all the story-tellers had forgotten, because they had not thought it important.

But now, at the welcome table, he remembers, because Lydia reminds him. Lydia reminds him that his Friend had loved women just like this. And the whole of the new world that is waiting for

Philippians 1:3–6 (RSV). But the whole Epistle is radiant with love and joy. Paul describes the church at Philippi as his 'joy and crown' (4:1) and instructs them famously, 'Rejoice in the Lord always; and again I say rejoice' (4:4).

In the Epistle (4:14–19) Paul thanks the Philippians for the practical help they have already provided, and mentions a unique 'partnership' (4:15) of 'giving and receiving' with them. But the terms on which he returns 'your messenger and minister' Epaphroditus with his letter are so obviously personal and intimate (2:25–30) that they cannot but suggest that such donations would continue.

For two millennia Martha has been compared to Mary to her disadvantage: the desire that women should sit in silence at Jesus' feet and enter into contemplation has never been met with a corresponding and necessary desire that they should stop serving men. Jesus' injunction to Martha has to be put into the wider context of their friendship and a genuine willingness by men to eat less elaborate meals: 'only one *course* is necessary' (Luke 10:42). Though neither Luke nor his Jesus thinks it appropriate that men should share the cooking! (See **Martha.**) In the context of women like Lydia, this can even be interpreted as an affectionate tease – since, obviously, both Lydia and Martha did find time to 'listen to the teaching', as well as supervise the hospitality.

Paul's angelic arrival must be reminded that before there was Paul there were long suppers, busy housewives, warm beds, comfort, friendship and women who listen before they act.

He tells the stories with a tenderness that will shine across the centuries, because in this first brave Christian household in Europe he learns how necessary, how important, a bossy, busy, middle-aged woman can be if she knows how to listen.

Umbrian Journey

Cast me a steady toplit mountain
fill golden city walls with towers cascading roses
circle with violets dot with lilies
buff the steep sides of houses
wide the casements palest limestone mark the pavements
rosy the light on the wide air softening
below the plain divided breaking
moulds lives and making

picture the moon the hillslope rounding
quattrocento idyll
write a cell one chair one table
candle at elbow

simple sufficiency

Rita
patron of desperate cases
cast out the rest

Rita of Cascia: 1377–1447
Marriage-survivor, counsellor, mystic
Patron of desperate cases
Feast: 22 May

❧

Born in Roccaporena, in Umbria, Rita, like many other young women, was married against her will and endured eighteen years of violence and betrayal at the hands of her brutish husband.

When he was murdered in a vendetta she entered the Augustinian convent of St Maria Maddalena in Cascia.

She dedicated her life to the care of the sick and to counselling those in need. Her intense devotional life resulted in the appearance of stigmata on her forehead in the form of a 'wound pierced by a crown of thorns' which lasted for fifteen years. Already venerated for her holiness and for miracles, she died of tuberculosis and her incorrupt body was transferred to an elaborate tomb which still survives. She was canonized in 1900 and a new basilica with a hospital, school and orphanage attached was built in 1946.

Rita's help is especially sought in connection with broken marriages, and at one time her popularity in Italy was gauged to be greater than that of Mary. Her cult flourishes especially in Mediterranean countries, and in South America, the USA and the Philippines. In Ireland her protection is also sought, and shrines occur in the Augustinian churches. In England she is particularly honoured at the Augustinian church in Honiton, Devon.

Metonymy: Holding on to the Pieces

❧

If we hold on to the pieces
the foot of Teresa the hand
of St Catherine the withered
face preserved by
wax and God's miracles
preserved – the complete
corpse of St Rita emitting
odour of primroses – is this
in longing to grasp
their likeness to us?

embodied and corrupted
preserved and still fragrant
their alien condition takes
on a greater unlikeness –
for example, Francis' letter, our only
tangible trace, title to the
saint's hand in which
holiness is earthed and embedded

interviewed holiness flees
the follower of the Saint must perform
as music imitates the composer's
perfect conception for
logic has small part in
grasping these lives
saintliness lies in the doing

philosophers are agreed we cannot
'incorporate saintly self-
renunciation and action
into standard cognitive discourse'
for hagiography, like fiction or poetry
will slip out the seams of metaphor
while we are fingering the relic

Thekla

Onesiphorus: Far off a file of camels moving northwards
over the Cilician plain
above a flicker of sunlight on white feathers
the storks
flying from Syria to build
their nests
upon the broken arches of the aqueducts and the
ruined columns of Ephesus.

Every springtime
dusty caravans move up over the hills
vanish suddenly into the darkness
of the pass. When Paul came
across the plain to our cities
to Iconium to Lystra and to Derbe
it was in the dust and heat of the day.
I left the fragrant gardens of our suburbs
the orange-grove the cypress and the lemon
I walked to the place where the main road forks
towards Antioch. I was a long time waiting
for the face of the one revealed to me
– sturdy – hook-nosed – beetle-browed –
who would bring the word to Galatia.

There in a dream as I waited
I saw a young girl
her long hair bound with precious jade
ornaments of coral and silver about her arms

Thekla: 1st century
Evangelist, teacher, patron of virgins
Cult suppressed 1969
Feast: 23 September

❦

'This dubious saint . . . enjoyed considerable popularity in the East and was commemorated for centuries in the West' (*ODS*).

The story of Thekla (or Thecla) was known through the *Acts of Paul and Thecla*, largely discredited as legendary as a result of its fantastic incidents and the attacks on it by, amongst others, the early church fathers Tertullian and Jerome. However, later scholarship has retrieved the original tale and closely dated it to the first century, the reign of Claudius or Nero; it was enlarged and revised towards the middle of the second century, *c.* 130–150. The original simple story was of a young girl of noble family, moved by St Paul's teaching to turn her back on her fiancé and family at the age of eighteen. From her upper-storey window in her home town of Iconium (modern Konya, in central Turkey), she heard Paul speaking all through the day and the night to a throng of men and women in the courtyard below. (The streets being narrow, the house opposite was only a few feet away.) When her family used their influence to have Paul put in gaol because she refused to budge from her post and would not eat or speak to them, Thekla bribed doorkeepers and guards with her silver ornaments and got into the gaol, where she spent the night at Paul's feet, listening to his talk of Jesus.

When Paul was thrown out of town she seems to have followed him. Arriving in Antioch, the capital of Pisidia, she attracted the attention of Alexander, the proconsul, who, moved by her beauty, attempted to embrace her. Striking at him, she tore his cloak and pulled off his wreath of office, an act of sacrilege against the Roman state. She was sentenced to be thrown to the wild beasts at the Venatio, or local festival, was later pardoned and returned to Iconium to preach the gospel.

Later accretions to the story include, amongst other things, variations on her punishment (sentenced to be burnt – a storm extinguished the flames); that a cloud covered her nakedness in the arena; that she baptized herself in

seated at an upper window
her face pressed to the bars listening
she strains to snatch the drift the
talk in the packed courtyard below
where people crowd the doorway to hear
the prophet Paul.

Slowly the caravans of traders
merchants women with water pots the
camels donkeys dust-covered families
make their way from Antioch.
The sun drops in the sky
and still I am searching their faces for the
bandy-legged messenger with the
countenance of an angel.

Many years go by and the tales grow like
families, as corn left to seed
sprouts new ears
but still burned in my memory
the girl who pursued the prophet Paul

I Onesiphorus saw in a dream
the steadfast young woman Thekla
true follower of Jesus the Christ
who wrung the truths of His teaching
from the lips of the prophet Paul,
who bribed the keepers of her house
and the prison guards so

a ditch which was full of seals; escaped in men's clothes to join Paul, who commissioned her to preach; was saved from rape by rocks parting to conceal her. The likelihood is that these additional heroic details of the narrative, which was enormously popular, belong to the same poetry of the imagination that created Margaret's dragon experiences and Katherine's wheel and, as we point out elsewhere, clearly point to popular needs. (See **Margaret of Antioch, Katherine of Alexandria.**)

The later discrediting of the *Acts* as pure legend seems likely to have been because Paul is represented as causing a disturbance to family life and ties, which the Church at that time was keen to encourage and not to be accused of disrupting. Thekla can be seen as one of the first in a long line of women who refused marriage to pursue a life of holy celibacy. (The tale devotes considerable space to the anger and pursuit of both fiancé and family, and their undoubtedly factually-based threatened violence.)

As well as disruption to family life, Thekla's story also lends strong support to women's participation in active ministry. The contemporary relevance of all this to the position of women in the Roman Catholic Church today hardly needs underlining: aspects of the history quickly suppressed, such as Thekla baptizing herself and Paul's commission to her to preach, were particularly to be disowned for the support they lent to the preaching and teaching ministry of women in the early Church.

The fourth-century pilgrim Egeria made a pilgrimage to Thekla's basilica and heard part of her liturgy there, indicating that the church fathers did not succeed in suppressing it – and the popularity of the *Acts* is attested by the eleven surviving versions (see **Helena**).

Professor Ramsay, the late-nineteenth-century scholar who made a study of all the evidence, concludes:

> *There remain even in the mutilated and rewritten tale some traces of women's rights and position characteristic of the Asian social system at that time, rights which were strongly opposed by the Church.*

Incidents from the original first-century story with apparently the strongest claim to historical probability include:

1. When Thekla is to be thrown to the wild beasts there is a near-riot among the women of the community. Iconium was a new Roman colony, where women were used to being held in high esteem, and where barbaric practices such as the Venatio were unknown.

she sat at his feet
harvesting his words so
he could not cast her off

Paul: *I know not the woman thou speakest of, nor is she mine.*

Onesiphorus: I Onesiphorus saw
how she followed the prophet
with long searching
how she refused to be ignored
and how the living God
loving her stubborn purity spared her
from the fangs of the wild beasts

She lived some say at Seleucia
at Myra or perhaps Iconium
witnessing and teaching
baptizing in the one true Way
until the day of her resurrection
at a goodly age

Thekla: In the Taurus the snow lies till May
In the night the words of his message
hang on the clear air
like mountain bells

Autumn was already advanced
when they embarked at Caesarea
for Myra en route for Rhodes
berth-place of the corn-ships

Was it here I found him
already a prisoner?
or at Seleucia of Isauria
where the legends say

2. The animals' refusal to attack Thekla and their protecting her: the lioness sent in to kill her instead kills a bear sent in to finish them both off. There are numerous historical examples of such attachments between victims and the animals.

3. The pardoning of Thekla by the governor, Alexander, instead of completing her sentence of death by sending in the wild bulls: this was said to have caused the Queen, Tryphaena, who had taken care of Thekla before the Venatio, to faint. Tryphaena and Alexander are both historical persons, and Tryphaena was the Emperor's cousin. While Alexander was invoking the death penalty in reality for disrespect, since Thekla refused to put up with his sexual advances, he risked offending the Emperor by his action.

Ramsay backs up his case with detailed evidence of the historical significance of Queen Tryphaena, her relationship to the Emperor, and the date of these events, all of which fit the local circumstances of the tale which belong to Galatic Phrygia, and date from the first century. In *c.* AD 130 the story was revised and enlarged to connect it with Acts and the epistles of Paul.

Ramsay teased out from the tissue of legends that had grown up over the first centuries around this enormously popular saint the original local, largely historically substantiated tale, including the details mentioned above. In his view,

> *Such an accurate representation of a past epoch would be utterly different in type from other forgeries . . . the tale must be founded on fact committed to writing by some person not far from the historical events . . . . [It] takes us into the midst of popular life . . . illustrating the spirit prevalent in Galactic Phrygia in AD 50.*

SOURCES

Acts of Paul and Thecla, second century. Of the eleven versions that survive, five are in Latin, the rest in Greek, Coptic, Syriac, Armenian and Slavonic.

H. V. Morton, *In the Steps of St Paul* (London, 1936).

Amy Oden (ed.), *In Her Words: Women's Writings in the History of Christian Thought* (SPCK, London, 1995).

W. W. Ramsay, *The Church in the Roman Empire* (Hodder and Stoughton, London, 1893).

I lived and underwent
perilous adventures at
the hands of robbers and
wild beasts where my shrine stands

and the rock split?
Did I catch up with you on the road of
powdered limestone chalk-white
devoid of shade or water

Or through the dark slit pass of Judas
in the high mountains where snow never melts till summer
wearing the square-cut cloak of woven goats' hair
or amongst the mulberry groves skirting Antioch?
Or in the city's heart, the

coloured fountains, marble columns, in the temple-
shade of the agora? In Antioch of Syria, city of a
thousand delights, unending revelry,
elegant, spicy, quick and crowded
on the wide main corso
in the shade of the covered colonnades
in the throng of merchants, actors
prostitutes, dancers, tipsters,
athletes, flute-players, wrestlers, boxers

did I catch up with you?
Did I catch at last the word I sought so far?

Paul: *I know not the woman thou speakest of, nor is she mine.*

Thekla's Prayer in the Arena

❧

L ook favourably, Lord, Saviour, companion of the poor, friend of the persecuted, on this your handmaiden, see how I am exposed, naked in me is uncovered the shame of women, remember me oh Messiah in this my hour.

And the governor summoned Thekla out of the midst of the wild beasts and said to her:

'*Who art thou? and what is there about thee, that not one of the wild beasts touches thee?*'

And she said:

I indeed am a servant of the living God; and as to what there is about me, I have believed in the Son of God, in whom He is well pleased; wherefore not one of the beasts has touched me. For He alone is the end of salvation, and the basis of immortal life; for He is a refuge to the tempest-tossed, a solace to the afflicted, a shelter to the despairing; and, once for all, whoever shall not believe in Him, shall not live for ever.

Who art thou?

I am the handmaid of the living God.

Put on these garments.

He that clad me when I was naked among the beasts the same in the day of judgement will clothe me with salvation.

When she had dressed herself the women of Antioch shouted 'as with one mouth'.

Thekla, to Paul:

I have received the washing, O Paul, for He that hath worked together with thee in the gospel hath worked with me also in my baptizing.

After which St Paul commissioned her to preach; later she retired to live in a cave at Seleucia for the remaining seventy-two years of her life.

Morning's Minion: for Hildegard of Bingen

Caritas
habundat in omnia,
de imis excellentissima
super sidera
atque amantissima
in omnia,
quia summo regi osculum pacis
dedit.

Before morning, before dawn, Abbess Hildegard wakes restless and anxious. She wonders quickly why and then she remembers and feels weary.

She was too old for one thing. Old meant tired. And her beloved daughters were all sheep, rabbits, mice, timorous mice — poor children. Not good enough.

'But, Mother . . .', they bleated, 'but, Mother . . .'

'Are you afraid of them? Afraid of those silly clerics? Are you afraid?' she had demanded. And of course they were. She was too perhaps — she paused to inspect the possibility of fear, but it was not an emotion she knew much about; she could not be sure she would recognize it.

'Oh no, Mother,' they whimpered, 'but, Mother . . .'

'Did I not bring you out of Babylon, and establish you here in the land which we were promised?' She was overplaying her hand and she knew it. Perhaps it was not surprising they were all like sheep when she led them like a shepherd. Diessenberg had not been Babylon — it had been home. The place of her childhood, the place of her uneventful, studious, contented years, before the visions had rocked her, shaken the foundations of her life, broken her free of contentment, forced her into joy, certainty and obduracy. Forced her into praise.

Hildegard of Bingen: 1098–1179
Abbess, mystic, scientist, author

Charity
abounds towards all,
most exalted from the depths
above the stars,
and most loving towards all,
for she has given
the supreme King the kiss of peace.

Hildegard of Bingen, *Divine Love*

Hildegard was brought up from the age of eight by Jutta, a recluse but also Abbess of Diessenberg. She took vows at fifteen and spent the next seventeen years in quiet study. Then (much like **Teresa of Avila**) she started to experience a period of intense visionary mysticism. In 1136 she succeeded Jutta as Abbess, and was ordered to write down her visions. The account, entitled *Scivias* ('sciens vias Domini' – she who knows the ways of the Lord), was given formal approval by the Archbishop of Mainz, and later with some reservations by Pope Eugenius III. The work was commended to him by his teacher and friend Bernard of Clairvaux (*c.* 1090–1153), who was an admirer of Hildegard's. Both of them were mystics and, moreover, committed to developing more affectual and personal spiritual disciplines.

Under her leadership the community grew to the extent that the abbey at Diessenberg was too small, and the whole community moved to Rupertsberg, near Bingen.

Like other visionaries Hildegard felt called to reprimand and advise rulers, of both Church and State. She was a prolific writer: theologian, poet, playwright and hymnodist. She wrote on medicine and natural history; and was also an accomplished artist and musician. Much of her work has survived.

In the later years of her life her community was placed under an interdict by the cathedral chapter of Mainz, for the offence of burying an excommunicant in the abbey cemetery. She appealed to the archbishop and

Now she was obdurate. She was old and cross. And stubborn. Stubborn had worked for over seventy years, she knew no other way.

'But, Mother . . .', and then, as though inspired, one of them had said, 'But Mother, why don't we do it in the night, quietly?'

And she had felt the rustle of relief, the slight exhalation of breath that filled the room, the tiny collective sigh of those who had, or thought they had, found a way through, a compromise. Compromise was another emotion she did not know much about.

'Do you think they'd fail to notice? That they wouldn't know?' She heard her own voice sounding haughty. What happened in Rupertsberg was known and not ignored in Bingen, in Mainz, in the whole Church throughout Germany. She was a seer and a scholar, a scourge of the mighty, a friend of the great: she was not ignored. They had their eye on her. Secretly she revelled in that.

'But Mother, he could ... he could pretend ... he could ignore ...'

He would too. It made good sense. That bishop was not looking for trouble. There had been bishops ... a hidden part of her knew that it had been fun, challenging bishops ... but that time was past, she was too old, and the present bishop too mingy. It made good sense. The good sense of it made her angry. She flared up:

' "Once you were darkness, but now you are light in the Lord: walk as children of light. . . . Take no part in the unfruitful works of darkness, but instead expose them. For it is a shame even to speak of the things they do in secret; but when anything is exposed by the light it becomes visible, for anything that becomes visible is light. . . . We are children of the light, children of the day. We are not of the night or of darkness."

'That is from Paul, daughters. If it right to give him burial, it must be right to do it in the light.'

It had sounded persuasive. It had been persuasive. Now in the dawn she regrets her anger; and regretting it, feels it surge again through her whole body. She reaches for the posy that she keeps beside her bed and inhales.

The rose is cold and this cold has a useful mixture in it. If you are hot-tempered or irascible, you should take the rose and garden sage and grind them to powder. And in that hour when the wrath rises in you, you should hold it in front of your nose. The sage comforts, the rose gives pleasure and delight.

was vindicated, and the community was restored to its diocesan status before her death.

Hildegard enjoyed an unusually high level of self-confidence, both in her literary and artistic work and in her political dealings. Marina Warner, in *Monuments and Maidens*, in relation to the re-emergence of the Wisdom literature into western Christianity in the eleventh and twelfth centuries, makes an interesting observation:

> *While Sophia/Hokmah, the beautiful bride, excited intense responses in both men and women, males showed a greater need to give her an historical character and to purge the erotic force of the scriptural metaphors. The incarnational tendency of the Christian imagination led the greatest thinkers to identify the bride/mother with Mary .... It is perhaps surprising that the cult of Mary is less marked in the texts of women writers .... The asymmetry springs from the erotic character of the imagery: votaries' relationship to Holy Wisdom was changed by the question of sex. In general, while a mystic like Bernard imagined the Bride as the object of his love, his contemporary Hildegard identified herself with the symbol of transcendence itself, not with its worshippers.* (emphasis in original)

This suggestion would seem to be supported by Caroline Bynum's study of thirteenth-century mystics where she proposes that, contrary to twentieth-century expectations, women who accepted their designated theological position, especially their supposed closeness to matter and body (as opposed to the immaterial and spiritual qualities of men), far from experiencing alienation and distance from the divine, felt empowered by their particular and natural intimacy with the *incarnate* (embodied) Christ (C. W. Bynum, *Thirteenth-Century Mystics*). There is considerable diversity in the ways women can and do use the available metaphors for self-empowerment. Clearly Hildegard was unusual in many respects. How much of this can be related to her being brought up in a women-only community from such an unusually young age is an interesting question.

Ephesians 5:8–13 and Thessalonians 5:5.

From Hildegard's *Apothecary*. The medieval medical system divided all substances into 'cold' and 'warm' and also into 'moist' and 'dry', thus making four possible 'humours' — cold moist, warm moist, cold dry, and warm dry. Medicine was based on balancing these humours in the body, usually by

Comfort, pleasure and delight. She rests one more short moment on her bed. To her comfort, pleasure and delight she hears a bird down by the river experiment with a short burst of notes, startling in the perfect silence, the first rustling movement of the dawn chorus. Nearer, in the orchard, from the fruit trees that they have planted comes a response, a long smooth trill, up, up, and at the breaking point the deeper note of the blackbird joins the harmony, the reply from the river side, and more and more, upward into glory and the coming of the day. Lauds sung by the birds as her daughters will sing it shortly, before they go out into the cemetery to do what has to be done.

Comfort, pleasure and delight. From the east comes Sophia, Hokmah, Holy Wisdom, dancing upon the dawn. Her belly is smooth, slightly curved, full, and deep in her navel a diamond dances differently, in counter-rhythm, to the refractions of light. Hildegard smiles in the grey pre-dawn – she does not reveal these details, although they are revealed to her: she may be bold, high-handed, rash, but she is not altogether stupid.

Her beloved friend Bernard, who is dead now, could describe the Holy Spirit as the passionate kiss between the Father and the Son, but he has certain advantages, being male. She is not altogether stupid: she has gone as far as she can:

The form of a woman flashed and radiated in the primordial root . . . how wondrous a being you are, woman, who laid your foundations in the sun and who have overcome the earth.

Once long ago she sent Pope Eugenius, who is dead now, a diamond: not as bright as the diamond that flashes from the belly of Wisdom, but a precious gift – with an edge to it, a cutting edge:

. . . if a man is fanatical, untrue and choleric, he should keep this stone always in his mouth and by power of this stone the evils will be turned away.

Then Eugenius III, Bishop of Rome, Father of the Church, successor to the Chair of Peter, by the grace of God Pope, had, with reluctance, approved her visions. Authorized her authority. Had she needed that? It made things easier, but were things meant to be easy?

Today was not going to be easy.

Today she was going to act on her own authority: the authority

taking in those elements that the patient was discerned as being deficient in – rather like homoeopathy – or in some cases leeching, purging or bleeding an excess of humours out. Many of the assignments seem arbitrary: Hildegard calls the rose cold, but lavender warm. Much of Hildegard's *Apothecary*, which was highly regarded in its own time, consists of recipes or prescriptions like this. The *Apothecary* is not a 'herbal' or 'book of simples' – as domestic medical cures were called – but a 'scientific' medical treatise. It covered not just obtainable local herbal and natural substances, but the humours and uses of minerals, precious metals and stones. This whole approach to medicine, made yet more abstract because the Church forbade practical anatomy (hence the low status of surgery, which was normally performed not by doctors at all but by barbers), was not seriously challenged for another two centuries, when Paracelsus 'burned the books' of medical-theological authority and started to pay attention to the actual medical practices of rural women. It is worth noticing that Hildegard was articulating here, not a radical woman's voice, but a scholar's. And, in her own contemporary terms, a wide-ranging and brilliant scholar within a highly male tradition. The diseases the *Apothecary* treats of along with anger include circulation of the blood, vapours, giddiness, frenzy, insanity and obsessions, rather than the more mundane indispositions of daily life. Her works of natural history follow the same abstract pattern, but are shot through with her very obvious love of the natural world – which is also reflected in the illustrations to the *Scivias*.

Bernard of Clairvaux's ecstatic language (including this extraordinary metaphor for the Holy Spirit) was highly eroticized and personalist. As Warner (see above) has suggested, Hildegard's use of the Wisdom literature, though equally ecstatic, was rather different: the glorification of the abstract notion of femaleness. The idea of woman (in general) as 'wondrous', as opposed to merely redeemed in Mary, was distinctly unusual. This quote from the *Scivias* indicates the boldness of her use of the Sophia tradition, which was increasingly available in the West at this period as the first Crusade (1099) brought Europe into closer contact with the Churches of the East and their traditions.

Pope Eugenius III was a student of Bernard of Clairvaux. He was Pope from 1145 to 1153 and his papacy marked the high point of Bernard's (and indeed Cistercian) influence. Eugenius was persuaded by Bernard to recognize the authenticity of the *Scivias*, even though the Pope never felt able

given her in the power of the Spirit, in the dance of Wisdom, in the song of Sophia, in the wind of Hokmah. In her own learning and visions — *Scivias*, one who knows the ways of God.

They will bury an excommunicant, in the full light of day; a man in the convent cemetery; a sinner in the sacred place. They will process — dressed in silk, in bright colours, in reds and golds and greens. They will wear their enamel crowns, painted like jewels, like tapestries, like stained glass and they will sing, and sing, and sing.

Then the clerks of the Chapter of Mainz will place the house under an interdict; they will because they will have to. From where they stand they will have to, there will be no other choices for them if they are to be true to their calling; just as she will bury him because, from where she stands, she has to, there are no other choices for her if she is to be true to her calling.

Provided she lives long enough she will win in the end. She always does. This is not the first fight she has had with them. She will be ruthless in pursuit of her own truth. She will have to be ruthless, partly because that is how she is, and partly because, although she has power, she does not have enough power to be generous, to give any ground, to spare any means at her disposal: because she is a woman, because she is not ordained, because she has nothing to trade, except her own vision of her own authority. She will appeal to the archbishop, to the heads of other religious houses, to the memory of Bernard, if necessary to the Pope himself. She will win: she won before over the silken gowns and enamelled crowns, the commitment to praise, not to penance. She had won theologically: 'God clothed the first humans in radiant brightness.' Christ had restored that brightness. Her nuns did not need sackcloth and ashes to expiate worldly transgressions:

Jesus has brought us to life in him, he has forgiven all our sins. He has overridden the law and cancelled every record of the debt we had to pay.

Here, in this abbey, under her rule, were women who in their very dress would signal their identity with the holy and the divine.

If she had won that one, she would win this far lesser, far more uninteresting fight.

In the meantime, however, they would be without the sacraments.

Almost she wavers. Almost.

to support it unreservedly. Eugenius was a correspondent of Hildegard's and she reproved him severely on some occasions. However, this particular anecdote is non-historical – the quotation is not from her letters but from the *Apothecary*.

One of the activities of the Rupertsberg community which caused the most anxiety to the local hierarchy – an anxiety which was more widespread, but the Chapter of the Archdiocese of Mainz were the immediate superiors who were expected to deal with the situation – was the lack of penitential and expiatory symbolism. Far from practising mortification and humility, the nuns all wore colourful silk dresses, and – most scandalously – attended the sacraments and received communion wearing enamelled crowns (presumably this means brightly coloured ones; not jewelled but gaudy and ornamental). There were various attempts to put an end to this practice, but Hildegard defended the style of her Rule with great vigour; and won. She also won the long fight in the last few years of her life to have the Interdict, placed on the whole community because they buried an excommunicant, lifted. This last is particularly interesting because it was not an internal or 'life-style' choice. An excommunicant could not be buried in consecrated ground, and no one but the bishop could lift such a verdict. An Interdict – the word means 'a forbidding' – put an abbey (or individual) outside the community of the local church, although it did not involve the penalties that followed from being declared a heretic: it was about discipline, not doctrine.

However, in the two centuries following the death of Hildegard there were numerous attempts to have her canonized and these were consistently unsuccessful despite claims of miracles both during her life and after her death. In the fifteenth century her cult was approved for local use, but she has never achieved universal canonization. This does suggest a continuing unease with elements of both her spirituality and her theology. Recently there has been an enormous revival of interest in Hildegard, especially in the USA: much of her writing has been republished, not as academic text but as popular spirituality, and her non-canonization has been used as 'proof' of the sexism of the church hierarchy. Although there has to be a large element of prejudice here – she was a major intellectual and a highly independent (not to say stroppy) woman – I would like to suggest that it is rather more complicated than this. Hildegard's theology underlay both her high level of self-confidence and self-authorization and the specific

In extremity she finds strength. The strength from the east, whence comes Sophia, Hokmah, Holy Wisdom, dancing upon the dawn. Her belly is smooth, slightly curved, full, and deep in her navel a diamond dances differently, in counter-rhythm, to the refractions of light. Hildegard smiles.

The community is the sacrament.

Women's bodies, with Our Lady's, bear the body of Christ.

Women are the symbol of transcendence itself.

Does she dare?

The dawn chorus reaches a climax. She is old, stubborn, ruthless, bold. How wondrous a being you are, woman. She dares.

practices of her community. Contrary to the orthodox teachings of the Church she was apparently singularly unworried by sin – and therefore by a need for penance, humility or self-abnegation. Her position was what would nowadays be called triumphalist. Christ had conquered – 'and all manner of things would be well'. I am using this quote from **Julian of Norwich** very deliberately: it seems more than coincidental how much Hildegard and Julian have in common. Of the major women mystical writers of the medieval period who have not been canonized it is these two who are currently attracting enthusiastic attention in the late twentieth century. They have (despite real differences) a remarkable amount in common. Neither of them has an orthodox position on sin: Hildegard's community did 'not need sackcloth and ashes to expiate worldly transgressions. She could surround herself in the abbey with women who in their very dress signalled their identity with the holy and the divine' (Warner, *op. cit.*). Julian believed that 'sin was behovely' (*useful* to God). Both of them felt able to use female and feminine imagery for the godhead; both of them justified this through unmediated personal revelation. The combination of feminism's profound worries over what excessive guilt has done to women and the influence of theologies (like that of Matthew Fox, for example) which effectively repudiate personal responsibility for sin is given historical ballast in the writings of these two women. It is hard at present to address the very important theological questions that these women's writings raise, precisely because of the long history of discrimination, but there are serious issues here about women's experience of Christianity, and about the significance of orthodox teaching on personal responsibility.

O vas nobile,
quod non est pollutum
nec devoratum
in saltatione antiqua spelunca,
et quod non est maceratum
in vulneribus antiqui perditoris.

Your body is a chalice,
its wine never drained
in the ancient cave dance.
The ancient foe could not ravish
nor scar your flesh.

Hildegard of Bingen, 'The Chalice'

The Magdalen Reading

&

Your fingertips pressed together
in concentration lips parted your
kneeling body erect you pray —
what is the book open beneath you
its pages banded in wide illumined margins?
On the ground centring the folds of your gown
the angel's swathed limbs, your ointment pot
emblem of your superimposed identities.
On your left, supported by the angel,
your saviour in his crown of thorns
fully human, fully stretched, hangs
nailed in miniature to his tree.
You make a triptych, virgin, angel,
Christ. Your young girl's form
centres the painting

Beyond you the fifteenth-century landscape unfolds
borrowed from a hundred Italian masters —
the crags the castle cottage arbours hillsides trees
the distant spire and mountain
Close by your draped kneeling figure two
giant snowdrops bend pendulous heads
Your face is so young so smooth your breast
barely swelling I would take you for
Christ's mother, your triumphant hair
neatly capped. As you pray you read
And on your young girl's form and on the

Mary Magdalene: 1st century
Friend and follower of Jesus of Nazareth
Patron of repentant sinners and of the contemplative life
Apostle to the apostles
Feast: 22 July

Revered throughout the Church's history as a penitent whose changed life testifies to the love and power of Christ, Mary probably came from Magdala, a town on the west coast of the Sea of Galilee.

Western tradition has identified her with Mary the sister of Martha in Bethany and, more enduringly, with the woman 'who was a sinner' mentioned by Luke.

This identification was strongly propounded by Gregory the Great, and has greatly influenced iconography and the popular cult in the West.

It is now widely accepted that these are three separate women.

The poem 'The Magdalen Reading' is based loosely upon a painting in the National Gallery. In Adriaen Ysenbrandt's *The Magdalen in a Landscape* (early sixteenth century), she is represented twice – in the foreground praying with the book of devotions open before her, and in the background reading propped up on her elbow in the front of a cave.

The next poem, 'The Magdalen', is based on the figure of the Magdalen in the East window of the church of St Mary Magdalene, Sternfield, Suffolk. The flesh is suggested because the outer robe has slipped while in fact her shoulder is clothed in an undergarment.

'The Pot of Ointment': in John 11:2 the identification is made between the unnamed Mary and Mary of Bethany, sister of Martha and Lazarus, but John is quite clear that Mary Magdalene is a separate person.

And, behold, a woman in the city, which was a sinner, when she knew that Jesus sat at meat in the Pharisee's house, brought an alabaster box of ointment,

And stood at his feet behind him weeping, and began to wash his feet with tears, and did wipe them with the hairs of her head, and kissed his feet, and anointed them with the ointment.

225

pot, the book, the saviour's loins, falls
the full light of meaning

And there,
what are you reading?
There, not once, but twice
Not only on your knees in prayer, but there
reclining at your ease, head
propped on hand, a tiny figure
in the cave of the past
as long-ago hot holidays
the child hidden in the uncut grass or
hands and knees on the attic floor
while rains and adults pounded
reads on entranced
captive in a secret world

The Magdalen

Your name presents you
mysteriously different, freed to
intercede, to read, to contemplate
the mystery of the Trinitarian God, your
friend, your liberator, your own
identity plaited through the centuries' eyes
sinner and contemplative, witness,
apostle to the apostles
That Northern European tradition sees you as
contemplative, not sinner

In this small church, one of many dedicated to you
the length and breadth of England, you glow
in Victorian-rich colour as the sun rises,

Was the story too good? That Jesus should say to Simon the Pharisee:

You gave me no water for my feet —
she washed my feet with tears, and wiped them with the hairs of her head.
You gave me no kiss
but this woman since she came in has not ceased to kiss my feet.
You gave me no oil for my head
but this woman hath anointed my feet with ointment.

You did not anoint my head with oil
but she has anointed my feet with myrrh.

Luke 7:44–46

That he should forgive her sins because she loved much; that she should be saved to go in peace because she had faith. Did they need to fasten these sayings to your name?

But in Luke 8, the next chapter, you are named, amongst 'certain women which had been healed of evil spirits and infirmities', 'Mary called Magdalene, out of whom went seven devils' – along with 'Joanna, the wife of Chuza, Herod's steward, and Susanna, and many others', who ministered to him out of their substance. With Joanna, with Susanna, and many other women, you, God's enablers, made possible the miracle of this ministry.

You were not always reading.

You it was who came, 'upon the first day of the week, very early in the morning . . . unto the sepulchre, bringing the spices which they had prepared . . . and found the stone rolled away from the sepulchre. And they entered in and found not the body of the Lord Jesus' (Luke 24:1–3).

Or, as John tells us, you alone, when it was yet dark, ran and told Peter and John, and when they had gone home, you stayed outside the sepulchre, weeping, and the angels sitting asked you why you wept, and when you turned round you saw him – and he asked you: 'Woman, why do you weep? Whom do you seek?' And she, supposing him to be the gardener, begged, 'If you have borne him away, tell me where you have laid him, and I will take him.'

For with you he spoke first.

But in the centuries' eyes you are flesh, and with that hair, you are sinner. Your beauty picked out for men's eyes to lust upon, for the painter must

Mary the witness of your Lord's suffering
and his Resurrection,
witness to the crucifixion,
the golden rope of hair hanging to your waist.
In this pane you face your risen Lord
Your gown has slipped to reveal
one shoulder, in the whole window, yours, the
only, unspoken, flesh

The Pot of Ointment

❧

If these are women, what matter if we make one of
three? Let one woman stand; one suffices.
The Roman Calendar may now reject
this economically woven plait
the Church knows better – this
trinitarian fusion three-
in-one two Maries one unnamed two
healed all forgiven all women therefore
one why
trouble to distinguish three only
women sinners all and as one
who greatly loved and gave her all
chiefly this emblem remembers.
Your cult proclaims all woman, of whom
sinner, saint, contemplative, man demands
spendthrift love

show off his art, and here they may feast the eyes without shame for the Magdalen's sinful flesh is by the male Saviour redeemed.

Or else they see you reading, your glory hooded, your breasts chastely bound.

THE GOSPEL OF MARY (SECOND CENTURY)

This was supposedly written by Mary Magdalene and survived (in part) in a Coptic papyrus; it was one of the Gnostic gospels accepted by some early Christians as canonical.

> *[Peter said:] Did he then speak secretly with a woman in preference to us and not openly? Are we to turn back and all listen to her? Did he prefer her to us? [Matthew said:] Peter, you are always irate. Now I see that you are contending against the woman like the adversaries. But if the Saviour made her worthy, who are you to reject her? Surely the Saviour knew her very well. For this reason he loved her more than us.*

SOURCE

Robert Grant (trans.), *Gnosticism: A Sourcebook of Heretical Writings from the Early Christian Period*. Reprinted in Amy Oden (ed.), *In Her Words: Women's Writings in the History of Christian Thought* (SPCK, London, 1995).

Josephine Butler

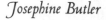

It was half past one in the morning of 21 April 1883. The Members of Parliament, and she would no longer call them honourable members, filed out of the lobbies. When she saw William Fowler, an old and faithful friend, she knew, for he 'was beaming with joy and a kind of humble triumph'.

There was nothing humble in her triumph. God said to her, 'Say unto Jerusalem that her warfare is accomplished.' She ran down the stairs from the Ladies Gallery, although a lady never runs, and she was weeping with joy, though a lady never weeps.

Parliament, on a free vote in the House of Commons, had repealed the Contagious Diseases Act (1866) by 182 votes to 110.

'When the Lord delivered Zion from bondage, it seemed like a dream; then indeed we were glad.'

Josephine Elizabeth Butler was not glad like that very often. For her God had done a cruel thing to her. She had been born in 1828 with every possible advantage, of wealth, and class, and intelligence, and beauty, and affection, and opportunity, and – there is no word for it – charm, lovability, attractiveness, the gift of friendship. Privileged.

'Nobly born, liberally educated, honourably wedded.'

An inheritance and an upbringing designed to inform the mind, perfect the charity, inspire the heart, and refine the sensibilities of any young woman.

The cruel trick was that it worked.

It worked in Victorian England.

Her informed and liberal mind believed in the equal citizenship under the law of everyone regardless of class.

Josephine Butler: 1828–1906
Christian feminist

❦

Josephine Butler (née Grey) was the national leader of the campaign for the repeal of the Contagious Diseases Acts. These were originally introduced in 1864 to combat a growing concern about venereal disease in the armed forces. They entailed 'examining' women under suspicion, licensing them if 'clean'. The details and effectiveness of these Acts is debatable. Butler objected to them on a number of grounds. (i) They were unconstitutional – they led to the imprisonment and forcible medical treatment of persons not convicted – or even charged – with an offence. *And* they introduced into law a new sort of discrimination against women, in creating a criminal offence which discriminated between men and women. (ii) They gave legal standing to the iniquitous 'double standard' of morality. (iii) They had a brutalizing effect on women who were prostitutes, and a petrifying effect on those who were not. (iv) A Christian government should not 'encourage' prostitution, by making it safer for men by punishing women – it was contrary to the will of God. The effectiveness of the Acts was never of any interest to her. Largely thanks to her work they were repealed in 1883. She spent the rest of her life involved in other national and international campaigns around similar issues.

A description of **Perpetua** from the *Passio Perpetuae et Felicitatis* but remarkably appropriate to Butler 1,700 years later (see page 155).

Butler was the daughter of John Grey of Dilston, the immensely respected, powerful, rich and well-connected leader of northern progressive Whig politicians. She was the seventh of his eight children and was highly educated, intellectually, and brought up in an international, sophisticated but morally serious environment.

Her charity taught her that such equality must be most directly expressed in law and in love on behalf of those for whom it was least evident — working-class prostitutes, the bottom of every decent Victorian heap of shit. 'I am not here to represent virtuous women: I plead for the rights of the most virtuous and the most vicious equally.'

Her inspired heart meant that there was no barrier to charity: it had to be both personal and political; both intimate and organized; both tender and intelligent; exhausting, unending, iron-cored, velvet-pawed.

Her refined sensibility meant that when she went into places where injustice and poverty and pain and squalor were present, she went into Hell.

The presence of injustice made her ill, because she could not be well where God was not. *That* refined. She was very often very ill.

She walked, she was driven, into the pit of Evil and she knew it was evil and she did not even have the comfort of the prude. She did not think that sex with a cash nexus was dirty, she thought it was desecration, a sin against love. The abyss was her own soul, and the uncaring blindness of the world, and she could not make herself blind. 'You know I am no "spiritualist", but my awful experience has taught me some things of which I scarcely dare speak — the power of the Evil One and his rage.'

She looked at her own portrait and said 'It is rather terrible. It bears the marks of storms and conflicts and sorrows so strongly . . . when I looked at [it] I felt inclined to burst into tears. I felt so sorry for her.'

Brutality brutalizes. She walked into the darkness knowingly, and much was forgiven her because she loved much.

What, asked the Royal Commissioners in 1871, enabled her to carry on with this heart-breaking, vilified, disgusting and unladylike work, despite her ill health?

The awful abundance of compassion which makes me fierce.

Butler wrote a biography of **Catherine of Siena** (1878). She obviously identified strongly with this other woman who (despite being a Roman Catholic, something that Butler found it hard to sympathize with) combined a driving political activism in a moral and theological cause with a burningly intense interior life. (They also shared chronic ill health.) They shared another characteristic: a gift for friendship, in a form more passionate than we usually mean by that word. People – men and women of all classes and backgrounds – fell in love with them, and it shaped their lives. **Teresa of Avila** had something of this: 'God made me pleasing', she said. It is not true that this 'charm' is simply a mark of God's favour – many saints are markedly lacking in it; but both these women were successful precisely in areas where women were most at risk. In acknowledging their effectiveness, this ability to love and be loved should not be overlooked: for both of them it clearly flowed out of the intimate relationship with God which caused them to love people: to listen, to be present to people. For many of her contemporaries the most scandalous thing about Butler was that she (and her husband) *liked* prostitutes; they were friends. Of all her beloved friends, the closest was undoubtedly her husband George Butler, a continual source of support to her, both practically and spiritually. He was an unusual Victorian husband – an 'Angel in the home' – and yet, like her, much loved by his friends. They were passionately devoted to each other.

Letter to Fanny Forsaith, undated, possibly 1895.

In 1894 her portrait was painted by G. F. Watts (now in the National Portrait Gallery). The quote is from A. S. G. Butler (her grandson), *Portrait of Josephine Butler*, pp. 186–7.

In 1870 Butler's National Association for the Repeal of the Acts had twice campaigned against a Government candidate in a by-election (the same candidate, Sir Henry Storks, who had been responsible for introducing the Contagious Diseases Act into Malta). Appealing particularly to the first-time voters from the 1868 Reform Act, which had given the vote to a new class – the skilled (male) artisans, who were particularly threatened by the Contagious Diseases Regulations – the Association had defeated Storks. (A strategy later developed by the militant suffragists: Emmeline Pankhurst and Butler were friends.) Worried, the Government agreed to appoint a Royal Commission. It met in 1871; and Butler gave evidence to

> *And yet we hear it said, 'Women who sell their persons are already so degraded that even registration for sanitary purposes can degrade them no further': henceforth they are to be no longer women, but only bits of numbered, inspected, ticketed human flesh flung by Government into the public market. As well might one say that a woman is irreclaimable who has experienced the bitterness of protracted famine as that she is irreclaimable when once she has sold her person for money.*
>
> *When you make a law which includes all unchaste women as 'common prostitutes' you err and you oppress; and when you say that fallen women have lost all truth, all nobleness, all delicacy of feeling, all clearness of intellect, and all tenderness of heart because they are unchaste, you are guilty of a blasphemy against human nature and against God.*

And in her passion, such a painful clear-headedness, that allows no simple solution, no placing the matter back in God's hands, no sentimental 'rescuing'. Nothing but to fight for her friends, whose lives were the price of injustice, male prejudice and self-protection, the double standard and the position of women in England in the nineteenth century.

The Commissioners asked her about the motives of women becoming prostitutes – seduction, starvation, parental negligence, wantonness? She agreed to them all. And then,

> *There is one most important cause of all, which is the absolute want of industrial training and paid work for women; for without them what is a friendless woman to do? . . .*
>
> *I will set a floodlight on your doings – I mean the immorality which exists among gentlemen of the upper classes . . . and the many dangers of the future which arise when men become willing to barter constitutional freedom for liberty in lust.*

And she never even had the comfort of the self-righteous.

But now, here, in the middle of the night, 'Regulation had received its death blow in Britain.'

They had prayed. God had answered those prayers. She and her allies went out towards the river:

it in March. Her submissions, even in the stodgy prose favoured by such things, were a *tour de force*.

'I am not accustomed to religious phraseology, but I cannot give you any idea of the effect Mrs. Butler produced, except by saying that the influence of the Spirit of God was there' (P. Rylands, MP (one of the Commissioners), letter to George Butler, 21 March 1871). On the recommendation of the Commission the Government did introduce a Bill to repeal in February 1872, but the Butlers, and most of the Abolitionist movement, rejected it as inadequate; and the Government withdrew it.

From a speech delivered at the Freemasons' Tavern, Manchester, 1870.

'Reclaimability' was at the heart of the issue. Butler theologically did not believe that it was possible for any person to be 'irreclaimable' and, in addition, she did not believe that prostitutes were uniquely in need of reclamation. 'Men who doubt the reclaimability of fallen women look upon unchastity as the one damning sin. The woman, on the other hand, looks on the hypocrisy as the one damning sin. Thus while one class of persons may be looking upon another class as utterly irreclaimable, the very class so judged may be holding the same view with regard to the judges' (Butler, *The Hour before the Dawn*, p. 34). The word is so foreign and distasteful to contemporary sensibility that it is difficult to read such debates sympathetically.

Butler was a very successful 'rescuer' (more contemporary distaste). The women she called her friends and welcomed into her house and home, her friends, her enemies — *everyone* acknowledged that she was loved by the women she worked with. It was not just practical aid — though her 'refuges' were 'frivolous' (the girls were encouraged to laugh) and useful (they were encouraged to train for decent work) — nor the fact that she was never interested in cleaning up the streets, but in empowering self-esteem. She saw in everyone she met — especially if they were poor or abused — a unique reflection of her God. No one, even her worst political enemy, who had met her ever questioned that there was anything evangelical, puritanical, bogus, self-seeking, exploitative or prurient in her relationships with these women. She met them exactly as she would meet any new acquaintance — and if it worked out that way they would (and did) die of syphilis in her best spare room.

Butler saw women's employment and women's education (in which she was involved before she began her main campaign), at all levels of society, as a democratic and republican issue. In addition, she saw no hope of

The fog had cleared away, and it was very calm under the starlit sky. All the bustle of the city was stilled, and the only sound was that of the dark water lapping against the buttresses of the broad stone terrace. I felt at that silent hour the spirit of the psalmist who said, 'When the Lord delivered Zion from bondage it seemed like a dream.'

Free at last. After seventeen years of brutal campaigning, she was able to turn her attention to the even more hellish matter of the international slave trade in under-age girls.

How, the Commissioners had asked her, could it be right for a lady to have such familiarity with the techniques of professional prostitution and brothel keeping? How could a lady of her social standing and breeding bear to contemplate such degradation and wickedness in members of her own sex?

'There is no evil in the world', she said, 'so great that God cannot raise up to meet it a corresponding beauty and glory that will blaze it out of countenance.'

The awful abundance of compassion had made her fierce.

reducing both prostitution and its griefs until society was prepared to give 'friendless' (here simply meaning unsupported) women a genuine alternative.

Butler: from a letter to Harriet Meuricoffre, dated Winchester, April 1883.

The campaign against the oppression of women, in particular the international 'white slave trade' and the 'purchase' and 'theft' of infants for prostitution, lasted the rest of Butler's life. It contained, frankly, some bizarre episodes: she was involved with the editor and journalist W. T. Stead in the research for his *Pall Mall Gazette*'s series entitled 'The Maiden Tribute to Modern Babylon'. But the evidence which the series, and other researches, produced is so appallingly painful – even now – that it is not surprising that a certain lurid element crept into the writing and the lives of those involved.

The attitude to women's sexuality has changed so much in one hundred years that it is easy to misconstrue Butler's work. (Easier in a way than some medieval woman more readily iconized because she did not wear a crinoline!) She was 'fierce' for the rights of women because they were oppressed, because she loved them and because she burned with an irreducible passion for justice. The presence of injustice made her ill, because she could not be well where God was not; she suffered a great deal because she did not value her health more than she valued justice.

The Church of England has declared her an 'Anglican worthy' – the nearest thing to formal canonization available.

A Woman of Genius

❧

All I wished to express
took the form of verse which
like a second Moses I
set adrift
naked
on the waters of the Nile
of silence so
exposed so orphaned
If
ever I write again
my scribbling will always find its way
to
the haven of your feet

Divine Wisdom

❧

In syrup an egg shrivels into shreds –
how well one may philosophize
when preparing dinner
a
simple narration of my inclination towards letters
(who heard by light of reason secret words
not granted woman to utter)
for that she stole from Divine Wisdom
to give to human reason
conferring ladyhood on who should be servant
for
Human letters are slaves
and must be censured when they take advantage

Sor Juana Inés de la Cruz: 1651–1695
Poet, philosopher, nun

The texts on the left-hand pages are composed mainly of words by Sor Juana, from the translation of the *Respuesta* by Margaret Sayers Peden, in *A Woman of Genius: The Intellectual Autobiography of Sor Juana Inés de la Cruz*, freely adapted and interwoven as verse.

Born Inés Ramirez de Asbaje y Santillana on a small ranch near the village of San Miguel de Nepantla sixty kilometres from Mexico City, Juana was for most of her life a challenge to the views of the Church of her time about the place of women.

Her appetite for learning, she tells in her autobiography, developed from as early as three years old. At her own request, she left home at the age of eight to go to school in the capital and was amongst the children selected by the viceroy to be educated.

Despite her poor Creole background, she was chosen because of her brightness and her beauty at the age of thirteen to be lady-in-waiting to the Vice-reine of Mexico. Within only two years she was celebrated and fêted for her beauty and her intellect by all the court, gaining a precocious reputation as the most learned woman in Mexico.

In 1667, before her sixteenth birthday, she retired from the court and entered the convent of St Jerome. This may have been partly determined by the licentiousness of the secular, and indeed in many cases of the priestly, life in Mexico at the time, which was a cause of great concern to the Inquisition in general and to Juana's Jesuit confessor, Father Antonio Núñez, in particular:

> *Aware of the singularity of her erudition, as well as her not inconsiderable beauty . . . [Núñez said] that God could not visit a worse scourge upon this land than to allow Juana Inés to remain in the worldly limelight.*

Juan de Oviedo, *Vida y Virtudes del Venerable Antonio Núñes*, quoted in Dorothy Schons

Eminence

Wherewith they crowned our Lord
obsidional made not from
gold nor silver but from the
leaves and grass flourishing
on the field who lifted
Satan's siege who sayeth
I have gone round about the earth
and walked through it
and as man's lot was thorns
and thistles so did they
to thee who bore thy crown
as eminence calling down
upon thy gentle figure every
butt of scorn of contumely
as figures of the winds
adorned with iron barbs
on crests of buildings
attract the animosity
of the air the fury of the
thunderbolt the lashing
wind and torrent oh
unhappy eminence exposed
to such uncounted peril

Schons concludes that Sor Juana was forced to flee the rapacious morality of Mexico City to secure her salvation as well as to pursue a life of scholarship. In the words of Juana's own autobiography:

> . . . *given the total antipathy I felt for marriage, I deemed convent life the least unsuitable and the most honourable I could elect if I were to insure my salvation.*
>
> *Respuesta de la poetisa a la muy ilustre Sor Philotea de la Cruz* (Reply of the poet to the illustrious Sor Philotea . . .), quoted in Schons

Amy Oden, in *In Her Words: Women's Writings in the History of Christian Thought*, comments that Juana wrote the *Respuesta* as a 'defense of her theological claims about human nature and purpose as well as a defense of her life of scholarly pursuit'.

Juana was advised on entering the convent by her confessor Father Núñez, who, with another patron, put up the necessary dowry. At the time the price of a convent dowry was the same as for a marriage, between one and four thousand pesos.

The convent allowed Juana time, space and resources to study and to write. She became widely known for her poetry, including many secular songs and plays, and was known as the 'Tenth Muse' of New Spain. However, most of her writings were published in the old country, Spain, probably because of the hostility of the Church and the Inquisition in Mexico.

Juana herself attacked the licentiousness prevalent amongst men in her day: 'Foolish men, who fault women for no reason. . . . In you are joined the devil, the flesh, and the world.' (Schons gives an example of that licentiousness – a notice in a contemporary chronicle comments on the fact that a priest who died was 'in addition to being gallant, of pleasing face and very wealthy, . . . a virgin'.)

The hostility that Juana inspired in the Church of her day is attributable not only to her writings and to the unacceptable dominance her intellect gave her, but to the general climate of misogyny and distrust of women. Extreme licence and extreme prudery reigned. The archbishop who was Juana's most implacable critic was heard to say that if he found any woman had entered his house he would order the bricks she stepped on to be removed. The perception of woman as snare and temptress was stronger in seventeenth-century Mexico than almost anywhere else in the Catholic world, including Spain, where Juana's publications were welcomed and found to be harmless by the Church.

Juana on her own nature

❧

'All the trivial aspects of my nature
which nourished my pride'
Pride in her command of logic,
rhetoric, physics, music,
in arithmetic, geometry,
architecture, history, law,
astrology without which
how to understand the Book
which takes in all books, the
knowledge which embraces
all knowledge?
'to have no
    obligatory occupation that would inhibit
the freedom of my studies
    yet a further circumstance
is required: a
    continuing prayer and purity of life
in the absence of which
    none of the rest is any use'
nor the sounds of a community
drinking chocolate, ordering ornate habits
in rich fabrics, instructing their
slaves, their cooks
    that would 'intrude
upon the peaceful silence of my books'

The decade of the 1680s saw Juana's flowering as a writer under the protection of her new patron, the newly appointed viceroy, who with his wife was a frequent caller at the convent. Convents at this time:

> *did not renounce worldly possessions . . . nuns held property in the form of cells, slaves, and clothes. They drank enormous amounts of chocolate and even kept their own cooks. . . . The celebration of religious feasts with special receptions for visitors such as friends and members of the family were not unusual.*

> Asuncion Lavrun, 'Unlike Sor Juana? The model nun in the religious literature of Colonial Mexico'

Juana's less than wholehearted attitude to her religious community – her fears that her 'obligatory occupation . . . would inhibit the freedom of my studies . . . the sounds of a community . . . would intrude upon the peaceful silence of my books' – is thus in one way at least fairly characteristic of the attitudes to religious life of her time. If she was not a model nun, Juana was certainly not an exceptionally irregular one, despite her prolific secular writings and contact.

However, her life pattern did not satisfy Father Núñez. Unable to persuade her to put her religious calling before her literary commitments, he finally broke off relations with her. Father Núñez's biographer says:

> *He did curtail as much as he could [their] circulation, her constant communication with the outside world, by word and writing. . . . he counseled her with the best arguments he could that, grateful to the heavens for the gifts with which it had enriched her and forgetting the world, she should place her thoughts . . . in the heavens themselves.*

> Juan de Oviedo, *op. cit.*

Núñez was both very powerful and himself extremely learned, and it is likely that his condemnation of Juana led to the opposition of the rest of the Church. Her output of secular poetry and comedies in particular aroused the hostility of the reforming archbishop, Aguiar y Seixas.

This is the background to the best-known of her difficulties with the Church, the unauthorized circulation by some clergy of her criticism of a Jesuit sermon given in Mexico City some years earlier. In 1690 her bishop, under the pseudonym Sor Filotea de la Cruz ('lover of God') wrote a stern but nonetheless appreciative letter to persuade her to mend her ways. What was accepted within the Catholic culture of the time, of course, was that

Once in my presence two young girls
were spinning a top when I began
to meditate on how the impulse continued
free and independent of its cause
even at some distance
from the child's hand
I ordered flour fetched and sprinkled about
so one might learn whether these
were perfect circles

Juana on the Annunciation

The Mother of the Word
Her reason became clouded and
her speech deserted her
She burst out
With doubts and questions:

And whence is to me? And whence
Cometh such a thing to me?

Of things one cannot say, it is needful to say
That they cannot be said.

Thus anticipating Wittgenstein
by more than two hundred years . . .

any cleric had the perfect right to instruct a woman in her proper behaviour. Nonetheless it is clear from the document that Juana's position as a leading, if not the leading, writer in Mexico, is part of the context out of which the bishop writes.

> *I do not intend with this judgement that your mercy alter your natural inclinations by renouncing books, but rather that you better them by occasionally reading the book of Jesus Christ.*

When Juana responded, in *Respuesta . . . a Sor Filotea de la Cruz*, in 1691, far from acknowledging her fault, it was to make a defence of her rights, of the rights of women, to think and write, a document which can be counted amongst the significant legacies of pre-eighteenth-century feminism. The *Respuesta* sets forth her life with remarkable frankness and details the persecutions she feels she has suffered as a woman intellectual and a writer:

> *. . . amongst the blossoms of this very acclaim emerged such a number of aroused vipers, hissing their emulation and their persecution. . . . the most noxious have been those . . . who in loving me and desiring my well-being . . . have mortified and tormented me . . . saying, 'Such studies are not in conformity with sacred innocence; surely she will be lost.' They have even asked that study be forbidden to me.*

Juana continues that her gifts were given her by God and that not even the admonitions of others nor her own meditations 'have been sufficient cause to forswear this natural impulse that God placed in me'.

In the years 1691 and 1692 Mexico suffered severe famine as a result of torrential floods and crop failure, followed by epidemics. In Juana's own convent ten nuns died. The prevailing view held that these visitations were a judgement on Mexico for its widespread moral laxity, licentiousness and sinfulness. Whether or not there was a connection between these events and Juana's own conversion, around 1692, Sor Juana Inés de la Cruz once more turned her back on the world of fame and letters, this time decisively.

She resumed relations with Father Núñez, dedicated herself to the religious life, sold her library, her musical and scientific instruments, her jewels, the gifts that she had been given by admirers of her works, and everything that she had to relieve the poor.

Of her life in the last two years Father Núñez said that she was not running but flying to perfection. She died after working day and night nursing the sick in her convent during the plague. In her 'petition . . . to the Divine Tribunal, begging forgiveness for her sins', she had written:

Juana defending her right to speak

❧

Moses thus inspired did speak
and God has granted me the mercy
of loving truth above all else
this natural impulse to be illuminated
by reason, and wisdom will not
enter into a malicious soul'

In your dream you conclude
quedando a luz mas cierta
el mundo iluminado y yo despierta
we acknowledge your part in that
leaving the world illuminated
by a more certain light
and we awake

I recognise that I deserve no forgiveness . . . knowing your infinite love and immense mercy, and that as long as I am alive there is time . . . withal as God knows for many years I have lived in Religion not only without Religion, but worse than a Pagan might live . . . it is my will once again to take the veil.

The conclusions reached by commentators about the ending of Juana's life vary as widely as their standpoints. Schons sees her as 'broken by the storms that had beaten about her', giving up the unequal struggle. 'She who had once been the object of hatred and jealousy died in the odour of sanctity, revered and loved by all.'

For Lavrun, 'the "model nun" overpowered the exceptional genius in the last years of her life', and it is the latter who is remembered: the Juana who 'would let herself speak with many voices; the one who would challenge long-held attitudes on women's behaviour with the power of her logic; the one who would allow her mind the total freedom of its own inquisitiveness'.

The latter comment focuses on Juana's exemplary quality for this book, bearing witness to the two sides of one of the impossible (binary) divides in women's lives: as writer, intellectual, imperfect religious *and* model nun, 'flying towards perfection', with no easy resolutions.

A saint of our times?

Wisdom 1:4

SOURCES

Main source: M. Sayers Peden (trans. and intro.), *A Woman of Genius: The Intellectual Autobiography of Sor Juana Inés de la Cruz* (Lime Rock Press, Salisbury, CT, 1982).

Asuncion Lavrin, 'Unlike Sor Juana? The model nun in the religious literature of Colonial Mexico', in S. Merrim (ed.), *Feminist Perspectives on Sor Juana Inés de la Cruz.*

S. Merrim (ed.), *Feminist Perspectives on Sor Juana Inés de la Cruz* (Wayne State University Press, Detroit, 1991).

Amy Oden (ed.), *In Her Words: Women's Writings in the History of Christian Thought* (SPCK, London, 1995).

Juan de Oviedo, *Vida y Virtudes del Venerable Antonio Núñes* (Mexico, 1702).

Dorothy Schons, 'Some obscure points in the life of Sor Juana', in S. Merrim (ed.), *Feminist Perspectives on Sor Juana Inés de la Cruz.*

Walpurgis: abbess, healer, traveller

⚜

May 1st. Springtime in the Hartz mountains. Bright flower-bespangled days and a sharp chill still waiting to pounce under the cover of darkness. In the villages the children process in costumes – witches, warlocks and little devils; their mothers watch, laughing. *Walpurgisnacht*. In the evening in the dark town, in Goslar, where there is a museum of the torture of women, there is laughter too – less innocent. There is laughter and drunkenness, and in the town square they burn a woman, in effigy; they burn the witch to celebrate the saint.

> *In Eichstatt, at the tomb of Walpurgis, the healing oil seeps out,*
> *each drop swelling out of the rock.*
> *Fat drop by fat drop.*
> *For twelve hundred years the oil of healing has seeped out of the rock.*

Walpurgis is a traveller; she never stops travelling, even though she was an enclosed Benedictine nun; even though she has been entombed in Eichstatt for twelve hundred years. Adventurer, pioneer, boundary transgressor. Out of place. Out of time. In tune.

It is a long road still from Wimbourne in Dorset to Eichstatt. It was a longer road when Walpurgis took it. Chuggering ox carts up over the green downs, and a dank ship's hold, and the farmlands of northern France, civilized and smiling right to the edge of the forest; and then the forest, the endless dark forest stretching away away to the north and the east beyond the known, into the longest coldest winters that hell can frighten a soul with, out there where the imagination fails and the darkness of contemplation falters. The endless forests of Thuringia, the Franklands, Bavaria, Frisia, Nordgau. Where the dark gods still hold the people in slavery. Wolves, snow, flood,

Walpurgis: d. 779
Abbess of Heidenheim, virgin

Walpurgis was one of the group of Anglo-Saxon monastics of both sexes, led by Boniface, who were involved in the mission to the Franks (inner northern Germany in general) in the eighth century.

Walpurgisnacht, 1 May, the feast day of the saint, is celebrated much like Halloween in Britain, throughout Germany, and particularly in the Hartz Mountains. Goslar, the principal town in the region, was a Red Cross hospital town during the Second World War, and was therefore not bombed like other cities in the area: its medieval 'charm' is enhanced by its witchcraft museum, housed in the ancient wall, which is predominantly a shrine to sado-masochism and gynophobia.

The rocks around the tomb of Walpurgis have, since her re-burial there in the mid-ninth century, exuded an oil which was regarded as miraculous. We do not know a great deal about Walpurgis's life or rule, but she did study medicine under Lioba at Bischofsheim and was known as a healer in her lifetime.

The eighth-century mission of Boniface (*c.* 675–745) was an extraordinary and extremely important episode of the pre-medieval European period; so much so that Boniface has been described as having had 'a deeper influence on the history of Europe than any other Englishman' (C. Dawson) — not merely for the (somewhat unstable) christianization of northern Germany, but because of the alliances he forged between crown and papacy, which made possible the emergence of the Holy Roman Empire; because of the educational and literary influence of his monasteries; and because of the authority he granted the pope in his firmly structured ecclesial developments.

hunger and pagan war bands always waiting, waiting in the dark forests and ready to pounce. A long road to danger and glory.

Walpurgis left Wimbourne with the blessings and sweet farewells of Tetta – abbess, mother, teacher, friend – and travelled first to Bischofsheim, to the blessings and sweet welcomes of Lioba – abbess, sister, teacher, friend.

She studied medicine, because it was useful, necessary even. She was a healer, it transpired, a healer and a leader and a teacher.

But before she was a healer, and a leader, she was a pray-er. Her life was a prayer. That was why Boniface wanted her, wanted them all. He sent to England for books, for money, for prayers, for church goods. He sent to Rome for authority, but he sent to England for help. He sent to England for nuns, for nuns to lighten the darkness with their singing, to hold off the forces of the forest. To pray. To pray. Without monasticism there could be no Church. Learning, healing, music-making, praying, praying.

Arriving was only the start of Walpurgis's journey. She was young, energetic, bold, clever. After only two years, because of her ability and the Church's need, she moved on to Heidenheim – the double monastery her own brother had founded.

The journey begins here, and it goes inward as it goes outward. To heal, to teach, to hold steady in fear, to give and to give, to pour out self into a darkness that consumes and consumes and still not be consumed so that there is still a source, a core of self, from which to pour out self. There, in the lonely place, the frontier, where danger lurks in every chance meeting, where rivers are hard to ford, conversions are hard to sustain, and where, in the end, they killed Boniface, there they all travelled inward, away from family, from ease, from arrogance. There they prayed on the very edge of the darkness, pushing into the darkness, which was forest and self and community, the darkness which was within and without.

And, sweet Jesus, it was fun.

Love and laughter. Friendship. Kinship. Work. More work. Letters, long letters. Gossip, theology, business. Boniface had gone to Rome, Boniface was back from Rome. Willibald was writing a tour guide to the Holy Land – 'I ask you!' Could we have prayers for the harvest? Should we crown Pepin as King in France? Has anyone got a spare

In 748, at Boniface's urging, Lioba (d. 782), a nun from Wimbourne, trained by the remarkable Abbess Tetta ('the mother of saints') and a relative of Boniface, led a group of about thirty nuns to join the mission; her rule was based on Benedict's, and stressed learning – all the nuns had to learn Latin – but subordinated it to the celebration of the divine office. The letters of Lioba and Boniface show one of the most attractive relationships between a man and woman, both people of considerable authority, long acquaintance, kinship, shared goals and obvious love. At Boniface's request they were buried next to each other. Lioba became a woman of enormous authority. It was at her request that Walpurgis joined her from Wimbourne, along – over the years – with other nuns, like Tecla (d. 790). Boniface looked to the English church for support throughout his life and the close connections, strengthened by a sense of racial community between Anglo-Saxons and north Germans ('who are of one blood with you' – Boniface, *Letter to the English People* (738), in *Works of Boniface*, trans. and ed. J. A. Giles, 1844), continued after his death.

The concept of the 'double monastery', with women and men religious in the same community, was common in Britain (particularly within the Celtic church). Because of the peripatetic character of Celtic priests, and particularly bishops, these houses were often ruled by an abbess (see **Hilda**). In fact Heidenheim's first leader was a man – Winnibald; Walpurgis became abbess after his death. It is the only known example in Germany at this time.

Many members of Boniface's mission were related, as Boniface and Lioba were. They came mainly from noble families in Wessex; when not actually kin, their families were known to each other. There is an element of 'old school tie' in their relationships. Walpurgis had two brothers working in the mission, Willibald (d. 786/7) and Winnibald (d. 761). Both of these two were, like their sister, highly educated and also, like Boniface, widely travelled. Willibald's *Hodoeporicon*, a guide to the Holy Land, is the first English travel book. Willibald visited both Palestine and Constantinople, where he lived for some years. He reformed Monte Cassino, Benedict's (480–550) own monastery; and at Boniface's request went to Germany to found a Benedictine house. His brother and sister were its first leaders.

Much of the sense of joy and energy which comes over in the letters of Boniface obviously sprang from this sense of easy intimacy, into which the

psalter? If anyone is going to England could they take letters? Boniface is dead. A gang of pagans murdered him on the banks of the river Borne.

A long way from Wimbourne.

Meetings chanced on the roadside as they criss-crossed the forests.

After long days of hard travelling, as evening fell, they would push their weary horses on the extra mile, the extra hour, through the dangerous darkness; and would stumble saddle-sore to the abbey gate already closed for the night. And inside, the nuns and monks would hear the approaching horses, and would not know whether to be terrified or happy. Whether the stirrings, the thump on the door meant worldly feast or heavenly banquet, until the bell rang out. *Deo gratias. Te deum laudamus.* For here even the extern nuns learn Latin.

And the Abbess Walpurgis, though still in her nightclothes, would offer the formal welcome of a Benedictine abbess, before flinging her arms round the visitor – Boniface, Lull, Willibald, Winnibald, Sturm, and so many others unnamed and unremembered – and feeling herself held in his familial and familiar hug. Mother, father, brother, sister, bishop, teacher, cousin, confessor, penitent, soul-friend, comrade, family beyond family in the place where there is no family, except that which they have made, again and new, in courageous love. So that welcoming and being welcomed is the journey, as Benedict himself had taught.

A long road from Wimbourne in Dorset where the hills curve down to protect the abbey, and where Tetta teaches her daughters, and turns them into saints.

But not the last journey. There is a stranger longer sadder harder journey, that brings Walpurgis here to Goslar, where in her name women are mocked and tortured. They are pagans still, these Christians; twelve hundred years and they, baptized, respectable, honourable citizens who laugh at their children's antics. Still they are pagans, baying beer-drunken in the night to silence their own fears. They do not believe in the holy oil of healing and hope that she gives them, but they do believe in the devil. And they have dragged her on a journey that has made her a part of it.

women were entirely incorporated. Anglo-Saxon attitudes to gender seem surprisingly modern and relaxed (*Selected Letters of Boniface*, trans. E. Emerton).

Boniface was martyred in 754, along with several companions, while preparing to baptize some converts near Dokkum.

The missionaries, especially the men, travelled extensively even by modern standards. Boniface and others were frequently going to Rome (in 718, 722 and 738 certainly); he also had major political commitments in France (he did indeed crown Pepin in 751). But they also journeyed continually throughout the missionary territories, in appalling conditions and at considerable danger. The letters record meetings, welcomes, comforts, exchanges. Their intimacy and collegiality has a tender affectionate quality to it, which speaks both of shared respect and long-term friendship.

This sense of a fellowship, a community, in which the women's work was clearly held in the highest esteem in its own right (not just as 'support') is one of the most attractive things about this group of saints. It is so sane and modern that it makes the supernatural element of the *Walpurgisnacht* associations preposterous, at the same time as it makes the misogyny of the witch-hating more painful.

It is not entirely clear how Walpurgis became so closely associated with witchcraft, or rather anti-witchcraft. In the medieval period the Church became more or less unable to see a difference between certain forms of religion and witchcraft. Indeed, this continued into the nineteenth century, when many religious practices – such as medium possession – in missionary territories were translated through the discourse of witchcraft (e.g. Nangas in Zimbabwe), rather than discourses of theology. Major, literary religions, e.g. Buddhism, Islam, etc., were not handled in this way, but tribal practice often was, and still is. In the 720s Boniface cut down a sacred oak tree at Geismar to prove that its gods would not be able to avenge such

And still in Eichstatt, at her tomb, the healing oil seeps out,
each drop swelling out of the rock.
Fat drop by fat drop.
For twelve hundred years the oil of healing has seeped out of the rock.

They buried her at home in Heidenheim in 779. A hundred years later they took her body on a journey and buried her again at Eichstatt. The miracles began, the healing and the hope. So they dug her up again, and broke her up and sent her relics all across northern Europe, as though she had not done enough travelling. To the Rhineland, to Flanders, to France. Disseminated. Seeding the north, instead of rooted in her convent, where like any enclosed nun she belonged.

And now they use her against women who heal, women who teach, women who travel, women who love women. They burn and torture women of power. And they call her first time, her life time, the Dark Ages. She could perhaps stop, she could withdraw into heaven, but she has lost the skill: now beyond her own history she pours herself out, drop by drop, seeping into the world. A terrible and hurtful journey, when surely she has earned some rest.

There are new bands of sisters. They meet in upper rooms. They do not look like Benedictines. They resist the toils of paganism. They are not much interested in Anglo-Saxon nuns, or holiness, or prayer. But Walpurgis is interested in them. There is a bitter irony here, but she is without bitterness: she laughs in the darkness, ready to travel with them on their long road, pouring herself out in the oil of healing, the place of pilgrimage, the remaking of the story of women's journeys. Witch, saint, friend.

sacrilege: he does not seem to have used any vocabulary of witches around this, but **Joan of Arc**'s childhood dancing around ancient trees was used at her trial to suggest she was not a pagan, but a witch. However, Walpurgis's translation feast fell on 1 May, a traditional fertility-cult feast day for early summer (May Day still carries some of these connotations in the UK). One of the goddesses possibly honoured on this day was Walborg, an Earth Mother, and the similarity of the names may have affected her cult (see *ODS*), and allowed the crop protection ascribed to the goddess to be transferred to Walpurgis (in Anglo-Saxon her name is commonly spelled Walburga). Some images of the saint show her with three ears of corn – a common attribute of crop goddesses (her more usual symbols are a phial of oil and a crown).

It is especially ironic that Walpurgis has had her life 'stolen' in this particular form, because a less superstitious, 'magically' oriented group of educated, sophisticated, affectionate and mature people than Boniface's mission team would be hard to think of: they are not representatives of the 'wild side' or the heart's shadow as so many women of holiness have been, but quite the opposite. This robbing of their lives' meanings is one of the most painful parts of the post-life life of women saints, and one of the hardest to represent.

Personal note: *I first encountered Walpurgis on* Walpurgisnacht *in Goslar, where I was invited by a group of feminists to read a 'pro-witch' story ('The Burning Times',* Telling Tales, *Journeyman Press, 1983) at a night-long counter-cultural gathering. The cheering and yelling at the effigy-burning in the street below was strange and emotionally frightening. This story for Walpurgis is also a gift to the women of the Hartz mountains and elsewhere who still live in the shadow of the witch-burnings, and an expression, as a Christian, of apology – in both senses of the word.*

Sanctuary

Grey stone apse belly trimly nested
the hills swell there
tipsy gravestones shoutover
wildflowergrasses haze passing turf
added sky to kiss early earth
buzzard plummets to rust roost
did you catch walls too turning
brimmed spirit *excellent girl*
lit in dontknow darkness
the raging worldbeyond holds off
traffics stop

here the veil
thins for a shining place
between
                    an
upland haven
shielded
by Christ-time yews
knit
in a caul
of centuries
devotion
unnumbered

Melangell: 7th century
Solitary, contemplative, founder
Feast: 27 May

THE LIFE OF MELANGELL

In Powys there was once a most illustrious prince by the name of Brychwel Ysgithrog,
who was the Earl of Chester. . . . When one day in the year of Our Lord 604, the
said prince had gone hunting to a certain place in Britain called Pennant, in the said
principality of Powys, and when the hunting dogs of the same prince had started a
hare, the dogs pursued the hare, and he too gave chase until he came to a certain thicket
of brambles, which was large and full of thorns. In this thicket he found a girl of
beautiful appearance who, given up to divine contemplation, was praying with the
greatest devotion, with the said hare lying boldly and fearlessly under the hem or fold
of her garments, its face towards the dogs.

Then the prince shouted to the hounds to get it but the more he shouted, urging them
on, the further the dogs retreated and fled, howling, from the little animal. Finally the
prince, altogether astonished, asked the girl how long she had lived on her own on his
lands, in such a lonely spot. In reply the girl said that she had not seen a human face
for these fifteen years. Then he asked the girl who she was, her place of birth and ori-
gins, and in all humility she answered that she was the daughter of King Jowchel of
Ireland and that 'because my father had intended me to be the wife of a certain great
. . . Irishman, I fled from my native soil and under the guidance of God came here
in order that I might serve God and the immaculate Virgin with my heart and pure
body until my dying day'. Then the prince asked the girl her name. She replied that her
name was Melangell. . . . The prince . . . said 'because it has pleased the highest and
all-powerful God to give refuge, for your merits, to this little wild hare with safe con-
duct and protection from the attack and pursuit of these violent dogs, I give . . . to you
. . . these my lands for the service of God, that they may be a perpetual asylum, refuge
and defence, in honour of your name, excellent girl. Let neither king nor prince seek
to be so rash or bold towards God that they presume to drag away any man or woman
who has escaped here, desiring to enjoy protection in these your lands . . .'

This virgin Melangell, who was so very pleasing to God, led her solitary life, as
stated above, for thirty-seven years in this very same place. And the hares, which are

tiptoe
footstep by
footstep
flower
by flower
piercing the gloom

the smooth roads turn off
up the wooded valley floor
before the trees
spread their dark cloaks
engyl a ffon Melangell
trechant lu fyddin Fall
beneath the enfolding hillside
a thousand years
sacred slope encircled
forgotten
gentle pasture
and quiet lives yet
mil engyl a Melangell
trechant lu fyddin Fall

older than the grave-slab
five hundred years before
Rhirid Flaidd raised
proud new walls
to clothe the marvellous shrine
fashioned with recent skill

engyl a ffon Melangell
trechant lu fyddin Fall
here the small the frightened find
shelter beneath your hem the cornered
strength to dare out

little wild creatures, surrounded her every day of her life just as if they had been tame or domesticated animals. Nor, by the aid of divine mercy, were miracles and various other signs lacking for those who called upon her help and the grace of her favour with an inner motion of the heart.

. . . The same virgin Melangell applied herself to establish and instruct certain virgins with all concern and care in the same region in order that they might persevere and live in a holy and modest manner in the love of God, and should dedicate their lives to divine duties, doing nothing else by day or night. . . . Whoever has violated the above mentioned liberty and sanctity of the said virgin has rarely been seen to escape divine vengeance on this account, as may be witnessed every day. Praises be to the most high God and to Melangell, his virgin.

Adapted and abridged from a seventeenth-century MS,
translated by Oliver Davies and reprinted in A. M. Allchin,
Pennant Melangell:Place of Pilgrimage

The Welsh can be translated as: 'One thousand angels and Melangell/Overcome the powers of evil' or 'The angels and the staff of Melangell/Overcome the powers of evil.' This is quoted in A. M. Allchin, *Pennant Melangell: Place of Pilgrimage*, from a 1723 parish register, and the phrase was probably 'proverbial in the valley and may well have been remembered from before the Reformation'.

The saint wields the staff of her authority as abbess to overthrow evil, and the linking of the angels and the saints shows the people's belief in the community of the angels and the saints – the belief that 'There is a great cloud of unseen witnesses who surround us with their love and prayer'.

The parish register entry, and the local folk name for hares, 'St Melangell's lambs', together with references to the saint and to the holiness of the 'high valley' in post-Reformation poetry, indicate the continuing memory of St Melangell locally – despite the disappearance from the liturgy of all the Welsh saints, with the sole exception of St David, when Wales submitted to the Book of Common Prayer.

Throughout the post-Reformation era, up until the church's recent restoration, local people still regarded Gwasg Santes Melangell and its unique twelfth-century shrine, standing on the spot where Melangell's sanctuary church was first built five hundred years before, as a sacred place and came from all around to bury their dead.

mil engyl a Melangell
the savagery of man
she watches and enfolds
trechant lu fyddin
evil   *mil engyl*
dismembering the
holy innocent
engyl a ffon Melangell
compelled to witness
be not overcome by evil

cotton-light and hooded
a young child
cannot die
a young woman
bound and gagged face-down
engyl a ffon Melangell
trechant lu fyddin
trechant lu fyddin
mil engyl a Melangell

Only love
overcomes

God's acre of the
smallest creature
through purity of faith her
thirty-seven years established
in the shining valley
ingathering grace leading the
amassed power
of compassionate souls
touch the bones of death
gentling in the name of
Christ whole

Since 1988, the ancient shrine of St Melangell and the church, Gwasg Santes Melangell, Pennant Melangell via Oswestry, have been restored. Since the saint's day in 1992, it has been used as a place of prayer and pilgrimage and a centre of healing and counselling for the terminally ill, with a special care for cancer patients. It is the hub of the Archdiocese of Wales's mission for healing, drawing people from all over these islands and beyond.

Melangell's Latin name was Monacella and she is remembered in St Omer, in northern France, where the Jesuits believed they held her relics, and where a play was performed in her honour on her feast day up to the beginning of this century. In the early eighteenth century the Jesuits actively promoted the cause of her cult and sought unsuccessfully to get papal recognition for it.

SOURCE

A. M. Allchin, *Pennant Melangell: Place of Pilgrimage* (Oswestry, 1994).

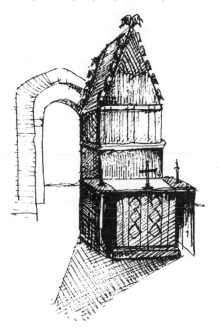

Margaret Clitherow

❦

Margaret, Maggie, Mother, Madam, Mistress Clitherow, Mama, Meggie, Mags, Margaret.

She is only just thirty; she is very young to have so many names. She will not accumulate any more.

The voices tell her, ask her, beg her, to plead. To plead Not Guilty. She is Not Guilty before the gate of heaven and she is not going to plead. 'Having made no offence,' she says, over and over again, 'having made no offence, I need no trial.'

Jesus was silent and made no answer.

She holds onto that against all the voices. They are not angry voices, they are respectful, friendly, supportive, loving voices. This makes it much harder.

In the stories it is never like this. Against a pagan emperor, against a rough soldier, a ferocious lion, a man who wants to have his wicked way with you, it is easy to be stubborn.

But here.

'Mistress Clitherow, you must answer to this court,' says Justice Clinch, and then breaking down, '. . . for heaven's sake Maggie, plead. Please.' That is not how the mighty and powerful, the cruel lord, the mean civil servant should speak. It is how your friends speak. It makes it very difficult. Because they are friends – she and John and Justice Clinch and Justice Rhodes – they were young together, young and a cut above the more humble citizens of York. They were justices now and John was a Chamberlain and her father had been Sheriff; and they all have fine houses in the Shambles with heavy oak beams and whitewash and carved staircases. She was with Mistress Clinch when little Jamie Clinch was birthed. She had petted Mary Rhodes's finger when the child slammed it in the linen kyst. Justice Clinch does not

Margaret Clitherow: 1556–1586
Martyr
Feast: 25 October (The Forty Martyrs of England and Wales)

✦

There are, sadly, very few saints like Margaret Clitherow. She was a young, bourgeois housewife, with several children and a happy marriage despite the fact that her husband, John Clitherow, a master butcher and 'a kindly and easy-going man' according to David Farmer, was an active Protestant. Her life does emphasize the point that women are most likely to find a space for their ministries at times when the churches are in confusion. She was married in 1571 and in 1574 became a Catholic.

Luke 23:9. Jesus refused to plead at his trial before Herod.

The trading families of York were intimately connected with each other, by both marriage and social intercourse. In addition Margaret was personally popular. 'Everyone loved her', wrote Father Mush, an early hagiographer, 'and would have ventured more for her than for themselves . . . her friends would run to her for help, comfort and counsel and with all courtesy and friendship she would relieve them.'

It is unusual, and unusually painful, to be condemned to death by your affectionate friends.

In 1576 the first priests trained overseas arrived in England; they were out-laws and needed assistance; as early as 1576 they were finding shelter in Margaret's house. Between 1577 and 1585 she was in prison several times. She said once, 'There is a war and a trial of God's Church. If God's priests dare venture themselves to my house, I will never refuse them.' In 1583, while in prison, she learned to read. On her release she opened a school for her own and her neighbours' children – strongly suggesting a real excitement in acquiring this 'unfeminine' skill.

In 1585 harbouring priests was made a capital offence. It was under this law that her home was raided and she was arrested in March 1586.

want to have to order her to be pressed. She is in prison now because They want to give her more time to change her mind – more time for all the people who love her to get at her.

And she likes Peter Clinch so much. He is a good man, pushed against a wall of Law as heavy as the pressing board. She is tempted, tempted to make his life easier.

Jesus was silent and made no answer.

'Margaret.' Father William wants her to plead. 'Margaret.' Father William wants her to plead too. For very different reasons. Father William, she knows affectionately, is jealous. He does not quite approve of women being martyrs – they should stay at home and take care of heroic priests, like him. She was after all his convert; not a Catholic born, not like him – and it does not seem quite fair that she, a woman, a wife of a prosperous Protestant, the mother of a lively brood, worldly, kindly, witty, happy, should nonetheless sneak into heaven before him.

But if she is going to be a martyr, Father William thinks, she should do it properly. She should plead Not Guilty, resoundingly and brazenly. He is worried that all her penances and mortifications and the clarity of the charge and her long record of encouraging Catholics, and harbouring priests and all the evidence against her will not be enough. If she will not plead, then she will die for defiance of the court, not for the sake of the gospel. Will she qualify as a martyr then? Will he have been the director of the soul of a saint? It would make up for the fact that he had failed to get himself arrested, that he had allowed her to bundle him into a cupboard, and left her and her outrageous family to deal with the pursuivants.

He wants her, he needs her, to do it properly. She is tempted, tempted to give him his fierce desire.

Jesus was silent and made no answer.

'Mother.' Henry in Douai, William longing to go. 'Mama.' Anne, little John, Katherine. They do not ask her to plead. They do not ask for anything except that none of this should be happening. She should come home. She should be laughing, their big house should be filled with happy laughter, the apprentices kicking their heels and teasing the little girls; the schoolroom should be full of children and

Pressing, the *peine forte et dure* – being slowly squashed to death under a heavy board – was the automatic punishment in England in the sixteenth century for refusing to plead at one's trial. This continued until 1741. In 1772 the law was changed so that a person refusing to plead was treated as guilty and punished accordingly. Since 1826 a person refusing to plead, unless insane, has been treated as though they had pleaded 'not guilty' and their trial proceeds in the normal way.

Margaret was canonized in 1970 as one of the Forty Martyrs of England and Wales, a supposedly 'representative' group selected from the 200 or so who had been already beatified. Just how representative this was may be asked: of the forty, thirty-three were ordained (thirteen seminary priests, ten Jesuits, ten priests from other orders) and seven lay people, three of them women. Very little is known about Margaret Ward, except that she was single and a servant, before the startling adventure that led to her execution: she smuggled a rope into Bridewell Prison which enabled William Watson, priest, to escape. But she was executed in 1588 together with four lay people and one priest. Ann Line, a widow in 'private vows', was also arrested while the priest celebrating Mass escaped. It is interesting that in all three of these cases the priests did leave their flock, and individual *women* took the responsibility.

None of the English martyrs were canonized until 1970. (More and Fisher were exceptions: they were canonized in 1935.) Relationships between the Vatican and Britain made canonization prior to the twentieth century too sensitive.

The Roman Catholic Church has canonized remarkably few mothers – Monica, Augustine's mother, is one (along with Mary). Other exceptions tend to be women who entered religious life after they were widowed (**Bridget of Sweden**), queens (Margaret of Scotland), or more occasionally martyrs (**Perpetua**). Margaret of Cortona had an illegitimate son, but her bizarre 'penitential' ill-treatment of him prevents her representing Catholic motherhood as normally understood. This disproportion seems to have *increased* in the last two centuries.

upstairs some poor scared priest on the run should be coughing over his Office inside the curtains of the big bed and looking forward to his breakfast. It is exciting when the priests come; and the boys slide down the long bannister; and their father enters the hall and yells for quiet and his wife; and she comes, running from schoolroom, or still-room, or nursery, and the children know that, although their parents agree about nothing, in truth they agree about everything important: that a house should be warm and hospitable and full of laughter and music and helping each other and cuddling and learning and blessing. They think they can stop it all, they think she will come home and everything will be all right, and they are too young to know that it is too late. She is tempted, tempted to preserve their innocence and their hope.

Mm . . . mm . . . mmm . . . murmurs the little one inside her. The one she must not listen to, the one whose sole hope she is, the one who will never get a chance . . . the one who is the only thing in the world that will turn John's love from her, because she is killing his child too, for her stubborn faith. She is tempted, tempted to do evil that good may come of it, even when the good is certain and dancing in her belly.

Jesus was silent and made no answer.

'Meg.' Surely no martyr of the early Church; no priest strung up at York Tyburn on the tree that is the door to heaven; no hero of the faith; no one ever before has had to answer for their faith before such a judge – husband, lover, friend, man of good will and kindness and passion and ah just yearning, desiring loving – saying 'Meg, dear heart, please. Plead. We might get you off. We might. For love's sake, my sweet love, my dear one, for my sake, plead.'

'Having made no offence, I need no trial,' but it comes out as a whimper, and she knows now the harshness in Our Lord's voice when he said to Peter 'Get thee behind me, Satan.' It is not anger, it is the melting, the tender melting of love that threatens her stubborn will.

'It is my turn, Meg. Everything, everything you have wanted: my house full of criminals, my bed empty on a Friday and goodwives preferring the meat of other butchers. William off to Douai, and Henry too and Anne for a nun I dare say, but please, be fair, be kind, you must give something. Your church cannot ask this of you.'

Is there an androcentric belief that motherhood is 'natural' to women, part of what John Paul II has called our 'feminine genius' (1996), and therefore not a possible locus of 'heroic' or 'supernatural' virtue? In September 1995 the *Tablet* reported an article by a Vatican official, Mgr Moll, stating that the Vatican was enthusiastic to find *married couples* to canonize: 'When marriage and the family are under the strain of heavy burdens there is a need for convincing examples. Staying together in good times and bad . . . shows a heroic degree of virtue.' Apparently, however, faithfulness to one's children does not.

The speculation that Margaret was pregnant again at the time of her death has informed her hagiographers, although I can find no original source for it. If true, the ethics of her decision become more complicated: certainly the contemporary teaching of her Church would expect her to have put this particular consideration very much higher than seems to have been the case in the seventeenth century.

Interestingly, Felicity of Carthage (see **Perpetua**) was also pregnant at the time of her trial. Her community proposed a rather startlingly different solution: since pregnant women were not sent to the arena in the early third-century Empire, her comrades prayed (successfully) for her to have a premature delivery. The attitudes to motherhood and its obligations, within Christianity, are socially constructed and do change.

Mark 8:33.

Margaret's oldest son had already been sent to France for his education, with the intention that he might proceed to ordination. Anne, her daughter, later became a nun. John Clitherow must have supported his children, financially at least, in these plans.

'It won't work, Johnnie,' she says softly leaning on him now. 'It won't work because then I would not be me.' She had not meant when she became a Catholic to take anything away from him. She could not have known that it would become who she was; and that not to go through this now, though she had not sought and did not choose it, would make her someone other than the woman whom he loved. It was fearfully simple. She had to stand to herself so that she could lean on him and weep because she could not give him this thing, this little thing, he had asked her for, he who asked for so little; she could not give it to him and still be the person who made his eyes fill with begging tears. And if she were not that woman then there was nothing for either of them to live for anyway.

It is this tough thing that is between them. When two people meet as equals in a world where they are not meant to do so, each must have a hard cold thing of their own. She knows this. She can only follow the wisdom of her own heart, believe that she will be saved by the truth, and hope that he will be saved by God's mercy, although the priests do not think so.

'Why?' he says at last. 'Why won't you plead?'

'They will ask the children – our children, and the serving girls and apprentices – to witness against me. I cannot ask them either to betray me or to perjure themselves. I cannot. It would damage them. John, don't you remember . . . ?'

He remembers and he understands. When they were young they had gone to see a witch trial. The witch's daughter had given witness against her mother. So much pain in both their faces. And three weeks later, courting by the river, they had found the daughter, her face bloated from the water, dead by her own hand, dead and damned, so she might as well have gone for a witch and not known the pain of her betrayal.

'I cannot, John. I love them. And the Law will not let you bear witness on your wife. It would have to be them and I cannot. I'll not plead.'

He looks away embarrassed. He had not thought of so much love. There is a hardness in her, there always has been and her penancing and popish fooleries have made her harder still. But the hardness is another name for an enormous softness, a cradling that has made all her stubbornness a gift to him for all these years.

John Clitherow's devotion to his wife is not a purely sentimental fantasy of mine: when he heard that sentence had been passed on her, 'he fared like a man out of his wits and wept so violently that blood gushed out of his nose in great quantities, and said "let them take all I have and save my wife, for she is the best wife in all England and the best Catholic too"' (Fr Mush).

He does not agree, but he consents, as he has always done, not because he is weak but because he understands the strength in her that would make anything less an insult. He looks at her, half-grinning like a little boy caught out with a stolen sweetmeat in his mouth, and he says, 'Having made no offence, you need no trial.'

'Thank you,' she says. And, now it is all dealt with, they laugh.

She says, 'I warn you, dear one, I shall be rude to them today. I want it to be today.'

He is startled by her clarity.

'This Friday', she says, 'is my day. How often does a butcher's wife, the mother of five noisy children, get to be a martyr? How often in all of history does the Annunciation and Good Friday fall on the same day? March 25th, in the year of our Lord fifteen hundred and eighty-six. God be thanked, I am not worthy of such a death as this.'

'That's a handsome line, Meg, my lovely,' he says, trying not to weep at the purity of the child who will go to heaven showing off, 'an excellent line; be sure to say it in your last speech.'

And because she loved him, she did.

Most convicted criminals were allowed to make a short speech from the gallows. Margaret Clitherow did, and this line is a quotation from it. I am not certain as to the answer to her second question – but she was executed on Good Friday, 25 March 1586. The last words of martyrs have been carefully recorded throughout Christian history – and, one suspects, quite often bowdlerized too. Their state of mind at the moment of death – ideally hopeful, forgiving and stalwart or victorious – was crucially important to 'calculating' the certainly that they were, indeed, constant unto death. The sometimes almost morbid detail in which their last moments were noted had a theological justification, which interestingly has passed into more general culture.

I see this Christian passion for martyrdom weighing heavily on women after the conversion of Constantine. Women, more confined to the home than men, had less chance to become martyrs; they were, for instance, prevented for centuries from exercising themselves in the mission field, or as crusaders, etc. Their attempts to identify with the sufferings of Christ on their own have led to some of the penitential excesses, the masochistic elements of Christian spirituality (cf. **Rose of Lima**). Not many women, unlike Margaret here or **Mary Fisher** or **Perpetua**, have lived in a time when martyrdom is inflicted externally.

The Empress Helena: c. 250–330
Feast: 18 August

❧

The Finding of the True Cross

❧

She seeketh out the holie Crosse of Christ
neere the place where our Lord was buried:
it was an auncient use
to burie the instruments of malefactors executed
neere the corpses
her souldiers and the Cittisens
digging therefore aboute the Sepulcher
at last found three Crosses and three
or foure nailes

Uncertaine which was the wholesome Crosse
and which the theeves the saint
called for a dead bodie then
they touched the corps first with one Crosse
then with an other, and nothing
was donne

But when the true Crosse touched
the dead bodie
life entered into it
and it rose up alive
to the glorie of Christ
and the admiration of all the beholders

Adapted from C. Horstmann (ed.), *Lives of Women Saints of Our Contrie of England.*

Once upon a time, literally a time, many times ago, time before time, in another epoch, in another world, the most important woman in the world.

A single task. A far-reaching task.

A task whose accomplishment underpinned the Passion of the Son: the adoration of the Holy Cross, its feast, the fourteen stations, the 'Vera Icon', the 'whole body of meditative prose and verse, Latin, and vernacular, spread throughout Western Christendom, all focused on the Saviour's sufferings through the veneration of the instrument of his death'.

When as an adult I first became a Christian I could not bear to think about, much less contemplate or meditate upon, the cross. 'Is it', my wise (Catholic) poet friend asks, 'the error – or heresy – of Christianity that it stops at the cross?' Like blocked momentum . . . .

Was this indeed her task, as it has been argued? Or was it just that 'she won renown as the mother of the first Christian Emperor'?

Mothers too can be saints. Look at Monica. **Bridget of Sweden**. Both mothers of saints, though Augustine caused Monica a pang or two . . . ('her patient treatment of him over many years'). They weren't all so lucky, the saints' children. Not Margaret of Cortona's.

Four saints in three acts, wrote one of the most famous twentieth-century non-mothers, non-saints. Gertrude Stein.

Hers was an 'egoity' of enormous proportion.

Is the renown of the saintly mother in proportion to the smallness of her ego? Emptied out. Dedicated. Patient. And loving. Of course.

Is it more difficult to be a saint and a mother than it is to be a mother and almost anything – a writer, a social worker, a dentist, a croupier?

What sort of renown does a mother win? Unless, of course, her son happens to be King, Pope or Emperor.

She was over sixty when she became a Christian, so she hadn't to tame her temper over sleepless nights and intolerable nappies, whatever they used in those days. An honorary mother. One dictionary records she was so devout her contemporaries thought she already was a Christian since childhood. Little transformation there? Or was it her courage? Her new life? The same dictionary eschews any mention of her part in finding the True Cross; 'She dressed quietly, gave generously to churches, to the poor, and prisoners, and made a pilgrimage to the Holy land, where she died.'

Not much to be sainted for, had she not been an Empress? But to the medieval imagination it was clear. She was a pilgrim. One who ventured, who risked herself and who spent herself unstintingly in charity.

> Then, another authority, there was:
> something about the workings of God
> wanting a different thing from each of us
> laborious or easy
> conspicuous or private
> something only we can do
> for which we were created
>
> Evelyn Waugh, 'St Helena'

– which, he said, was, for Helena, the finding of the one true cross.

finders keepers

Aged about sixty she set off
on pilgrimage to the Holy Land.
She went to seek the one true Cross
for the adored son, Constantine
Emperor of Rome, born at Nish in Serbia,
first Christian ruler of all the West,
preoccupied with affairs of state,
reconciling the warring halves
of his domain.

Alone she had settled at Trier.
Day followed day –
the boy who grew up to be Emperor
too busy for her.
Each day unrolled slow as the one before,
as the one after. The dust heaped up in her heart.

One sleepless night, maybe, between
two and three, the lowest hours of the blood,
her own Annunciation came.
The painters saw it, the heavy well-planed cross
hanging ominously above her head
guided like an errant missile by cherub-angels,
very literal, very wood. How she saw it
we do not know.
From her undertaking came
a history as enduring as her son's.

You can stand in the cathedral
on the foundations of the palace
where the Empress Helena received the faith
and was given a vision of the Cross
and in obedience made the long journey
to Jerusalem – that is all we know. We know
nothing of her life but a few bare facts.
Except her vision. And her courage.

❧

When she was forty did she wonder for what particular reason she was created? When she was left for a more advantageous union. Forty then as forty now for a woman whose husband has found someone younger, brighter, whose hair is supple gold, whose limbs are lithe, her connections more to his liking, oh yes, for that someone it is easy to be gay and full of zest, but for her who is left, too young to be old, too old to be young, forty is forty by far. The oldest age.

At forty they may stop and talk to you, exchange brief news. They do not pull up a chair, open a bottle of wine and gaze into your eyes.

Who in the court would notice such a woman?

Except her son.

The year Anno Domini three hundred and twelve. A lonely woman, neither young nor old, discarded by her ambitious husband, embraces a new faith.

❧

They say that in Adana, on her way to Jerusalem, she built a fine bridge spanning the Sarus river of which one arch still stands.

You can see coins which Constantine had minted in her honour.

They report she travelled throughout Palestine and the East, much beloved for charity, humility, her care for sick and prisoners.

She died, they say, in the Holy Land. Or in the East, in the great city of Constantinople? Or in Izmit/Nicomedia? They say. They say. So was she 'a lonely resolute old woman with a single concrete practical task clear before her'?

Her tomb never became a great centre of pilgrimage. She herself never seems to have attracted great personal devotion; but she was a popular saint. Numberless churches are dedicated to her; numberless girls baptised with her name; she appears everywhere in painting — sculpture — mosaic.

Without her aid. Without her aid. Dreams. Helen. Elen. The road traversing Wales named after her. Maps of forgotten legends; princely and spiritual power married.

Discussing Helena, the novelist Evelyn Waugh, quoted above, goes on to assert that her significance for the Christian faith at the beginning of the fourth century was that, at this time, 'Everything . . . that was capable of interpretation could be refined and diminished except the unreasonable assertion that God became man and died on the Cross', which her 'discovery' made real, made material, to the faithful.

She has fitted, in a homely and substantial way, into the family life of Christendom.

'Homely.' One of Julian's words. 'Homely' fitted with 'courteous'. That is different from 'homely . . . substantial . . . family'. I see a broad-hipped woman, hair tied back, mopping her brow. Labouring, in laundry, pantry, cookhouse. Drawn by (is it?) Courbet. Further: 'There is little of heroism or genius in any of this. She was not poor, she did not suffer.'

What does he know? Of suffering? They were always right. Authorially. Authoritatively.

'Where one may ask lies her sanctity?'

Interrogation. What are these voices? What is this 'little church', this 'far—nigh'?

. . . an act of will, grounded in patience and humility . . .
Others faced the lions in the circus.
Others lived in caves in the desert.
She was to be St Helena Empress.

> Homely. And substantial. In family life, obedience, humility, service.
> The phrases laid like a stole upon her.
> In benison.
> In dismissal.

Born at Drepanum in Bithynia, possibly an innkeeper's daughter, Helena married the Roman general Constantius Chlorus, who divorced her when he became Emperor in 292 in favour of a more advantageous match.

Geoffrey of Monmouth (d. 1154) claimed she was of British origin and the daughter of Coel, king of Colchester, of 'Old King Cole' fame.

She was believed to have been instrumental in the finding of the True Cross in Jerusalem, to which she made a pilgrimage when she became a Christian at the age of sixty. (The story was related in the ninth century by the poet, Cynewulf, in 'Elene'.)

The cross was believed to have been discovered in Jerusalem during excavations for the foundations of her son Constantine's basilica of the Holy Sepulchre on Mount Calvary. The stem and title of the cross were venerated in Jerusalem in the fourth century.

The holy woman and pilgrim Egeria wrote of the True Cross in her travel journal of her pilgrimage to the Holy Land in 404–17. (She also visited the martyrium of **Thekla**, near Seleucia, and heard readings from the *Acts of Paul and Thecla* at a service there.)

The cult of the relics of the True Cross spread to Rome and the basilica of Santa Croce was built to house the relics. Other accounts have them brought from the East to Hautevilliers near Reims in 840, during the iconoclastic period, when the Orthodox Church destroyed its icons.

SOURCES

C. Horstmann (ed.), *Lives of Women Saints of Our Contrie of England* (Early English Text Society, London, 1886).

L. Ouspensky, *Theology of the Icon*, Vol. I, trans. A. Gythiel (St. Vladimir's Seminary Press, Crestwood, NY, 1992).

Evelyn Waugh, 'St Helena', in *Saints and Ourselves*, Series I (1953), ed. P. Caraman SJ (Hollis and Carter, London, 1953).

The Prayer and Contemplation
of the Very Devout Religious Woman and
Great Handmaid of God, Sor Maria of the
Order and Habit of St Dominic

⁓

'Oh most kind and sweet Mother of God and Mother
of sinners
Oh devout Mother who wished to be Mother to sinners
Mother of torments and pleasure
Mother of pain
Mother of repose
Mother of repose for those in pain and Mother of pain
for Him who was all repose, you
who were Mother of pain for Him'

Who, in sixteenth-century Avila, would listen
To any woman were she not in ecstasy?
Who mimicked the Passion so completely
Not a limb could be moved
This body's pose absorbed her Lord
Melted in her lover's embrace the Beata
Fed and absorbed Him, no
Other, for, they found, they said,
Closure of her digestive tract
While her side opened to bleed the
Copious wound of Christ

Sor Maria of Santo Domingo
Born Aldenueva, Spain, c. 1470–86, died Piedrahita, 1524
Tertiary, reformer, abbess

*Many have rashly judged this handmaid of God and the miracles he works in her. . . .
this handmaid of God possessed nothing of her own and had only what is given her.
. . . [she] established and nearly completed in a short time a very large house and costly monastery. She maintains just under two hundred holy women. . . . she keeps them
with much penitence and has them go without shoes and keeps them very happy, content and plump.*

From the introduction by her confessor to the *Book of Prayer of Sor Maria of Santo
Domingo*, trans. and ed. M. E. Giles

Sor Maria of San Domingo was an illiterate peasant woman, a Dominican
tertiary, whose exact date of birth, sometime between 1470 and 1486, is
unknown. She came from the village of Aldenueva in Barco de Avila.

She was known as Beata, which means holy or blessed woman, a term
often used to refer to women who quit the world to live either alone or in
a small community.

In the sixteenth century these women could be seen as the spiritual
descendants of the beguines (cf. **Marguerite Porete**), although the reasons
for their choice were probably severely practical – usually because they were
unable to pay the dowry necessary to enter a convent, which was still
mainly the preserve of the aristocracy.

Their homes could be a small cell, a room or a house, often near the
parish church, 'sometimes a bridge or tower'. The medieval anchoresses' way
of life was not dissimilar (cf. **Julian of Norwich**), but the anchoresses were
more regulated, more enclosed and were wholly devoted to the contemplative life, whereas the Beata embraced the active life as well.

Like **Sor Juana**, Sor Maria proved to be a goad to her church authorities,
but in her case it was her activities in urging strenuous reform of the
Dominican institutions while she was still only a lay Dominican which
aroused fierce criticism. Having initiated local reforms, in 1507/8 she went

The Meditation on Mary and the Passion

❧

See how she goes to the little window
to see if the fresh morning comes
with happiness and with sorrow
she sees his blood-drained body

    Now my Beloved has taken away
    What he gave me in His sorrow
    My Beloved who put such roses
    in Your sacred hands
    who put these fragrant lilies
    here at Your head and feet
    You took them for you were gentle
    all perfect white and coloured
    to these sinners who mourned you
    you accepted their gift
    to make them glad, to heal them

And as she weeps her Son
kneels before her, He Himself
adoring the Father and Himself in her,
He reveals
what He placed in her through her
faith in Him

    Oh my sweet mother
        you see Me here now risen
    Behold here your sweet husband, my mentor
        Rejoice, and weep no more
        My love and my Lord
    whom last I saw
    in the hands of the executioners

out on the road with a group of men and women to take the message to Toledo. Attacked by members of her own order for her meddling, her extensive raptures aroused the scepticism and disapproval of others.

So marked were these raptures that when taken up in them – they occurred frequently – she could take no food, and it was believed her whole digestive tract closed up. Her imitations of the Passion sent her into such trances of ecstasy that her limbs became completely rigid in the pose of the crucifixion and could not be moved. While in these states she was able to answer the questions of the most learned theologians and to enter into discussions of which she would later have no recollection.

While Sor Maria was at the Spanish court in Burgos, in 1507/8, the fame of her visions and ecstasies drew many to the court. It was reported that she was able to go into a trance on request, and her detractors claimed this was done to accommodate the schedules of the court ladies, conveniently at prime rather than matins. Despite these accusations, the primate of Spain was convinced by her 'living doctrine'.

Like **Catherine of Siena**, Elizabeth of Hungary, Margery Kempe and many others, she saw herself as mystically espoused to Christ, addressing Mary as her mother-in-law. Her ecstasies, besides re-enacting the Passion in her own body every Friday, included 'ecstatic communion', receiving the Host without any priest officiating (a clear challenge to the authority of the Church), and stigmata – also a not unusual phenomenon amongst medieval mystics: on Holy Thursday 1509 she apparently bled from the side where Christ was wounded.

The phenomena reported by her confessors and examiners were in the well-marked tradition of the ecstatic espousals of Christ, which were a feature of medieval religious life. Along with other aspects of women's mystical testimony – and women were far more likely to be visionaries than men – the mystics' erotic bond with Christ served to empower women to speak with an authority they would never otherwise have had.

More problematic for Maria's defenders than her ecstasies were her relations with her confessor and other priests – the former admitted he spent nights alone with her, even lying on top of her bed, so fearful was she of the devil. Similarly, her passion for fine clothes:

> *Beyond the propriety of her rule . . . a cap on her head, little bracelets on her arms, a collar . . . little French hats & skirts of fine scarlet cloth . . . a purse of red satin, coral beads & gold, silver ornaments, and games such as chess, and dancing . . .*

humbled on the cross
torn from my hands
who in his pain
accepted my poor cloth
nothing more had I to give
never dreaming my Beloved
    I should anoint your body
    so precious and so delicate
    with my tears
I knew not
where to look for you
when even the beloved disciple
saw your head bowed
    and hung his head

❧

Oh sister see how our Beloved comes
  with hoe in hand
behold our task
to till the soil

what is this hoe he commands we grasp
Penitence by which we cleanse
the garden of good conscience
and through this garden flows
a channel to swell the flowers
and green the grass of virtue,
the channel of our will conformed to His,
held and buckled to His precious side

and when the soil is tilled
our passions conquered
the precious hoe keeps watch
over the garden of the quiet soul
that it may continually by the Beloved
be refreshed and warmed

Her supporters claimed that there was never anything frivolous in her life without there also being something holy in it, particularly in her innocent amusements. Both she and her confessor swore their consciences were clear with regard to the night-time vigils.

By 1509, her reputation had spread to Italy, and that year a commission was set up by the Pope to investigate her case. This resulted not only in the clearing of all charges against her, but in Pope Julius II approving the Beata and exonerating her of all blame. The Pope's tribunal consisted of one archbishop and two bishops (all Spanish) — Archbishop Alonso de Fonseca of Santiago, Bishop Alfonso Carrillo de Albornoz of Avila and Bishop Pascual de Ampudia of Burgos.

Supported by many influential people in the Church and at court, towards the end of her life she founded and became abbess of the monastery of San Domingo at Aldenueva, in the town of Piedrahita near Avila, which she ruled, apparently much loved, until her death in 1524.

Although never considered as a candidate for canonization, she exemplifies the lengths to which women went who stubbornly and intransigently stuck to their guns in defying the normal protocols of the Church, seeking an opening for their voices, stressing their vision and the incarnation of the Passion of Christ within them.

Like Catherine of Siena and many others, her words come to us through the intermediacy of her male confessors.

SOURCES

Main source: *The Book of Prayer of Sor Maria of Santo Domingo: A Study and Translation*, trans./ed. M. E. Giles (State University of New York Press, Albany, NY, 1990). *The Book of Prayer* was discovered only in 1948.

The texts are adapted from Sor Maria's words as reported by her confessor.

Margaret of Antioch

⚜

'Dear Wendy,' I wrote, 'you'll hear from me with the S. Margaret narrative by the end of the month – I'm having some difficulty not turning it into a kids' story or a super-hero comic strip. Or a pantomime farce.'

Margaret of Antioch, virgin, dragon-tamer, matron of women in childbirth, fairy-tale princess, dream, myth, martyr, pray for us.

This is an old story. We bright children of the Enlightenment have killed and banished the dragons; we have killed and banished the virgins too. In this new shining rational world there is no place for Margaret or her dragon: no one wants the shadow, the dark magic which is as old as the caves in the hills where the dragons dwell.

It is not easy to kill a dragon, but it can be done, and there are many handy manuals to teach an aspiring hero the tricks of the trade. Sharp swords are less effective than psychoanalysis, on the whole; and analytic logic and the scientific method are excellent weapons against the dreams of the early dawn.

It is very much harder to confront a dragon, to tame a dragon, to challenge a dragon and to live with the consequences of doing so. It is hardest of all to love and accept and endure the darkness and the heat and the fear. There are very few manuals for this because it can only be done by those who have pure hearts and sharp wits and the wisdom to know themselves.

Once upon a time, long long ago and far far away, out in the dream lands – so long ago indeed that the sensible Pope Gelasius in AD 494 was already able to say that this whole story was a load of make-believe, apocryphal, childish, and not to be trusted – there was a woman called Margaret. Her heart was like a songbird's in the morning and she was as lovely as the lilies of the field.

Margaret of Antioch: no date
Virgin and martyr
Feast: 20 July

❦

Although she had more churches dedicated to her than any other saint in England (256 according to Arnold Foster in 1900) except the Virgin Mary, Margaret has no historical reality. Her first mention in England is in seventh-century litanies, and then in the Anglo-Saxon calendars of the late tenth century. The earliest English lives, of which there are three in Old English and one in Latin, date from before the Norman Conquest in 1066. Although the main diffusion of her cult into Northern Europe seems to have taken place with the Crusades, nonetheless her cult was established, in England at least, well before the medieval period: the chapel dedicated to her on the site of Westminster Abbey proves this, since the Abbey was completed by 1065. The Second Vatican Council, in the reforms of 1969, removed her name from the Universal Calendar and suppressed her cult.

From the ninth century onwards, however, her popularity grew. She was believed to have come from Antioch in Pisidia (rather than the better-known Antioch in Syria) and was venerated from the early fourth century, as a martyr who had died in the 'great Persecution', of Diocletian and Maximian. It seems likely that the many stories which grew up round her name were derived from a variety of sources – including the legends of Marina of Alexandria (Margaret is called Marina in some of the early texts), and of the beautiful actress Pelagia from the Syrian Antioch, who was surnamed Margarita (Margaret) because of her pearls. *Marguerite* is the French word for both pearl (a symbol of purity) and daisy (a symbol of innocence) – hence the name itself carried many of the connotations that the saint came to represent. The transposition or confusion of details from one saint's story to another was not uncommon, as E. Delehaye has shown in *The Legends of the Saints*. The important thing was to embellish the martyr's story with the romance of the marvellous – and indeed the Eastern – and create a narrative which was both edifying and inspirational.

The story says she lived during the reign of the Emperor Diocletian. The story says she came from Antioch in Pisidia, from that harsh coast where Artemis, protectress of virgins, comforter of women in labour, hunted with her bitch pack and accepted with a disengaged smile the great temple offerings of Ephesus.

The story says that her father was a priest of Artemis; that he knew something of the deep powers of the turning world, but that he used his knowledge against the little people and demanded their money, their livestock and even their children to appease his fierce mistress with rivers of blood.

But Margaret laughed at him, and when she heard about a different God who sacrificed only himself, and blessed children, and gave bread and wine to the people, she became a Christian. All priests should be tested by laughter, because corruption cannot endure mockery. So when his daughter laughed at him and refused point-blank to accept his authority over her, he threw her out of the house and drove her into the wilderness. And she lived by tending sheep in the wilderness with the wild beasts, and angels ministered to her.

One day Olybrius, the grand governor of Antioch, went hunting in the wilderness; he espied Margaret. Seeing her innocence and her loveliness he was jealous and immediately wanted to destroy both. So he had her captured and brought to his palace. He wanted to marry her, but she laughed at him too, and said she had already made her choices and they did not include giving up her God and replacing him with a somewhat vulgar and certainly brutal man.

Not surprisingly he was furious, and having failed to realize that those who laugh easily do not fear easily, he tried various and assorted means of torture to get her to consent. It says a great deal about the brain-numbing effects of tyranny that, having discovered that torture works extremely effectively in intellectual and political cases, tyrants immediately assume that it will also work in the task of inspiring sexual desire in young women. By and large it does not, and it certainly did not in Margaret's case. She merely laughed all the more and sang the taunting hymns of her faith, about how tyrants would be put down from their thrones and the humble and meek would be raised up.

Olybrius was surprised, shocked and threatened. He was humiliated. He was furious. He ordered her to be burned alive, now, at once

The growth of Margaret's popularity can be traced in the history of her supposed relics. They were brought from the East to San Pietro delle Valle, near Bolsena in central Italy, in 908. In 1145 they were 'promoted' to Montefalcone Cathedral. By 1212 Venice had obtained possession of them (the Venetians were famous, or infamous, in their enthusiasm for relic collection — most notably the bold theft of St Mark's relics from Alexandria in the early ninth century, which is unashamedly illustrated in the mosaics in the colonnade of the present cathedral). For Venice to have obtained Margaret's remains suggests her enhanced status.

In 1222 the Council of Oxford declared her feast day (20 July) a major festival on which no work, except essential agricultural tasks, could be performed.

By this time the veneration of Margaret had reached its peak but she retained her popularity throughout the Middle Ages. She was one of the Fourteen Holy Helpers (a collective cult most popular in Germany from the twelfth to the sixteenth century). Her legend taught that in her last tortures she promised that (i) those who write or read her history will receive an unfading crown in heaven; (ii) those who invoke her on their death beds will enjoy divine protection and escape from the devils; (iii) those who dedicate churches or light lamps in her honour will gain anything useful that they pray for; (iv) pregnant women who call on her will escape the dangers of childbirth and so will their babies.

She was the patron saint of women in labour. With our contemporary desire for 'role models' or exemplars, it may seem strange that women should have sought the aid of so improbable a virgin at this time; but to the more iconographic imagination of the medieval mind the image of Margaret walking (or in other versions bursting explosively) out of the dark stomach of the dragon made rich sense of this connection. Moreover, at the point of this extreme — and too often inevitable — consequence of non-virginity, the mythically competent have often sought comfort in such opposites. Artemis, the virgin huntress of the Greeks, was also the guardian of women in childbirth: it is interesting that the early Church chose (though how consciously is impossible to know) Ephesus, the great shrine to Artemis, as the place to declare Mary 'Theotokos' — the bearer, the mother, of God. At a time when childbirth was genuinely life-threatening these connections were perhaps easier to make. The readings and meanings

and in public, in the market-place of Antioch, for all the world to see. She was dragged out and bound to a stake; the bundles of wood were lit, were thrust in around her feet and Olybrius waited with impatience and a fierce joy for her screams to begin.

But at that very moment, a passing dragon espied her with delight. Virgin flesh was not easily come upon in those days, and a virgin already garnished with terror was an unexpected treat. Even as the flames leapt up around her the dragon swooped across the market square, while the crowd fell back appalled, and opening his huge mouth, like a salmon to a fly, he snapped Margaret up. Without missing a wing beat, he bore her high above the city and flew on. He was just shifting this succulent morsel around his mouth before grinding her bones, when he heard an extraordinary sound; he heard a gurgle of laughter. So shocked was he, and flying so fast, that he gulped and swallowed her whole.

A terrible fear, or a terrible joy, now fell upon the dragon. He flew on, his great red-and-gold wings beating the dry air of the eastern Mediterranean, while the blue sea and the white islands danced beneath him. And at last, when they were many miles from Antioch, he circled widely, descended and alighted on a small mountain, on soft green grass beside an olive grove.

When the dragon had flighted across the market-place of Antioch and Margaret found herself swept up between the huge teeth, she had laughed like a child from surprise and relief and because of the brief glance she had of Olybrius, almost swallowing his own moustaches from fear and shock. But now in the belly of the dragon, in the hot, dark, noisy pit she learned what fear was.

Fear is physical – but she had not been afraid of torture. Fear is pain, and it is isolation and it is losing all control and having no further choices to make, and having no one to admire you in the making of them. It is darkness, and nothingness, and madness.

It is more: Margaret had been brought up in a household where true magic has been corrupted and abused, and therefore rightly feared as dangerous. She knew, without any consolation, that she was at the mercy of everything which is least merciful, most ancient, most worthy of fear. Terror was upon her, and the fear of annihilation, of not being, of having gone out beyond the living, and being alone there. And she gave herself over to dying and despair.

of virginity can be more complex than we have been prepared to admit (see **Godiva**) and always carry both a political and a subversive reading. For instance, it has been suggested that along with saints like **Katherine of Alexandria** or Juliana, Margaret's popularity was based on the enthusiasm of the medieval Church to promote priestly celibacy and the religious life – 'the glorification of the virgin-life sublimated all earthly desire in the joy of the mystic communion with Christ' (Mack).

However, it seems just as plausible to suggest that Margaret's story had popular appeal *as a story*: it had all the classic ingredients of a folk-tale – the confrontation of beauty and virtue with the powers of darkness, which can be traced back to Judaic and proto-Babylonian myth, if not to universal mythological themes (see Marina Warner, *From the Blond to the Beast*); at the same time it was 'legitimated' by its religious context. Mack compared the Latin (clerical) and English (vulgar) versions of the early stories and points out that the English-language stories contain far more detail and emphasis on the tortures and temptations than the Latin does – they are 'shockers', they are titillating. In the *ODS* Farmer comments on the 'pious fiction' of the legends. This seems to miss the point entirely. This is a key hagiographical work: it incorporates into Christianity a number of deep cultural archetypes; it is a powerfully pro-woman story at one level, while acceptable to patriarchal authority on the one hand and male desires on the other. Feminism has explored the liberating potential of fictions that touch such imaginative chords. Wyschrogrod (*Saints and Postmodernism*), for example, has suggested that in a post-saint age the search for prototypes of extraordinary moral standing must be looked for in fiction. The medieval period may have been lucky in having hagiography as a specific genre that could combine this necessary fictionality with a conviction of objective worth and cultural approval.

Dragon slaying, taming or expelling was for centuries an activity that women saints were renowned for. **Martha**, the biblically attested sister of Mary and Lazarus from Bethany, for example, slipped her biblical leash in hagiographic legend, and evangelized Provence. She is often imaged with the dragon that she tamed at Tarascon by sprinkling it with holy water. Elizabeth the Thaumaturge, a saint of the Eastern rite, dealt with her dragon by spitting on it and then trampling its head. **Perpetua**, the earliest of these saints, but in some ways the most modern, *dreamed* a dragon on whose head she had to stamp in order to climb to heaven.

And in the instant that she opened herself to dying, to being without choices and without defences and without shame, she heard the whispery voices of the wild beasts in the wilderness:

'Yea, though I take the wings of morning and fly to the uttermost ends of the sea, yet thou art with me.'

It was true, as she knew, that dragons were huge and fierce and wild and mysterious; but it was also true, as she also knew, that not everything that was huge and fierce and wild and mysterious was necessarily evil. Her God had made the dark at the same moment as the light. God had made the shadow and the wildness and the ferocity and the passion. Weary from crucifixion he had none the less walked quietly through hell and harrowed it and brought back as trophies all the things Satan had claimed and had been given by those who fear the dreamlands. In the dark, then, there were new joys, and the dragon was the same as her wild longings, her ferocious and stubborn courage, her desire to fly. Her heart soared as she knew that this was just a new adventure, an adventure through fear and darkness into the greater darkness which might, just maybe, just might, be even more beautiful than the light.

So when she felt from within the descending and landing of the dragon she waited eagerly for what might happen next.

The story says that so great was the delight of heaven in her courage, so great was the power of her virginity and her faith, that she broke through the wall of the dragon's sides in the same power as Christ had burst from the tomb; that the power of Christ burst the dragon asunder and destroyed it, as death itself had been destroyed; that Margaret sprang again into the world as a child springs from the womb and that the explosion was as lovely and brilliant as the birth of a new star in a new galaxy.

The story says, quite differently and otherwise, because it *is* a story, the story also says that the dragon, awed by her chastity, by her courage and by her endurance, opened his huge mouth, freely and tenderly, and that she struggled out through the great red throat, through the tight entrance-way between the teeth of fear, and stepped free and safe onto the gentle green grass of the sunny island. That she came to birth here, from the dragon's belly and the dragon's mouth,

Elizabeth Stuart, in *Spitting at Dragons*, p. 125, points out that women dragon-slayers, unlike their male equivalents, are not armed or mounted for this task, but perform it from their own interior authority.

reborn in faith and joy. And breathing the sweet mountain air, seeing the olive trees of peace rustle their silver leaves, she knew that she was one of the few in all history who could safely look a dragon in the eye and so she did. And then she gathered flowers and made a daisy-chain, a garland, to lead the dragon, her new friend and spectacular pet, out into all the illuminated and flower-strewn pages of Christian manuscripts, and the tiny leaded jewels of stained-glass windows, and all the dangerous and fearful places of birthing women's hearts.

The story says that after this she converted hundreds and thousands of people to her new faith, to the God who gives us power over dragons and fathers and Emperors and our own fears.

The story says that, in the end, they executed her. They cut her head off because of her faith. Even the dragon could not save her. The story says they killed her. Of course they did. What else could you do with a young woman whose father is a priest, but disowns her; who lives as a shepherdess in the desert; who turns down an offer of marriage from a prince; who is rescued from his wrath by a dragon; who is swallowed alive by a dragon and bursts free in a triumph of faith?

Beautiful, young, stubborn and powerful – you can't let a woman like that live. Better send her virginal and laughing to be a martyr in heaven.

Look, this is what the story says. It is a story. Pope Gelasius said we did not have to believe it. It is too much even for *The Golden Legend*, that bizarrely optimistic volume which can record as fact more things than you or I have ever dreamed of. *The Golden Legend* has no trouble at all with thaumaturgy, gender-shifting, bi-location, psychokinesis, monster management, cosmically disruptive births, levitation or magical origins, but even *The Golden Legend* falters here, cannot quite accept the dragon, wonders if perhaps this is slightly less than authentic, slightly not scientifically provable.

But the faithful do not care. They love St Margaret, they seek her assistance, they dedicate themselves, their children, their churches and their treasuries to her. She is their friend. She meets their needs. She makes them laugh and rejoice and praise and celebrate. Her cult spreads, from nowhere to the whole of Europe.

Joan of Arc, another awkward virgin, hears her voice, challenging and inspiring her to act. She also gets burned.

St Margaret, virgin, martyr and metafiction, pray for us.

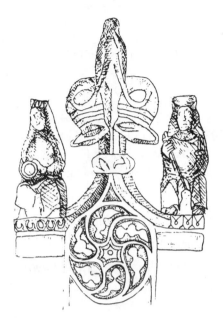

The *Golden Legend* (*Legenda Aurea*) provides the best-known of the many medieval lives of Margaret. It was originally compiled by James of Voragine, Archbishop of Genoa, who died in 1298. It reflected a romantic and narrative approach to the lives of the saints, clearly influenced by concepts of chivalry – so that imagination and beauty were emphasized more than the majesty and power of God and the devout human qualities of the individual saint which had dominated eleventh- and twelfth-century hagiography. It became an immensely popular work throughout Europe, and was translated into English and published by Caxton in 1503 – it remained a 'bestseller' up to the Reformation.

Margaret's emblem in church imagery is first and foremost the dragon, sometimes represented as tamed and led, sometimes chained or pierced and writhing at her feet. Occasionally she appears popping out of the dragon's mouth; sometimes she carries her girdle or a long cross and, at Caher in the South of France, she is shown keeping a flock of sheep.

Julian's Three Requests

She asked for three graces by the gift of God:
The first was to have mind of Christ's passion.
The second was bodily sickness.
The third was to have of God's gift three wounds.

Julian Speaks out of a Moment of Fullness, of Fullness Alike of Knowledge and Love, a Moment in Which All Is Given

I saw God in a point
        and
fulfilled my heart most of joy
so I understood it shall be in heaven without end
to all that shall come there

And he showed me
a little thing
the quantity of an hazelnut
lying in the palm of my hand
and it was as round as a ball
It is all that is made

It lasts and it ever shall last, for
God loveth it
and so hath all thing being
by the love of God

For as the body is clad in clothes, and the flesh in the skin, and the bones in the flesh, and the heart in the body, so are we, soul and body, clad and enclosed in the goodness of God.

Julian of Norwich
Born at the New Year, 1343
Died some time between 1416 and 1426
Theologian, author, anchoress

❦

Julian received her revelations on what seemed to be her deathbed, aged thirty, on 13 May 1373; she then recovered and lived on for many years as an anchoress (see below). She was much sought after for spiritual guidance – in her autobiography Margery Kempe speaks of the 'holy dalyawns' she had with Julian about the special grace given to her, Margery, by God, 'for the anchoress was expert in such things and good counsel could give'. Julian lived to be more than seventy, according to the testimony of medieval bequests. She is named after the church to which her cell was attached.

She realized the full meaning of her visions after twenty years' meditation and reflection, in February 1393: this is the approximate date of the composition of the 'Long' text; the 'Short' text being written down soon after she originally received the visions.

Both texts are unique in being the compositions of a woman in the vernacular Middle English written before 1400. They are steeped in the Bible, and Julian's only 'heresy', which prevents her acceptance as a saint by the Roman Catholic Church, is that she does not accept hell.

However, in her insistence upon faith, and the nature of grace, the Trinity and many other aspects of Christian dogma, Julian is entirely orthodox.

> . . . *There are no miracles or cult of Julian, and no Life. It is her message that matters and that is, that the Cross of pain is also the Cross of glory, that the Cross reveals the love of God.*
>
> *To Julian the Crucified says not, 'Are you sorry your sins crucified me?', but, 'Art thou well pleased that I suffered for thee?', and she says simply, 'Yes'. For her the Cross is the revelation of the Love that is God; and having faced steadily all the implications of this, in the end she can write, 'Love was our Lord's meaning.'*
>
> Benedicta Ward, 'Julian the Solitary', in *Signs and Wonders*

Palimpsest: Of Julian the Woman

❧

Very little is known of her
not even her Christian name
and she is not alone
she had probably been married
and if she had borne children
they too were dead
and she is not alone
writing of the motherhood of God
in a tradition of writing about the life of
prayer for women
she is not alone
    But for I am a woman, weak, feeble and frail,
    should I therefore not tell you
    of the goodness of God
    since that I saw in that same time that is his
    will
    that it be known?

Writing in deprecation of her womanhood
she is not alone
if this were a device
presenting herself an unlettered woman
of Christian humility
and to emphasize grace
later after twenty long years
in her cell she destroyed those words
no longer needing to work
by the world's rules
disregarding her critics for
her supreme message

Very little is known about Julian of Norwich, not even her baptismal name. . . .
Before 1413 she became an anchoress at St Julian's Church, Norwich. . . . [she] was
not a nun or an anchoress at the time of her revelations. She mentions that her
mother, the parish priest and a small boy were present at her sick-bed, which would
have been impossible if she were an enclosed religious. She had probably been married,
for unmarried laywomen of thirty were virtually unknown in medieval England . . .
we may deduce that she was a widow . . . and that, if she had borne children, they too
were dead by 1373.

Alexandra Barratt (ed.), *Women's Writing in Middle English*

In the East Part of this Church-yard stood an Anchorage, in which an Ankeress or
Recluse dwelt 'till the Dissolution, when the House was demolished, tho' the
Foundations may still be seen: In 1393, Lady Julian the Ankeress here, was a strict
Recluse, and had two Servants to attend her in her old Age. This Woman in those Days
was esteemed one of the greatest Holynesse.

Francis Blomefield, *Norfolk*

The earliest manuscript that survives of Julian's writings, from the mid-
fifteenth century, also contains a translation of **Marguerite Porete**'s *Mirror*
of Simple Souls, writings by Richard Rolle, such as *The Fire of Love and the*
Mending of Life, and part of **Bridget of Sweden**'s *Revelations*. It is held in the
British Library.

Other medieval devotional and/or mystical writings probably known by
Julian, who was an extremely well-educated woman, include *The Chastising of*
God's Children; Walter Hilton; *The Cloud of Unknowing*; and other spiritual classics by the early Fathers such as Jerome and Bernard. There are affinities in
her writings with Boethius, Chaucer, the *Ancrene Wisse* and many other
important medieval works. She shows close knowledge of, for example, St
Augustine and St Gregory, and of William of St Thierry, all of whom were
known in her day only in learned circles.

Julian was well placed for borrowing devotional books – in Norwich the
cathedral's Benedictine priory library was one of the finest in late medieval
England, and across the road from her cell attached to St Julian's church the
Austin friars too had a good theological library. Other communities in
Norwich included Franciscans and Carmelites: all evidence of the intellectual vigour of the place. Julian's greatest source of reference, however, was
the Bible. Her modern editors believe she made her own translations from
the Vulgate, especially of the Gospels, the Epistles, Hebrews, Psalms,
Wisdom and Deutero-Isaiah.

that there is no anger in God
tosses off the pettiness
of man's concern
now the anchoress is widely known an
expert in all such things
her good counsel is sought
and she is not alone

Now they know –
   'She knew it would be impolitic to set
   herself up as a bluestocking'
who know –
   'she herself had little use for
   bluestockings.'
      for of all things heaven deliver them
from those whose stockings are coloured
as their minds by the learning they claim for
their sole/soul
preserve
'I do not permit a woman to teach'

and in those years Julian impelled by the power of
God's presence she
assumed authorship a
woman writing from woman-depths and
all shall be well and
all manner of things shall be well

swept away hellfire and was consigned by the
Church to oblivion, for what power could
'little church' have in the face of such
gentle teaching?

Her Trials by the Devil

❧

And in my sleep at the beginning me thought the fiend set him in
my throat and would have strangled me, but he could not. Then
I woke out of my sleep, and . . . the persons that were with me beheld

She was clearly a learned woman, though she wore her learning so lightly, as shown by both the breadth of her reading and the skill of her arguments, her understanding and deployment of philosophical concepts, and her grasp of rhetorical devices. We do not know how or from whom she acquired her learning, nor anything about her parents, the circumstances under which she was enclosed, or who were her associates and directors.

In her desire for suffering in imitation of Christ Julian was representative of the devotion of her times as we know it through many anonymous unpublished prayers of the period, and particularly of the dominant Franciscan spirituality of Western Europe. However, her spirituality always emphasizes the counterbalancing joy of God and offers a predominantly hopeful note – as T. S. Eliot quotes her in *Little Gidding*: 'And all manner of things shall be well.'

Like **Marguerite Porete**'s *Mirror of Simple Souls*, Julian's *Shewings* remained a significant text for men and women religious long after she herself was forgotten.

Other quotations in 'Palimpsest' come from the editors of Julian's works, E. Colledge OSA and J. Walsh SJ, *A Book of Showings to the Anchoress Julian of Norwich*.

Another aspect of the 'temper of the times' associated with the great upsurge in Franciscan spirituality in the early fourteenth century was the influence of 'Franciscan' visual art, especially the crucifixes, to inspire the pious. The apparitions these inspired – crucifixes that spoke, or moved, or bled – were relatively frequent occurrences and they shape the background to parts of the Visions, such as that in which Julian writes of seeing the blood flowing from underneath the crown of thorns.

These representations – statues, images, objects – were important in so far as they were sources for the pious, taking them as far as human wits may encompass – 'als farfurthe as man ys witte maye reche', as Julian puts it. In other words, she makes the distinction between the object and its function and its power to represent the holy mysteries to limited human minds.

In the second of the three graces Julian had asked for – to experience in herself Christ's passion, bodily sickness and the three wounds – she had her 'bodely sight in the face of the crucifixe that hyng before me'. The details that follow, of the spitting, soiling, buffeting of Christ upon the cross, conform to the traditional pattern of the five mockings of Christ. (The

me and wet my temples, and my heart began to comfort. And on a little smoke came in at the door with a great heat and a foul stink. I said: Benedicite dominus! Is all on fire that is here? And I knew it had been a bodily fire that should have burned us to death. I asked them that were with me if they smelt any stink. They said nay, they smelt none. I said: Blessed be God! For then I knew well it was the fiend was come to tempt me. . . . I took power that our Lord had showed me on the same day with all the faith of Holy Church . . . and soon all vanished away, and I was brought to great rest and peace, without sickness of body or dread of conscience.

Mother Julian

❧

widowed we suppose and orphaned of her children
to the property of motherhood belongeth
kind love, wisdom and
knowing, and it is good

The mother's service is nearest,
readiest and securest,
for it is most of truth.
This office might not
could not, nor never anyone
has done to the full,
but he alone.
But our very mother Jesus, he,
all love,
beareth us to joy and endless living,
blessed must he be

YOU HEAR the reporter said
his face turned to
low stone I have never
heard such a sound and
be comforted

spitting Jew was a Passion symbol in medieval art.)

Julian goes on to describe how she saw the face of Christ, one half first, beginning at the ear, caked over with dried blood, 'till it closyd in to the myd face', and then saw the same in the other half of the face, 'and then it vanished evyn as it cam'.

While for her modern editors this is apparently a highly confusing description, to anyone familiar with modern art, Julian's account, recalling the portrait techniques of the Cubists, hardly seems so problematic.

Julian goes on to say that she wanted to see the Passion more clearly and was answered in her reason that God should be her light,

> For I saw him & sought him. . . . And thus I saw him & sought him, & I had hym and wantyd hym; and this is & should be our comyn workyng in this life . . . he will that we beleve that we see hym contynually, thow that vs thynke that it be but little; & in the beleue he maketh vs evyr more to gett grace, for he will be seen, and he will be sought, and he will be abyden, and he will be trustyd.

Julian's message is clear: God *wants* to be known by us, and seeks every means to discover Herself to us.

> Thus was I lerid, that love was Our Lords mening. . . .
> And I saw full sekirly in this and in all, that ere God made us, he lovid us: which love was never slakid no never shall. And in this love he hath don all his werke, and in this love he hath made all things profitable to us. And in this love our life is ever-lestand. In our making we had beginning. But the love wherin he made us, was in him fro withoute begynning, in which love we have our beginning. And all this shall be seen in God without end, which Jhesus mot grant us. Amen.
> 'I keep thee full securely.'

Julian's message of hope radiates from this security, and from her firm belief 'that if a man or woman was genuinely turned to God for however long or short a time, even if it were for a single day of service . . . he should experience all three degrees of delight'.

Moreover, the fullness of her understanding of the Triune God, and within the Trinity, of the nurturing, caring, mothering Christ, is balanced by her vision that temptation will be permitted by God, who nevertheless protects her creatures through the ordeal, and that suffering is allowed because, while not good in itself, it is a means to come closer to God.

this pain entered unseen
along the street to the
school doors fall wide open
how cradle this slaughtered
grieving   I am the ground
of thy beseeching

I keep thee full securely
god of the cross, hear this
morning's mourning
children massacred
in-gathering

> 'Our heavenly mother Jesus
> may not suffer us that are his children
> to perish.'

L ove was his meaning.
 Who shewed it thee?
Love.
What shewed he thee?
Love.
Wherefore shewed it he?
For love.

Hold thee therein.

The Anchoress' Rule

❧

love your windows as little as possible
see that they be small
let the cloth upon them be twofold
black cloth; the cross white
within and without

If we could indeed apprehend the closeness of God in the homeliness of Julian's metaphors:

. . . he is our clothing, for love wraps us and winds us, embraces and encloses us . . . .

we should indeed become part of Her. It is through the love of God that everything in creation lasts as it does:

. . . because God loves it, and so through the love of God, does every thing have its existence.

Since God is the maker, the lover, the keeper, if we try to find our peace in this 'little thing', in this world, we can never find 'ease of heart or soul'. We must be *noughted* through love – only then can we receive spiritual peace.

J. A. S. Morton (ed.), *The Nun's Rule, Being the Ancrene Riwle Modernised.*

The *Ancrene Riwle* dates back to the thirteenth century, a hundred years before Julian. It gives a good idea of how austere the life of the anchoress was: every detail was laid down for their way of life, and when they entered their cells, they were literally walled up, only to leave their enclosures in their coffins. They were, however, allowed maidservants – bequests are recorded to Alice, a servant of Julian's. A window would open onto the church or a place that people could reach to talk to the anchoress and seek spiritual advice, as Margery Kempe did.

The anchorites' cells were attached to churches in the middle of towns or villages, as Julian's was to the church, it is assumed of St Julian, in

make the sign of the cross
on mouth   ears   eyes   breast
nor are you to preach to any man
'I do not permit women to teach'

ye shall not possess any beast
except only a cat

because no man seeth you
nor do ye see any man
ye may be well content with your clothes
be they white, be they black
only see they be plain, and
warm and well-made – the skins
well-tawed, as many as you need
for bed and for back
next your flesh no flaxen
nor iron haircloth hedgehog-skin
no scourge thereof or leather thongs
nor lead nor briar
let your shoes be thick and warm

in summer ye are at liberty
to go and to sit barefoot
to wear hose without vamps
wear drawers of haircloth
very well tied, the strapples
laced tightly, reaching your feet
if ye would go without wimples
wear warm capes and over them
black veils. have neither ring, nor
broach, nor gloves, nor ornamented
girdle. have your hair cut four
times a year, to disburden your head
wash yourselves wheresoever necessary
as often as ye please

Norwich. It was considerably harder to be an anchorite than an ordinary religious, and separate ceremonies, initiated by the bishop, marked the enclosure. The anchoritic life was defined as a living death, hence the symbolic importance of the walling up of the door to the cell from the outside. A second door led into the parlour, where privileged visitors and her confessor might meet with the anchoress; this was also home to her 'maidens', or maidservants. The anchorites saw themselves as the weakest of Christians for whom it was necessary to flee the world to save their souls, to avoid sin.

The anchoritic movement provided an outlet not only for those with a calling to the solitary life, inspired by the tradition of the desert fathers and mothers, but also to those who were poor and uneducated, and therefore debarred from gaining access to the convents.

There was a strong anchoritic tradition in the British Isles. The only woman anchorite who became a subject of hagiography was Christina of Markyate: she fled from a rejected suitor to live as a hermit in the woods, but ended her life in a convent.

SOURCES

A Book of Showings to the Anchoress Julian of Norwich, ed. E. Colledge osa and J. Walsh sj (Pontifical Institute of Medieval Studies, Toronto, 1978).

Alexandra Barratt (ed.), *Women's Writing in Middle English* (Longman, London, 1992).

Francis Blomefield, *Norfolk: An Essay Towards a Topographical History of the County of Norfolk*. Quoted in Colledge and Walsh.

Robert Llewelyn (ed.), *Julian: Woman of Our Day* (Darton, Longman & Todd, London, 1985).

J. A. S. Morton (ed.), *The Nun's Rule, Being the Ancrene Riwle Modernised* (Kings Classics, London, 1905).

Benedicta Ward, *Signs and Wonders: Saints, Miracles and Prayers from the 4th to the 14th Centuries* (Variorum Press, Aldershot, 1992).

Medieval texts adapted from the mid-seventeenth-century MS Sloane 2499, quoted in Barratt, *op. cit.*, and from Paris, BN Fonds Anglais 40, also mid-seventeenth century, quoted in Colledge and Walsh.

Maximilla, Prophet and Priest

❦

I am pursued like a wolf out of the sheepfold; I am no wolf: I am word and spirit and power.

Let a woman learn in silence with all submissiveness. I do not permit a woman to teach, nor to have authority over men; she is to keep silent. For Adam was formed first, then Eve; and Adam was not deceived, but the woman was deceived and became a transgressor. Yet woman will be saved through bearing children, if she continues in faith and love and holiness with modesty.

I do not permit women to teach.

Woman is the work of Satan.

I am pursued like a wolf out of the sheepfold; I am no wolf: I am word and spirit and power.

For as many of you as were baptized into Christ have put on Christ. There is neither Jew nor Greek, there is neither slave nor free, there is neither male nor female; for you are all one in Christ Jesus. And if you are Christ's then you are Abraham's offspring, heirs according to the promise.

'Peter, thou hast ever been of a hasty temper. Now I see that thou dost exercise thyself against the woman [Mary Magdalene] like the adversaries. But if the Saviour has made her worthy who then art thou to reject her? Certainly the Saviour knows her surely enough. Therefore did he love her more than us. Let us rather be ashamed, put on the perfect Man as he has charged us, and proclaim the Gospel.'

Maximilla: late 2nd century
Montanist prophetess

Maximilla, quoted from Eusebius, *Ecclesiastical History*, 16, 17. Maximilla, with Priscilla and Montanus, were the founding prophets of the heresy called Montanism. Most of the little we know of her has to be gleaned from unsympathetic 'orthodox' sources like Eusebius.

I Timothy 2:11–15.

Severus (a Marcionite), quoted by Epiphanius, *Panarion*, XLV, 2:1.

Galatians 3:27–29: reconciling these two Pauline texts remains problematic. Fiorenza sees this second quote as presenting a 'pre-Pauline baptismal formula' ('Word, spirit and power: women in early Christian communities' in R. Ruether and E. McLaughlin (eds), *Women of Spirit*, p. 31, thus meriting priority over the more dubious Timothy quotation. But they remain the main proof texts of the pro- and anti-women's authority factions within Christianity.

Gospel of Mary (second-century Gnostic text), quoted in *Papyrus Ber.*, 18:1–21. The Gnostic Gospels present alternative narratives of the life of Christ. Our knowledge of them has been extended by the discovery of the Nag Hammadi texts – which Elaine Pagels has written on extensively from a feminist perspective. Although Gnosticism appears superficially more pro-woman than orthodoxy, it is predominantly anti-material (dualist) and esoteric – neither of these attitudes in the long run is likely to work to women's social advantage.

The reason for this silence imposed on women is obvious: women's teaching in the beginning caused considerable havoc to the human race; for the Apostle [Paul] writes: 'It is not the man who was deceived, but the woman.'

Oh Eternal God, Father of our Lord Jesus Christ, the creator of man and woman, who replenished with the Spirit Miriam and Deborah and Anna and Hulda; who did not disdain that Thy only begotten Son should be born of a woman; who also in the tabernacles of the testimony and in the temple, did ordain women to be keepers of Thy holy gates . . .

Those disciples of women, who chose as their master Priscilla and Maximilla, not Christ the spouse of the Bride, appeal to the following women prophets: the daughters of Philip, Deborah, Miriam the sister of Aaron, Hulda and Anna the daughter of Panuel. But these women prophets did not speak in public nor in the assemblies.

I am pursued like a wolf out of the sheepfold; I am no wolf: I am word and spirit and power.

What a muddle, eh? What a wrestling, confused and difficult time, for the early Church; and no fax machines, no E-mail, no telephones. No postal services, but bad roads, and not much literacy. Long attenuated channels of communication that do not work very well, and only work very slowly. By the time you learn that what you are teaching is all wrong, it is too late. How do you say to the newly baptized, the newly baptized and already committed – they have left their homes, or given away their money, or set out as missionaries to new places, or given up their work, or been fed to the lions and are now venerated as martyrs who have gone the long and hard way to the great victory banquet of heaven and whose blessings lie sweet upon their communities: how do you say, more simply, to your neighbour whom you have converted and who is now wrapped in the love and joy of their new faith: how do you say, sorry, but we have just learned that we got your baptismal formula wrong; or we were not authorized

Didymus, *On the Trinity*, III : 41 : 3.

Apostolic Constitutions (fourth century), III, 6:1–23, rite for the ordination of women deacons. See Louis Bouyer, *Women's Ministry in the Early Church*, for the context to this and other ordination rites for women in the first four centuries. Bouyer makes clear that the early Church did not have a unified view of the appropriate role for women within the official ministries any more than it had – as these quotes make clear – a unified view of woman's ontological relationship to humanity, perceived as male.

Origen, *Fragment on 1 Corinthians*, para. 74.

(Or – to sum up – there was considerable diversity of opinion about the role of women in the early Church!)

There is a more general tendency to treat the Church in the way that fundamentalists treat the Bible: to assume that 'orthodoxy' and its smooth development were somehow both 'natural' and inerrant. (This affects both the Catholic churches and the Protestant churches, who believe that it is possible to reconstruct the 'primitive' Church free of all the accretions of Rome – 're-formed' rather than 'new'.) Even the earliest documents of Christianity, the Epistles, make clear that there was variety and tension, particularly about church order, from the very beginning: e.g., I Corinthians 1 : 12; Galatians 2 : 11–21. Luke in Acts plays down all differences as far as possible, but even he is unable to suppress the major debate of the Jerusalem Council about the relationship between Jews and Gentiles, for example.

Modern historical scholarship has enabled us to have a much clearer picture of both the early Church and the society in which it was taking root. The debate about the role of women was ferocious – it is important to

to baptize; or we have wrongly interpreted Paul; or we're not doing that like that any more? You cannot say it. You do not say it. And someone has gone off to the Gauls, or the Syrians, or just round the corner and now there are too many people who were taught wrong and are teaching wrong and it is impossible to sort it out. And there are local churches, individual charisms, determined bishops, international aspirations, rich pickings in Rome, persecutions, personal differences and within all, and – it must be believed – through all this, there is the deep power of the Spirit, blowing where it listeth, blowing hope into sad hearts, humility into proud ones, authority into those unused to it, power to work miracles into people who better know how to count small change. A muddle.

Poor Maximilla. The question is not – do women prophesy?
    They do. Obviously they do.
    Maximilla is prophesying.
    She is seized with the Spirit and she prophesies. And the fruit of her prophecy is salvation, for they flock to hear her and believe. For the Lord has done a new thing and poured out the Spirit on all flesh, on all who confess his name. But still behind her is a great weight of reassurance, in case she doubts, although she does not doubt because she has been baptized, but should she doubt Paul and Peter and Justin and Irenaeus and the whole biblical tradition, all make clear that women can be filled with the power of Spirit and can prophesy. And prophets . . . everyone knows that prophets are second only to apostles, and may speak with authority and may baptize and celebrate and dream and speak.

    Miriam, Deborah, Anna, Mary.
    The four daughters of Philip, the deacon. Amnia in Philadelphus.
    Theone, Stratonike, Eubulla, Phila, Artemilla, Numpha, Myrta.

But Maximilla is a woman. Everyone knows that Paul does not permit a woman to speak; she must keep silent. . . . But the Lord Jesus said to Mary of Magdala, 'Go tell the brethren. Teach them, tell them a new thing, tell them I am ascending to my father and your father; to my God and your God.' He told her to speak. Paul told her to be silent.
    Poor Maximilla.

remember that the Epistles were just that, letters written to specific communities about their own structures and theologies, not generalized sermons: if something is specifically criticized or forbidden we can be reasonably certain that it was happening (if women are told not to teach, it implies that they were in fact teaching – and so on).

But it is now evident that beyond the books finally chosen for the biblical canon (the official writings of Christianity) there was a great deal of theologizing going on, and the disputes lasted well into the fourth century: formal sanction to an exclusive canon of the present 27 books of the New Testament was not given until the Synod of Carthage in 397.

Provided that women accept that 'development' is not necessarily 'degeneration', the non-canonical writings and the early history of the Church can provide a great deal of inspiration: there clearly was a genuine impulse towards equality for women in certain parts of the early Church. How we *use* these texts to claim our authority now is a crucial question. At the imaginative, creative (prophetic) level Michèle Roberts's novel *The Wild Girl* uses the Gnostic gospels as a resource for women's spiritual empowerment; and, in her inspiring fiction *The Illusionist*, Anita Mason represents the doctrinal chaos in the early Church as a human struggle for power and holiness.

From Acts 2:17 (see Joel 2:28–32).

Paul: e.g., I Corinthians 12:2–16 (even though he is fixing limits on women's behaviour, he assumes their prophetic ministry); Peter: Acts 2:17, 18; Justin Martyr (*c.* AD 100–165): *Dialogus contra Tryphonem* 88; Irenaeus (*c.* AD 130–200): *Adversus Haereses*, III, 11; *Didache*, 10:7; 13:3; 15:1ff.

A selection, by no means exclusive, of women prophets whose names are mentioned in the documents of the first three centuries of Christianity – from both 'orthodox' and 'heretical' traditions. The first four are biblical: Miriam, the sister of Moses and Aaron, is explicitly called 'the prophetess' (Exodus 15:20), as was Deborah, who was also 'judging Israel' (Judges 4:4); and Anna (Luke 3:36). The reputation of Mary, the mother of Jesus, as a prophetess was based on the Magnificat (Luke 1:46–55), but was universally accepted in early Christianity.

John 20:17, 18.

Miriam, Deborah, Anna, Mary.
The four daughters of Philip, the deacon. Amnia in Philadelphus.
Theone, Stratonike, Eubulla, Phila, Artemilla, Numpha, Myrta.

And her own dear Priscilla; her sister and fellow companion, her beloved. The Christ in the form of a woman had come to Priscilla telling her that where she lay was a holy place and here, here, soon, here in these very days, here, now, Jerusalem would descend out of heaven to this very place.

Here on the holy mountain the Holy Spirit, the Paraclete, still spoke directly to the children of Christ and led them further, deeper, more mysteriously into the Truth they had been promised.

Miriam, Deborah, Anna, Mary.
The four daughters of Philip, the deacon. Amnia in Philadelphus.
Theone, Stratonike, Eubulla, Phila, Artemilla, Numpha, Myrta.
Priscilla.

Maximilla. The Spirit spoke to her, Maximilla.

She was pursued like a wolf out of the sheepfold; she was no wolf: she was word and spirit and power.

The Spirit spoke directly to Montanus, to Priscilla and to her. The three of them, the trinity, the sign. And in their trinity none was afore or after the other; none was greater or less than another; but the whole three persons were together and co-equal. It was the sign. They were the sign. The sign of renewal and hope.

They came, she and Priscilla and Lucius Montanus, from Pepuza in Phrygia, and they were driven by the Spirit to ecstatic utterance. They proclaimed a new 'Church of the Spirit'. The Spirit spoke in her, and when Lucius had died the Spirit commanded her to continue – and it did not matter what they said, she had no choice but to obey first and before all the commands of the Spirit, the Holy Spirit, the comforter, sent to her, to them all if they would, by the power of the resurrected one, born in Spirit and in Truth. She was obedient, she was humble, she

The four prophet daughters of Philip the Deacon are mentioned once in the Bible (Acts 21:9) but Eusebius refers to their great fame (*Ecclesiastical History*, III, 31).

Amnia: The Montanists claimed her as a prophetess; Eusebius (*op. cit.*, V. 17) does not deny her prophetic standing, but claims her for orthodoxy. The other names are all mentioned, as prophets, in the *Acts of Paul and Thecla*.

Montanism, a rather successful second- and third-century 'heresy', was based on the belief that the Johannine promise that 'the Holy Spirit, whom the Father will send in my name, he will teach you all things' (John 14:26) meant that the revelation of God in Christ was not complete. The Montanist movement was founded in Phrygia by Montanus and his two equal companions, Maximilla and Priscilla (or Prisca). They claimed that the Holy Spirit spoke directly to them. Their pronouncements were written down and gathered as sacred documents similar in standing to the words of the Old Testament prophets, the sayings of Jesus and the letters of the apostles. Since Maximilla and Priscilla were proof that the Holy Spirit spoke through women, the Montanists admitted women to all the church 'offices' including baptizing and celebrating the Eucharist. They proclaimed the imminent Second Coming, and demonstrated a contempt for 'the World' and an extreme asceticism – including fasting, martyrdom and total sexual abstinence.

In one of their more famous oracles Priscilla was visited by Christ in *female* form, announcing the descent of Jerusalem upon the place where she lay.

Montanism was in many ways analogous to the contemporary Charismatic Movement. However, Montanism has two particular features of interest here: in the first place it was open to women's ministry – authorizing itself by establishing a 'prophetic line of succession' parallel to the growing apostolic line (which was exclusively male); and in the second place Montanists did not accept that the Old and New Testaments marked the limits of revelation. They believed that contemporary spirit-filled interpretations, visions and prophecies could have the same status as those enshrined in the canon of the Bible – a pressing issue at that time, as the process to establish a fixed canon of Scripture was gathering impetus.

was the instrument of the Holy Spirit of the Lord Jesus.

What was she to do? She was called to speak the tongues of wisdom. She was called to obey. 'If you love me feed my flock', so she broke the bread and fed the people and they believed and were saved.

What was she to do? She was called by the Spirit in whom there was neither male nor female, to proclaim the day of jubilees, the coming of the Lord, who came to them already, as woman, as man, as spirit and word and power. She knew the power, it drove her, drove her out of her frail body and into the heavenly places and gave her words like Isaiah was given.

What was she to do? It was driving her mad.

She was not a wolf. She was not a work of Satan. She was Maximilla, a Phrygian woman, called by the Spirit, called to a radical obedience beyond the point at which she was answerable to any man, even Christian men, who denied her right to teach because she was a woman. She could not, she might not, she was not permitted, to bow to them, to their commissions and lies and indictments and commands. The Spirit drove her, harsh and hard. She was a servant, as all the prophets were, of God the most high, and she must speak.

What she said was only what Paul had said: We are not of this world, we are not bound by the law; we are free. We despise the law and the world that made it. We are willing to stand here that our freedom be not compromised.

They slander us, they who should uphold us.

They say we murder babies; that we mix their blood in the cup of sacrifice.

They say we urge the faithful to kill themselves.

They say I am mad.

They say they know I am mad because I speak the words the Spirit gives me, and break the bread that Christ gives to all, and I call the people to holiness, like John at Jordan.

And they would make her mad in the end, if they could.

But she knew better. She was not called to suffer in silence. Silence was not her calling. Her calling was to call, to call out, in bitterness and in truth.

I am pursued like a wolf out of the sheepfold; I am no wolf: I am word and spirit and power.

During the life of Montanus the cult grew astronomically. After his death, however, Maximilla became the leader of the movement. She was persecuted by other sections of the Church, her Spirit was repeatedly 'tested' and various commissions were set up to prove she was a fraud. Since her opponents had some difficulty finding serious problems with the group's doctrinal positions, they resorted to the most extreme slanders – which, inevitably, focused on its women leaders. The old charges of sexual immorality, the abandoning of husbands and the murder of children played a substantial part, along with the Pauline injunctions against women teaching.

In her plaintive cry – 'I am pursued like a wolf out of the sheepfold; I am no wolf: I am word and spirit and power' – Maximilla articulated the dilemma that confronts all women, however orthodox, who wish to act within the official (ordained) ministries of the Church. Her reference to the sheepfold cannot be accidental. The precise duty laid on Peter in John 21 : 17 – 'Feed my sheep' – and the frequent gospel references to shepherds suggest that she knew exactly what she was saying. She was claiming her right to leadership within the community, based on Spirit-filled prophetic authority as equal to (not in preference to) apostolic authorized authority.

At this key moment in Christian history she lays down the terms of a conflict that has continued ever since – the conflict between 'charismatic' and 'apostolic' authority. On the whole women have profited, in terms of access to leadership functions, in unsettled times, when the power of the Spirit to 'break through' has been valued by men. Women nearly always seek self-authorization from internal movements of the Spirit, whether expressed as the Holy Spirit, like Maximilla, the Inner Light, like **Mary Fisher**, or direct mystical experiences – **Joan, Catherine of Siena** *et al.* The modern approach of arguing that the tradition itself authorizes women has not yet had a chance to prove its efficacy.

In a sense, all Christian feminists have to be Montanists in order to survive within Christianity. In particular we must believe that we are authorized 'in the Spirit' regardless of whether the 'official' Church recognizes it; that we have a 'radical obedience' to an internally revealed truth, over and above our obedience to orthodoxy.

While our charisms are not, on the whole, those of manic convulsive ecstasy we do nonetheless claim that the biblical revelation cannot be complete because it is inevitably patriarchal, and that subsequent revelation,

Maximilla, bloody-minded and joyful,
Maximilla, heretic, prophet and priest,
Maximilla, word and spirit and power,
Prophesy again in these times for us your children.

particularly about women's ministry and interiority, may be accorded an authority as high as Paul's and Matthew's. We can and will draw our own authorization from sources whose authority we require the rest of the Church to acknowledge. Although we do not act from ourselves alone, we are not 'wolves'. There comes a point when our obedience requires us to say to the Church itself, 'It is time you remembered that although I am a servant, I am not your servant', as Ursula le Guin puts it in *A Wizard of Earthsea*.

We must believe that the ministry of many women is destroyed not because of its doctrinal content, but because the ministers are women.

Bridget of Sweden

The son of God told his spowse
seynte Birgitte what must be in our howsyses
cloth of dedes of mercy –

let these treasures be our incarnation
guard we in owr house peace to God
and to owr neighborr
works of mercy be compassion
helping of wretches
and abstinence that is from euyll desyris and luste
but rich in treasure

foremost the linen
cloth of peace that wrapped our Saviour

that is so soft, so easy to the
bare body, in the summer bridal
fresh,
– linen that growyth of the erth –

summer through the flax fields deepen
haze under the East
Anglian pale washed sky a bluer rim
against the low lands slow unfolding
clipped to steely Northerns the coast
century by century
towing cities abbeys flax-fields his-
story

Bridget of Sweden (Birgitta): 1303–1373
Visionary, patron saint of Sweden
Founder of the Brigittine order
Feast: 23 July

❧

Material taken from *The Revelations of Saint Birgitta*, ed. W. P. Cumming (Early English Text Society, 1929), from the Garrett MS, mid-fifteenth century, Princeton University Library. There are six other extant MSS in the UK of Birgitta or Bridget's life.

Note: In the *Revelations* Birgitta speaks of 'linen cloth of peace and patience and woollen cloth of deeds of mercy, and silken of abstinence from evil'.

Birgitta's homely language and imagery come across in the medieval English translation. Her *Revelations* were extremely popular, and, revealingly, she was one of Margery Kempe's helper saints.

Born in Finstad, near Uppsala, daughter of a rich governor, Birgitta experienced visions from the age of seven. Her father, 'seeing that she was as comely as Esther', married her to a man 'noble, rich and prudent', at the age of thirteen, against her will; her husband was eighteen.

They postponed consummation of the marriage for two years: when they finally began to have sexual intercourse, it is recorded that they prayed for a child pleasing to God on each occasion. Finding she took pleasure in sex, Birgitta struggled with her desire; she whipped herself secretly to compensate for her 'marital pleasure'. In Lent she slept on the floor.

Birgitta had four sons and four daughters, the fourth of whom, Catherine, was canonized one hundred years after her mother. It was said that Catherine as a baby refused to take milk from the wet-nurse, or from her mother, after either had had sex.

After eight children were born, Birgitta and her husband lived together celibately until his death in 1343 or 1344. She then turned over the management of her estate and family to others, having received a vision in which

into the intransigent gulping
ocean

blue —
of pacyence and of pece spun
it leseth nott hys couloure

— cream white she wore it
late for her rescuing stepped
up between flower-columns
hand-in-hand Beloved to her
dedication — the ofter it
is wesh the clenner it is —
and she/he shall be as
one

Blessede be you, my God and maker,
Ihesu Criste
that I haue not well lyved in my days
and that I haue do lytell to thy wyrshyp.
Ther-for thy mercye ys moste
do with me after thy mercy

❦

Our Lady Saint Mary spoke to Saint Birgitta and said:
  'Fasten to the rock of the Passion of my Son as Saint Lawrence fastened it to him. . . . And when he was stretched out upon the coals, and when his grese melted and ran into the fire, and fire enflamed all the members of his body, he looked up to heaven with his eyes and said, "Blessed be you, my God and my maker, Jesu Christ. I know that I have not well lyved in my days, and that I have done little to thy worship. Therefore for thy mercy . . . I pray thee do with me after thy mercy." And with these words the soul departed from the body. Look my daughter he that loved my son so much and suffered such pains for his worship, yet he felt himself unworthy to get to heaven. How then are they worthy that live after their own will? Therefore behold the passion of my son and his saints; for they suffered not so great things

Christ told her he had chosen her to be his bride, and went to live as a penitent at a Cistercian monastery.

Shortly afterwards, in 1346, she founded a strict double monastery at Vadstena in Sweden, which was ruled by an abbess. Any spare income from the monastery was given away; the rule promoted extreme frugality in everything, and the buildings were ordered to be plain and not luxurious, but because learning was encouraged, the monks and nuns might have as many books as they wanted.

Birgitta continued to experience visions which instructed her to go to Rome, where she sought approval for her order. She set off for Rome in 1349, with her confessors, and never returned to Sweden, living in Italy and making many pilgrimages.

Birgitta entered fearlessly into the politics of the Church and Empire of her day, denouncing corruption and writing letters of advice and reproof to kings and prelates. She exhorted the Pope in exile in Avignon, Clement VI, to make peace between France and England, and to return to Rome, and she worked vigorously to re-establish the papal seat there.

In 1367 Urban V finally gave way to pressure from her and returned to Rome, but found the conditions there so bad that he returned to Avignon within three years. Birgitta warned him of the consequences of such a move. He died that year.

In 1370, three years before her death, the Order of the Brigittines of St Saviour received papal approval. Two years later she had a vision which ordered her to go to Jerusalem, where she experienced further visions. Growing rapidly weaker, she returned to Rome where she died in 1373.

The Brigittine nuns at Syon were known for their scholarship and their rare library, thanks to Birgitta's encouragement, in which expenditure on books was never stinted (see above). A convent at South Brent in Devon claims unbroken continuity with Syon Abbey, which was founded by Henry V.

Her life, the *Vita Sanctae Birgittae*, was written by her two confessors within four months of her death.

According to *ODS*, Birgitta was canonized for her virtue, not her revelations. Since most women mystics had to rely on confessors or spiritual directors to transcribe their message, the *ODS* objection, arguing the fallibility of her *Revelations* because of their editing/interpreting is strange, to say the least.

without cause, but for to give others example of living, and for to show how straight a reckoning my son shall ask of sin, that will not that the least sin be without amendment.'

There is also nothing so light than to Joy of the good of his neighbour and to will to him as himself. This linen cloth aweth to be to the naked body; for to the heart wherein God will rest, peace from sin must cleave most nigh and most principally amongst all other virtues. For this is the virtue that brings God into the heart and holds him when he is brought in. This peace springs out of the earth as linen; for very peace and patience springs of beholding of a man's own frailty. For if a man that cometh of the earth behold his own feebleness, how soon he is wrath and heavy if he be offended, hurt or diseased, if he think thus, he ought not to do to another that he may not bear himself. . . . For then peace loses not its colour, that is to say, its stableness. But it is the more stable and sad. . . . And if it happen that peace be fouled in any wise by unpatience, then the oftener and the sooner it be washed by penance, the whiter it is towards God; and the more it is troubled and oftener washed, the gladder and readier it is to bear and to suffer.

Godiva

She woke in the morning feeling wonderful. She had gone to bed fearful that the eyes would find her out in the night. But she woke strong and clean. Smiling. Powerful.

For the first time in her life she had taken a choice. She was changed for ever by that choice. She had chosen the hard thing and she had done it. It had changed her. She had been ignorant, where she had prided herself on being innocent. There was no going back, she had learned too much about herself: her vanity, her pride, her lust, her meanness, her anger. How many layers of contradiction there were in a brave act, and yet when it was done it was still a brave act.

When she pleaded with him it had not been brave: it made her feel good to plead and be rejected. She had not known that either and when she had wept she had been perfectly sincere. She had pleaded with him not to tax the townspeople further and he looked at her coldly and said,

'My Lady, it is very easy to be generous with what is not your own.'

It was cruel to shame her so, for indeed he was her husband and she owned nothing that was not his. But her shame, her sudden silence, stirred an anger in him:

'Easy to give what is not your own. Easy charity to the poor when your own belly is fed, Madam; easy nursing of the sick when your own bed is made for you with fine linen. Easy to earn a pardon on their behalf and walk proud in the town as a saviour. But you only give what is mine. You never give what is yours.'

She locked her chamber door. Once a month, cold as a nun doing Lenten penance, she paid him his marital due so that he had no complaint against her. She believed this was holiness, and rose before the sun did and he, turning in a drugged and desolate half-sleep, would see her beautiful fat plait, a rope for his neck, her back turned to him as she knelt at her prie-dieu.

Godiva of Coventry: 11th century
Benefactress of the poor

The legend of Lady Godiva is well known. She was the wife of Leofric, Earl of Mercia. In 1043 they founded a Benedictine monastery in Coventry and endowed it generously. They also built a church at Evesham, where she was subsequently buried. The earliest account of her ride is in Roger of Wendover's Latin Chronicle from between 1188 and 1237, where he describes Godiva as, 'a true lover of the Mother of God'. Her will contains probably the earliest mention of a rosary in England. The 'peeping Tom' element, however, was not introduced until the seventeenth century. A full discussion of the historicity of the tale can be found in *Godiva of Coventry*, edited by Joan Lancaster. In his chapter in the book H. R. Ellis Davidson concludes that the story 'is basically founded on fact, although the facts were not precisely related by Roger of Wendover and other early chroniclers', since elements of folk story, local tradition and memory of her exceptional piety, had been introduced. (Her situation, in short, was like that of many canonized saints from the same and earlier periods.)

The twentieth-century Catholic Church has a bizarre preoccupation with women's sexuality – or ideally their lack of it. The present Pope has canonized or beatified 272 people and so far as I can determine none of the *women* selected have been non-virgins.

Virginity has, of course, had different meanings at different times. For example, Peter Brown in *The Body and Society* has suggested that the stress on virginity in late antiquity was a radical anti-state posture. In the absence of contraception, the refusal by women to have sex was a refusal to act as 'good citizens' in an empire with a falling population: virginity here was a prophetic, eschatological and political act.

The I've-taken-a-vow-so-I-can't-get-married virgins so immensely popular in the twelfth and thirteenth centuries were women who were using their virginity to create a form of autonomy (and given the improbable circumstances, it is as likely that other women were using them to create their

'I have nothing but your love, my Lord.' She thought that was sweet, was prudent and charming and elegantly submissive. Now she knew it was sardonic. Taunting.

It was effective too. He was angry; she was virtuous. 'You have your honour, your dignity and your goddam mousy modesty. Will you give that for your beloved poor, so their wicked lord won't hurt them? Will you?'

Quite suddenly it was serious. Perfectly serious. She hesitated because it was serious. She had no idea what he would ask of her. She had to look into her own heart and ask herself 'Will I?' Ask urgently because whatever he demanded it would not be easy. 'Will I? Oh God, will I?' Then she saw the cold faces of the townspeople, people labouring under the burden of poverty uncomforted by a good Lord, and a long winter setting in. Would he ... would he take her in public? Would he drag her to his room and make her watch while he did unspeakable things with his wanton? Would he ... her limited imagination failed her.

'Yes, I will,' she said. Softly.

He laughed. There was a challenge now. His pride and hers were both at stake.

'Easy speaking, my lady,' and he laughed. He swilled his cup, tossed off the wine and then not looking at her, not looking at anything except the empty cup in his hand, 'Ride then, ride through the city, naked. Let them see. Let them see their sweet lady naked. For them to gawp at.'

He had chosen well. He saw the dark blush spring on her chest; her eyes dilate. He had never seen her naked himself.

She stood up. 'Tomorrow my Lord, after Lauds is sung.' She made a deep courtesy and in silence left the room. They had gone too far, both of them. She held her head high and did not start to moan until she had reached the shelter of her own bed.

She could not.

He had her white mule, saddled, waiting. She came down into the courtyard wrapped in a cloak.

'Madam,' he bowed.

He lifted her into the saddle and held out his hand for the cloak. For one moment their eyes met. Shame and pride.

own forms of autonomy). These marriage-resisters were seen to proclaim the sacramental freedom of marriage over against the rights of fathers; independence of choice over chattel status.

Virginity was also treated, at various times, as a way for women to claim spiritual equality with men; a way of evading parental control; and a difficult but necessary sacrifice in order to make time for other more interesting activities. All these options are represented elsewhere in this book.

Basically, however, the situation has changed: while virginity remains a perfectly legitimate and healthy personal choice, it really does not create a radical new space or theological challenge.

Hence my interest in Godiva. We urgently need some stories to counterbalance this single, and increasingly meaningless, emphasis on 'female purity', which I think puts women's psychological well-being and even lives at risk. As a commentary on this Godiva story, here is the story of Maria Goretti, who was canonized as recently as 1950.

Maria Goretti was twelve years old in 1902. She lived in Ancona. Her father, an agricultural worker, had died two years before, and Maria looked after her little brothers and sisters, so that her mother could go out to work. A young neighbour harassed and threatened her for sex. This is a horrible, but regrettably common, event. She rejected his advances; and then resisted his attempt at rape. He stabbed her repeatedly and she died in hospital the next day.

A contemporary hagiographer, David Farmer, in *The Oxford Dictionary of Saints*, concludes: 'In canonizing Maria Goretti the Roman Catholic Church also honours innumerable others who in similar circumstances preferred death to dishonour.'

This is pretty sick-making: as the world turned towards the supposedly modern, did no one notice that her childhood had been stolen already through the death of her father and the financial needs of her family? No priest, no church chose death rather than the dishonour of allowing her poverty and vulnerability to exist. No one, in 1950, in the aftermath of a world war in which women were raped, as they are in all wars, and seduced and betrayed and deserted, no priest, no church seems to have thought of the pain the canonization might give to such women, who had failed for one reason or another to prefer death to rape. They said Maria was a martyr, a martyr to chastity and a Christian way of life: a brand-new category of martyrdom; a martyr to no universal truth or any central dogma.

She raised her fingers to her throat and her hands were shaking so violently that she could not undo the clasp. He reached up and helped her, but he did not take it off for her, that she had to do herself. He had not forced her; it was her choice.

She dropped the cloak onto his arm. An evil little wind bit into her and her nipples tightened, pricking up hard and cold. There was gooseflesh on her arms. She sat very straight with her eyes down. The blush he had seen last night now covered her whole upper body like a rash. Her legs were mottled, purple from the cold. She bit her lip against the tears and pleadings. Charity was not easy.

He slapped the mule's rump and it moved forward through the open gate. She felt a rush of sensations – the shame, the cold, the shame. And a new and peculiar feeling where her hidden hair was twitched against the leather, the creaking saddle against her thighs, her woman's secret parts. The cold, the shame, the strange rhythm under her bottom, the shame, the new shame of that rhythm, the shame, the cold.

As she went down into the town, she discovered a new shame. If she must do this, why had she not done it when she was still young and lovely? Naked was shame enough; but a blotchy nakedness, with her breasts saggy and the white skin of her belly soft and scrunched from childbearing – that was too much shame. She could have borne it, she thought, if she could have ridden out in the fullness of her loveliness and they had stared in awe. But to be naked and pitied. It was too much. And her vanity shamed her too. She tried to think of their need, but she could see only their pity, that their lady was old and ugly with goose-flesh and wrinkled skin, like a fowl ready for the spit.

And because there was all the shame, noisy in her head, and because her shame kept her head down and her eyes fixed on her hands, at first she did not notice the quiet. As the mule turned towards the market she realized that it was very quiet. Perfectly quiet. Curious, she raised her head a little. There were no gaping crowds, no laughing children, no leering, jeering men. The street was empty. Every shutter closed, every door set to.

This was their gift to her, she knew, the only gift they could give her, and she must know that it was not an easy giving for them either. This gift of quiet and shuttered windows and a wasted day.

Maria Goretti died because she believed that her Beloved would rather have her stabbed, bleeding, mutilated, dead, than 'deflowered'.

All this raises some questions.

Does the Church also *dishonour* every woman who fails to persuade her rapist to kill her; who under such hard circumstances makes a different choice?

Who, indeed, are these 'innumerable others . . . in similar circumstances'? Surely and necessarily they are *women*? Is Farmer, here, unusually, allowing women a 'universal humanity' lest the perpetrators of these innumerable atrocities be too easily identified?

If her attempted rapist had failed to kill her, or the doctors had saved her life, what would be her status in the eyes of the Church? If her rapist had been successful, had hit her sharply over the head, for example, rendering her unconscious and had then raped her, what would be her moral standing? If he had turned her unconscious body over and penetrated her anally, but not raped her, would she be a virgin? If she had given in quickly, or after a long fight, or because her baby sister was screaming with terror, would she have gone to heaven? What does any of it have to do with her, poor child? How can you be a heroic martyr if it all depends on the whim of a crazed, power-mad, mean, misogynist man?

What 'dishonour' accrues to the victim of a vicious crime? Are the murdered dishonoured? The robbed, the falsely imprisoned, the assaulted, the attacked, the abused?

Why? Why should the Church *honour* anything so idiotic? Why is 'virginity' regarded as a 'virtue' *at all* since it lacks all the normal qualities: it can be stolen from someone without consent; it can be destroyed by accident, by horseback riding, by normal bodily functions; the failure to maintain it cannot be fully repented of; it cannot be prayed for, deepened or restored through grace? Why should we be expected to rate that silly bit of skin above the life of Farmer's 'devout but cheerful' young woman?

Devout but cheerful! But. BUT. *BUT.* Is devotion usually in contradiction to good cheer, to joy and happiness? What is the mean meaning of that 'but'? I think perhaps that little casual word gives away a game I do not want to play.

What does this say about God? Our God, who, the psalmist says, will uphold the righteous? How can women be asked, women be asked, expected, required, to 'love' a God, who under these and innumerable similar circumstances would rather see us dead than uphold our innocence? Why

Tears sprang to her eyes, but she might not weep because if there were tears on her face when she returned to the castle he might think she regretted her love. She had no regrets, only gratitude and love and friendship. She held her head high although there was no one to see.

That was before she felt the eyes. She felt them, full of lust and spite, long before she knew what had changed. The blush which had slowly ebbed leapt back.

The eyes. She had to cross the market square. She must cross it, inch by inch, at the steady jogged pace of the mule. She had to travel towards the eyes, straight towards them across the wide wide square. The eyes were watching her, were devouring her, were gaining power from her shame, were delighted, piggy, greedy.

Her head was still high with the love she had received. She looked straight into the eyes. And because the eyes held her she could not help but see also the shaking, the rhythmically shaking shoulders. She could not help but know what the hands she could not see were doing.

She had not known the first thing about shame. She was besmirched, filthy, beaten, defeated. She took one hand from the reins and tried to cover her genitals.

The rhythm of the shoulders was the same rhythm as the rhythm of the saddle against her own body. She was vile. She deserved this, and more. Who had she believed she was in her pride? Who could love her? Not her husband. Not the people. Only the greedy consuming eyes and the greedy demanding rhythm that told her that a woman's place was to have no place; that to act or to fail to act, to choose or to accept, that under all those things there was only this foulness, was only wickedness and filth.

Briefly she found her anger. She would have him flogged; she would tell her husband and he would burn out the horrible eyes with a red-hot poker. Then her rage hit a terrible knowledge: she could do nothing. To punish the eyes which had looked would be to repudiate the generosity of the eyes which had not looked. They had had the right to look and they had generously not used their power. And they had so little that to deny their right to be generous, to make her so precious a gift, would be a terrible sin. She could not deny their love to satisfy her dignity.

should we imagine that the God who became incarnate and who died on the cross so that we might have life more abundantly likes dead sex toys? Does God really think the life of a twelve-year-old is less valuable than a small piece of skin – more precious in the sight of God is the unbroken hymen of a child, than a laughing loving living woman? What sort of God is this? (The answer, whisper who dares, is – a male God.)

(And none of this should be allowed to stand over against the courage of a young woman who – her bloody-mindedness hidden in all the tellings of her story, including, I fear, mine – chose her own way over other people's definitions.)

There are probably other women who, like Godiva, were prepared to use or risk not just their bodies, but their bodies' meanings – their desires, self-esteem, chastity, modesty, honour – for the good of others: only when they are celebrated will the celebration of virginity have any true content.

Easy charity, he had sneered. Now she had learned what hard charity was. It was hard.

She had to pass below the eyes, just a few feet away. She straightened her back and thought of the long winter and food for her friends and rode on. And her ride became a procession, a tiny moment of honour and glory. She rode under the castle gateway, still blushing with shame and with her head held high.

He was standing barely inside the gate. He had the cloak ready and almost tenderly he wrapped her in it and lifted her down as though she was precious. She could see his bafflement, his wonder and his pride.

'They did not look,' he said.

'No,' she said.

'They love you,' he said, almost curious.

'Yes,' she said.

There was a pause.

'I . . . ,' he started. He was trying.

'I have been too proud,' she said; 'pride and I called it modesty. We could do better, you and I, my Lord.'

She knew then what the rhythm of the creaking saddle meant and was not ashamed, but amused. He took her hand and led her, with the formality extended usually to a royal messenger, back into the hall.

It was not perhaps altogether surprising that she feared she would see the eyes when she slept, but that in fact she woke strong and clean, smiling and powerful.

For each time we honour a woman who prefers her chastity to her life, we should also honour one who rides humbly into her own city, stripping herself of dignity, of modesty, of the protection of social convention and even of self-esteem, for the love of the poor and the oppressed. For so did he in whose name she rides.

Blessed is she who comes in the name of Lord. Hosannah in the highest.

Edith Stein: Sister Teresa Benedicta a Cruce, ODC
Born 12 October 1891, Breslau
Died August 1942, Auschwitz
Carmelite, philosopher, teacher

The Mystery of Redemption Lies in Remembrance

At last I have read through your life. I started on Monday, a dour Monday in February, sitting in the library muffled up against the cold, the curtain drawn against the door to exclude the draughts. The day was uncompromisingly grey, heavy. I did not begin at the beginning:

> Edith Stein was born in Breslau, Germany, on October 12, 1891, the youngest of eleven children of a devout Jewish family whose family had been merchants from Silesia 'nurtured on the spirit of the psalms'.

When finally I began to read – for I had been avoiding you – I plunged into your life as a philosopher, and read on and on, through your work with Husserl, your early search for truth, until I reached the point where the biographer described the impact of your friend, Ellie Reinach, on you at the time of the death of her husband in the First World War.

And I thought, is that all? One woman bears the loss of her husband with courage and serenity, even a kind of inner joy, and this sceptical philosopher is bowled over? Just this causes her to begin combing Christianity, reading the New Testament, plunging into worlds unrecognized by philosophical research?

But of course it is never one cause, never one impetus.

What previously she had seen as coincidence, on retracing her past Edith began to see as evidence of a pattern weaving her into her new awareness. By 1917 this had become concentrated into a pressing need to discover the truth about Christianity.

Baffled, but filled with respect and admiration for your intellect, I followed your patient search for this new truth like a detective story, fascinated by the interweaving that continued over the years 1917 to 1922 between the winding path to faith and the demands of philosophy.

You were baptized into your faith on New Year's Day, 1922. For the next eight years, turning your back on the academic world, you taught at the Dominican sisters' school in Speyer and worked on your translation of Aquinas.

I don't remember how far I got that day. As I write this it is the Monday in Passion week, the first of April, and it is impossible to deny Spring any more. The days of reading your life were the fag end of long winter darkness, the first winter of a new life, a winter of small, unexpected joys. And later, perhaps, will come renunciation.

Renunciation. The ultimate oblation, the clearest choice. The action of laying down your life, consciously choosing to remain with your people, not to accept the escape route offered you to America.

Through the days of living with your life, a bitter north wind I could not keep out of the old house or out of my bones blew relentlessly. I read each day till the small light faded.

From the difficult temper tantrums of a gifted two-year-old, through the achieving, quiet, but well-loved schoolgirl, the period when you suddenly left school at thirteen, apparently unable to cope with the demands of life, then your return eight months later and from then on your unstoppable progress through all the hoops of the German education system, your certificates, degrees, right up to the higher doctorate – through all this your life was on course to accelerate through the academic world and reap rewards as probably the first woman professor of philosophy in Germany, the leading phenomenologist after Husserl's death. But the Holy Spirit moved you otherwise. The rational, the logical, proved insufficient.

Through your life I can trace the pattern of transformation by which gradually God came to take up more and more and more of you. The exacting demands of your mind could not let this quest run second.

After baptism into the Catholic Church when you were thirty-one, you went to teach and live in a convent for eight years, abandoning academic ambition while you produced your translation of St Thomas Aquinas' *Disputed Questions on Truth*, considered to be a 'key text in Thomas's thought'. And this after years as one of the leading exponents of phenomenology, as Professor Husserl's assistant, at Göttingen University and then at Freiburg.

It was at Göttingen that you had heard Max Scheler, a phenomenologist and Catholic convert, speaking on religious questions. I wonder what Scheler said all those years ago, about 'The Nature of the Holy', which proved to be 'the first push along the road to conversion'.

Scheler convinced you that humility is at the foundation of all moral endeavour – whose sole purpose is to lead the individual to the loss of self in God – and on to new resurrection.

There can be no resurrection without self-abandonment. Without submission. The resurrected life must first pass through death.

Is it humility or huge pride that leads to such sacrifice?

The choice for you, you said, in choosing Christianity, was the choice between life and death. Only Christianity could give you the freedom to abandon yourself completely to God, to make a conscious sacrifice of your self for the annihilation of your people.

Your teaching career in Germany was halted by the Nazi persecution. The pedagogical institute in which you worked in Münster 'relinquished' you. Nurturing your hope of entering a religious life you confronted the darkness in lectures, letters and writings. The reality of what it could mean, carrying the cross, as a Catholic Jew, drew closer.

You did not suffer the Jewish persecutions silently. You wrote tirelessly of the dangers facing Germany and the countries of Europe. You wrote to the Pope, imploring for an encyclical against the Nazi persecutions.

Silence.

In 1934, despite your mother's great grief and anger, you entered the silence of Carmel. As your spiritual director at the Benedictines put it, you ran 'singing for joy, like a child to its mother's arms, never doubting'. It was a 'life absolutely transformed by the love of God, down to the last detail'.

Of that joy you wrote in a letter to your sister,

I know well that all I have written you is colourless. But in comparison with the full-ness of grace that each day brings, a poor miserable human soul is so tiny. Yet com-pared to what that soul can nevertheless comprehend, all words are inadequate. And when one has to write about this to so many people, one is afraid of making the sacred into something banal.

By the late 1930s it was no longer safe for you to remain in Germany.

The nuns transferred you to the convent of Echt in Holland for safety. Just before you left you had been working on St John of the Cross, the *Dark Night of the Soul*.

After the Church in Holland took a stand against the Nazi pol-icies, Catholics were amongst the first to be picked up in that coun-try. Both you and your sister were hunted down in the convent and taken with other Jews, Catholics and religious in the death trucks to Auschwitz.

To attain life you accompanied death.

What does it mean to read the life of one already beatified – whose early life was one of exceptional achievement, but who placed all of it at the feet of the cross to follow the way of Jesus? Can I, can we, identify with such renunciation, drenched as we are in our belief in the need to affirm womanhood, to claim our place, our pressing need for our voices to be heard?

What truth/s can feminists find in this story? Can Edith Stein's life speak to us at the end of the twentieth century?

Is the fact that her renunciation was so complete that it led to the gas chamber, that her path was to live out to the full the horror of the sacrifice – not, as Christ was, a Jew by Jews murdered, but a Jew by so-called Christians murdered in the company of her people, by those baptized and confirmed into the faith she had embraced – is that bitter irony luminescent?

Does it diffuse hope or savage anger at the waste of another, talented life?

Writing of the experience of a group of Franciscans in the concentration camps, one who had survived recalled the depth of the darkness, the sense of abandonment, the death in their hearts which seemed to make it impossible they should ever praise again. And yet, bound by their discipline, saying their office, out of that darkness came momentarily light, came from he knew not where but from God himself, inexplicable joy.

Is there joy in your story, in its dark ending?

Having refused the offer of an invitation to escape to America, your eyes were open, there was no turning back. Your lot lay with those European Catholic Jews who were amongst the early victims for their church's defiance.

Whatever the dangers, the difficulties, your trust in God grew, affirmed by a sense of 'resting in God' that from time to time visited you. Your power of acceptance and patient waiting sustained you.

Your Damascus road moment had been reading **St Teresa of Avila's** life. From St Teresa you learned of the choice between life and death, the honesty required in recognizing one's own sin, which arrests one in death, and the freedom needed to offer oneself to God.

It became clear to you that the two greatest challenges imposed on the human person are honesty and freedom. And from Teresa you learned of the meaning of interior prayer, where resistance to God begins to be healed and transformed. It was her name you took for your baptismal name, and kept as the first of your names when you entered Carmel – Teresa Benedicta a Cruce: Teresa, Blessed of the Cross.

It was the chapter on the power of prayer in your life that drew me first, and the expression of that prayer in action; the lectures you gave on the role of women, on 'Foundations of women's education', on 'The ethos of women's vocation'. You saw women's mature life, shaped by Christianity, as a source of healing to the world. You spoke of the need to become

broad . . . tranquil . . . emptied of self . . . warm and transparent . . . only hearts that are emptied and silent can be penetrated by grace . . . before they can be ready to assist others, women need to be anchored securely in their own depths.

You wrote of how we need to 'live every day in recollection and prayerfulness ... to find breathing spaces, moments in which [a woman] can return to herself and rest in God'.

In the convent you practised two hours of silent meditation each day. For you solitary prayer was the indispensable preparation for the visible events of the Church's history. You saw the Christian calling primarily in terms of the individual's transformation into God: 'The more recollected a person lives in his innermost soul the greater the power he radiates outward and the greater the influence he exerts on others.'

You considered that a mystic is simply a person who has an experiential knowledge of the teaching of the Church – that God dwells in the soul.

That God dwells
in one habit and aprons
with one small veil
that
the mystery of redemption lies in remembrance
who
identified herself with Esther

On 4 August 1942 you wrote to Mother Ambrosia (Antonia Engelmann), of Echt Convent, from Westerbork barracks in Drente where the Nazis were holding the convoy of trucks bound for Auschwitz:

Now we have a chance to experience a little how to live purely from within. Early tomorrow a transport leaves . . . what is most necessary: woollen stockings, two blankets . . . I would like the next volume of the breviary – (so far I have been able to pray gloriously) . . .
PS. 1 habit, & aprons, 1 small veil

The spirit of Carmel is love: 'All one can do is try to live the life one has chosen with ever greater fidelity and purity in order to offer it up as an acceptable sacrifice.'

'To arrive at being all, desire to be nothing' (St John of the Cross).
It is the richness of your life that speaks to me. Your death appals me.

It is through your letters that I reach you. Here there is meaning-
in-life. Not theology, though that too, not hagiography, though the
stuff of that is here, and not myth, though your life is rich enough for
myth. I mean, things like friendship, keeping the threads between loved
ones, once inseparable, now distanced, still knotted: loving and caring,
laughing and crying, sharing accounts of differing realities that live and
dance on the page, such human truth I find in your letters.

Not dragons nor pearls nor rocky caves nor three loaves to last a
lifetime, not leaf-shaped boats miraculously bearing saints across
stormy seas, not heads struck off and carried to appointed resting-
places or replaced on necks, not beasts tamed, springs gushing blood
or dripping oil. Not miracles nor magic, visions nor visitations, not
angelic communion – just the ordinary details of your extraordinary
life. Of cakes and pupils, veils and prayers, sickness, hopes, and above
all friendship, radiating out of the letters, counselling, encouraging,
affirming.

*If you imagine me at my place in choir, then please without the white mantle . . . [see
me] rather in the old brown habit, very small, [seated] on the floor. Just so, my
meditations are not great flights of the spirit, but mostly very humble and simple.*

When I raise my eyes from your words, the sun is out, shining
through the small-paned window, so warm in this light-filled library,
under the dark old ceiling beams. Pools of light on the pale wooden
floor.

The pink and white tulips on the window sill have found strength
to greet the first touch of spring, lifting up their heads on drooping
hothouse stems. Miraculously.

Unable quite to leave you, I linger over your letters, rich in the life and
liturgy of your church, and feel a now-familiar envy at the complete-
ness, the steadiness, the warmth that emanates from and embraces you.

In one letter you wrote to a friend, 'One can spend a silent Advent
here, as secure as an unborn child waiting for the great day of new birth.'

The gift of your life to this reader is birth, not death.

Which we are to learn is one.

Edith Stein entered the Carmelite convent in Cologne on 12 October 1934 and took as her religious name Teresa Benedicta a Cruce. She made her simple vows on Easter Sunday 1935, and her solemn vows in 1938.

While in the convent she was encouraged to continue with her philosophical work, and in the summer of 1936 she completed *Act and Potency*. Her other works of this period include her major work, *Finite and Eternal Being*. She also wrote *Ways of Knowing God*, *The Symbolic Theology of the Areopagite* and *The Science of the Cross*.

Edith Stein placed great emphasis on the example of great women of prayer who had preceded her; two saints whom she particularly drew upon were **Bridget of Sweden** and **Catherine of Siena**.

She was beatified on 1 May 1987. At the ceremony, Pope John Paul II wore for his chasuble her clothing-silk from her profession as a Carmelite. It had survived the destruction of the monastery under Allied bombing in October 1944. Ten years later, since this piece was written, she was canonized.

SOURCES

L. Gelber and R. Leuven (eds), *Life in a Jewish Family* (1986).

Waltraud Herbstrith, *Edith Stein: A Biography*, trans. B. Bonowitz (Harper & Row, New York, 1985).

Edith Stein: A Self-portrait in Letters, 1916–1942, trans. Josephine Koeppel OCD. Vol. 5 of *Collected Works*, ed. L. Gelber and R. Leuven (ICS Publications, Washington, DC, 1993).

Edith Stein, the Hidden Life: Hagiographic Essays, Meditations, Spiritual Texts, trans. Waltraud Stein. Vol. 4 of *Collected Works*, ed. L. Gelber and R. Leuven (ICS Publications, Washington, DC, 1992).

County Clare, 1996

I. BELLHARBOUR

Here nailed to the old beam
small crosses gathered each saint's day
February first ends winter.
Now the hut collapses the roof timbers fall
now the sweet hay stacked up to the old range
the cupboards and shelves an old
refrigerator piled in a corner
dung heaped to the sky through low-slung roof
-branches and the laths falling
Still St Brigit's crosses nailed neat to the beam.

On first of February, in hope of spring
schoolchildren hand out the crosses,
since before time when
past the soft Clare winter
only the winds and the rains blow

Brigit of Kildare, Mary of the Gaels: c. 452–c. 527
Abbess of Kildare
One of the patron saints of Ireland
Feast: 1 February

❧

Daughter of a Christian slave, Broicsech, and Dubthach, her mother's pagan master, Brigit was born near Kildare, possibly in Uinmeras, between Rathangan and Monasterevin. She chose a life of virginity dedicated to Christ at an early age, on a plot of land granted by the king of Leinster, and founded the Cell-Dara (Kildare), the church of the oak. She lived there with a group of similarly dedicated companions, a community of women religious who kept a sacred fire burning day and night. (Extinguished by papal orders in the thirteenth century, it was relit after popular unrest.)

Archaeological finds show that there had been a fire burning near the site in the Iron Age, lending credence to the theory that Brigit and her fellow women religious converted from druidic religion to Christianity.

The community was served by Conleth as their priest and after Brigit's death a double monastery of men and women was founded.

The shrines at Kildare were sacked by the Vikings in 836 and all the relics destroyed.

A monastery survived at Kildare until the Reformation.

An office of St Brigit survives in more than two hundred manuscript breviaries and many manuscript lives, on the Continent as well as in Ireland.

In Ireland more churches are dedicated to Brigit than to St Patrick.

It is she that helpeth every one who is in a strait and in danger; it is she that abateth the pestilences; it is she that quelleth the anger and the storm of the sea. She is the Prophetess of Christ; she is the Queen of the South; she is the Mary of the Gael.

She is guardian to the poor; she protects the harvest, she increases the yield of cow and sheep; she lights the fire in the hearth of the croft which is never extinguished.

2. NEAR LISCANNOR

As evening turns towards Compline
An old woman walks slow
down the hill.
She greets my companion and enters the shrine
to make the rounds.
Head swathed in the hot sun she
six times makes the round
stopping to tell the rosary before
the glass-coffined statues.
We see her no more.
Up the worn stone steps
a grove of trees shades the well-mouth
spattered with coins
cards and texts.
Above on the hillside she stoops to talk
where lie in their common home
lie in their muddle
the communion of saints and sinners

If you make the rounds,
if you say the prayers
your wish will be granted.
They say,
My companion informs me. Twice.
In case in my English stupidity
   I miss the point.

She is patron of studies and learning.

Although born a bondmaid, she was never sold in bondage; she dedicated herself to the religious life; when the time came for Brigit to take the veil, Bishop Mel used the form for ordaining a bishop. When one objected the bishop said he had no power in this matter: 'That dignity has been given by God unto Brigit beyond every other woman.'

Born without sin or travail like the Virgin Mary, Brigit is Mary of the Gaels, midwife and bride of Christ:

A fair birth fair dignity which will come to thee therafter from thy children's descendants, who shall be called from her great virtues truly pious Brigit; she will be another Mary, mother of the great Lord.

(This prophecy is part of one ascribed to druid Moccu Mugairne)

The Book of Lismore, from the lost Book of Monasterboice and other MSS, fifteenth century, in Whitley Stokes (ed.), Lives of the Saints from the Book of Lismore

As well as four early saints who wrote of Brigit, the medieval biographer of Brendan told that

when on his sea-voyage the saint found the sea-monsters honoured Brigit beyond all other saints, because she never took her mind from God.

She never washed her hands or her feet, or her head among men. She never looked at the face of a man. She would never speak without blushing. She was abstinent she was innocent she was prayerful she was patient . . . she was glad in God's commandments.

Denis O'Donoghue, *Lives and Legends of St Brendan the Voyager* (1893)

Besides the story of her ordination, other legends of Brigit's life feature her in clashes with authority and with other Irish, male, saints such as Patrick and Brendan, legends such as the drying of the cloak: Brendan came to visit Brigit on the plain of the Liffey, for he wondered at the great name she had for doing miracles and wonders. As she came in to welcome him, she laid her cloak to dry on the rays of the sun. When Brendan laid his cloak to dry, it at once fell off.

That these saints were contemporaries . . . or even met, is extremely unlikely; the stories reflect struggles between the followers of their various traditions . . . valuable accounts of the sexual dynamics of the time.

Mary Condren, *The Serpent and the Goddess: Women, Religion and Power in Celtic Ireland*

3. LISCANNOR, KILDARE

Your statue shows not the
  Queen of air, fire, patron of arts,
hanging her cloak on a sunbeam
pouring out ale to overflowing
making the butter come right.
Your modern plaster-cast statue shows
an old woman cloaked in brown
black eyes looking out blind
from her dead white face.

In the palm of her hand
she cups a crude child's toy
her abbey, Ireland's foremost, of Kildare.
So she mocks you
She the virgin,
founder, nun,
circumscribed
made over in the new
Roman tradition
patron saint, properly accoutred,
properly connected.
Of Mary of the Gaels
the honey of her poetry her
hospitality her prophecy
only the wind over the limestone pavements
lifting the shining petals of
bloody cranesbill
Bishop Brigit Queen of Fire
  nursemaid of the Christchild

An unknown author of the tenth or eleventh century attributed to Brigit this wish-prayer: 'I Should like to Have a Great Ale-Feast for the King of Kings; I should like the Heavenly Host to be drinking it for all eternity.'

> *Every day and every night*
> *That I say the genealogy of Bride,*
> *I shall not be killed, I shall not be harried,*
> *I shall not be put in cell, I shall not be wounded,*
> *Neither shall Christ leave me in forgetfulness.*
>
> *No fire, no sun, no moon shall burn me,*
> *No lake, no water, nor sea shall drown me,*
> *No arrow of fairy nor dart of fay shall wound me*
> *And I under the protection of my holy Mary,*
> *And my gentle foster-mother is my beloved Bride.*

Alexander Carmichael (ed. and trans.), *Carmina Gadelica*

In the nineteenth century, Alexander Carmichael collected many charms for healing both animals and people from the crofters of the Western Hebrides, most of which invoked Mary, Brigit (or Bride as she is more often known), Patrick or the archangel Michael. Examples include the charm of the sprain, for healing a horse's leg. There are other poems or hymns which invoke the womanhood of Bride or her praises for protection. House-blessings invoking her protection are still used.

Brigit's unchallenged position in the establishing of Christianity in the fifth and sixth centuries in Ireland alongside St Patrick is the more remarkable in such a patriarchal society, and arguably suggests a strong continuity between the druidic priestly caste and the new saints.

The descriptions given to her are local, earthy, poetic and mysterious all at the same time – she is: Bride of the mantles/ of the peat-heap/ of the twining hair/ of the augury/ of the white feet/ of calmness/ of the white palms/ of the kine.

She is: Bride – woman-comrade/ woman-helper/ woman mild/ own tress of Mary/ nurse of Christ – and to recite her genealogy and her praises is to invoke powerful and magical protection:

> *I am under the keeping*
> *Of my Saint Mary:*
> *My companion beloved*
> *Is Brigit.*

County Kildare, 1995

❧

walking
away from the small town
a hot clear morning
long-ago saints look out
past the neat hedged-bloodstock
primed paddocks
enclosing wealth
on the hoof
a small field
neatly mown strip
against meadow beyond
your saccharine statue
in its embrasure
a small stream
winding japanese-fashion,
stones, a little bridge
playing an air on
domestic calm
orderliness
no one but us

the stones
the stations of the cross
we stumble through
the credo, the
Hail Mary, station by
station
the well is clear, a few coins
scattered   sins
cast off   blessings
invoked
selves left behind or simply

There are also charms for the wells of Brigit of which there are many in both Wales and Scotland.

RUNE OF THE WELL

The shelter of Mary Mother
Be nigh my hands and my feet,
To go out to the well
And to bring me safely home,
And to bring me safely home.

May warrior Michael aid me,
May Brigit calm preserve me,
May sweet Brianag give me light,
And Mary pure be near me,
And Mary pure be near me.

The richness of these nineteenth-century Hebridean songs and prayers shows how Brigit's presence was part of the everyday life of the crofting people:

Love this is that which Christ wrote
When stretched upon the tree
Mary mild be by my hand
May Brigit calm be by my head.

⚜

It has been said that there is a 'mountain of material on Brigit's cult . . . and an exceedingly small molehill of facts about her.'

A question that has frequently been asked is how did the foundress of a small and apparently insignificant Irish community achieve such widespread recognition and a lasting position not just amongst Irish saints? In the Celtic pre-Christian mythology, Briganta (Brigit) was a major figure, a goddess associated with poetry, fire and fertility, associated with the festival of Imbolc. The figures of the pagan goddess and the Christian saint became superimposed in folk experience.

luck invoked and the
blessing of Bride
nursemaid of Christ
Mary of the Gaels

as the man said
it is not feeling that
matters only the
   being there the
devotion

   follow the
footsteps, the
        doing

and after   surprising us
the peace of God
stole
our hearts, your
heart and mine
in the midst of the
searching,   twining

The oral material of poems, legends, blessings, other-worldly experiences, miracles, etc., composed so near Brigit's own time, do give some indication of the impact she had made on her society and her time. But as with all such material, the processes of reading involve deciphering faint traces, sifting scraps, inference and the construction of a metatext of meaning from those ciphers, scraps and traces, a process that we have called reading *otherwise* or, more usually, between the lines.

Analogously with fictional characters, as Edith Wyschogrod has pointed out, it seems clear that it is through the imagination that the affective power of the saints' lives is released in the contemporary world. In a sophisticated reading context, in which readers are used to decoding the doubling strategies of narratives, and situating themselves in different relationships towards those strategies, the impact made by a legendary saint such as Brigit will depend crucially on what readers bring to the texts.

The original texts here bear most heavily upon an experience of reading *place*, rather than texts, as indeed do similar texts for the other Celtic saints.

SOURCES

Alexander Carmichael (ed. and trans.), *Carmina Gadelica* (1900–1971, 6 vols, various editions. Selection republished by Floris Books, Edinburgh, 1994).

Mary Condren, *The Serpent and the Goddess: Women, Religion and Power in Celtic Ireland* (Harper & Row, San Francisco, 1989).

Daphne D. C. Pochin Mould, *The Saints of Ireland* (Dublin, 1964).

K. H. Jackson (sel. and trans.), *A Celtic Miscellany: Translations from the Celtic Literatures* (Penguin, 1951).

Lady Gregory, *A Book of Saints and Wonders*. Reprinted by Colin Smythe Ito, Gerrards Cross, Bucks, 1993 (first published 1906).

Whitley Stokes (ed.), *Lives of the Saints from the Book of Lismore*, ed. with translation, notes &c. (Anecdota Oxoniensa, Oxford, 1890).

Keep taking the tablets — for Teresa of Avila

Last night I saw a dark angel.
Keep taking the tablets.

Was it dark for my sins? For my blindness? For my protection? From its nature? And it spoke . . .
Keep taking the tablets.

And I was frightened. I was very frightened. It meant me harm. I feared it meant me harm. I feared perhaps it meant me harm. Perhaps it would mean me harm if I was frightened. And I was frightened.
Keep taking the tablets.

This morning early, early in an apricot-coloured dawn while the birds were singing, this morning The Blessed Virgin Mary in her courtesy came to visit me; she was accompanied by twelve virgins, twelve martyrs and both the women Doctors of the Church.
Keep taking the tablets.

Oh, and the angels. Did I mention the angels? So cream and gold and wings, wings that filled up the background as clouds do the blue sky; as their singing, their continual singing, filled up the background — and still against the background of their singing it was silent. Was it silent singing? So I could hear clearly when the Blessed Virgin spoke to me.
Keep taking the tablets.

I was happy. I was very happy. Consoled, empowered, freed.

Keep taking the tablets. We will not (yet) speak of schizophrenia, we will call this a psychotic episode. Keep taking the tablets.

The same tablets? The very same identical tablets? For terror and for joy?

Teresa of Avila: 1515—1582
Doctor, virgin, foundress
Feast: 15 October

⁂

Born in Spain, into a prosperous family with a *converso* background (Jewish converts to Christianity, often under some compulsion), Teresa entered the Carmelite order in 1535. Although dogged by ill health (possibly psychologically based), she developed a strong contemplative prayer life – accompanied by extreme mystical phenomena. Despite this she decided to found a new religious house in which the primitive Carmelite rule would be more rigorously kept. St Joseph's at Avila was her first house – and during her lifetime she founded sixteen more 'reformed' houses; and also persuaded some of the Carmelite friars to join the reform. The political and practical ramifications of this were considerable: at the height of the difficulties John of Cross (her protégé, and the first male member of the reform) was kidnapped and kept prisoner by the unreformed monks. She also had to deal with a great deal of suspicion from the Inquisition. She wrote a number of key works on the religious life, contemplation and mysticism – for example, *The Way of Perfection* and *The Interior Castle* – and an autobiography, *The Life* (originally to reassure the Inquisition as to her orthodoxy).

Bernini's famous statue *St Teresa in Ecstasy* shows her in a sort of post-orgasmic swoon, and this – along with some of her own reported experiences – has led to a sexualizing and psychoanalysing of her in very interesting ways. Her writing, however, suggests someone of energy, charm and great good sense and intelligence. In 1970 the Second Vatican Council named her and **Catherine of Siena** as the first women Doctors of the Church (a title given to those canonized for their theological work).

One of the 'tests' of divine authenticity that Teresa applied to visions was that those from God always made the recipient feel happy: a sensation the devil could not imitate.

353

Mother sits in her cell – gaunt with austerity, with age, with pain and sickness and weariness, weariness in her bones; and still – a miracle – so pleasing. So beautiful and so delightful. God made the velvet glove for this iron hand – the finest quality velvet, like a fat cat's purr, to wrap this adamantine steel.

Mother is writing . . . writing . . . writing. Mother is always writing.

Visions – visions concern her today. Visions and locutions and ecstasies and raptures. Visions she says – and she should know, having dealt with them in herself and in others for a very long time – most certainly happen. (Equally certainly sometimes people lie. No matter.)

By and large visions come from one of four sources.

(i) They come from the devil. The recipient should be grateful. A very learned Dominican once told her, 'Whenever we see a representation of Our Lord it is right for us to reverence it, even if it has been painted by the devil himself; for he is a skilful painter, and, though trying to harm us, he is doing us a kindness if he paints a picture in so lifelike a way as to leave a deep impression on our hearts . . . Just so the good or the evil is not in the vision, but in the person who sees it, and depends on his profiting by it and upon his humility.'

(ii) The poor recipient is mad. She ought to keep taking the tablets – the tablets, in Mother's mind, are enough food to eat, enough work to do and firm discipline applied with a warm affection.

(iii) The recipient has an overwrought imagination. 'It should be remembered that the weakness of our nature is very great, especially in women . . . so it is essential that we should not at once suppose every little imagining of ours to be a vision; if it is one, we may be sure that the fact will soon become clear.'

(iv) They come from God and that is good; it is also simple for 'that becomes clear from the great blessings that they bring to the soul'.

It is best to find out, writes Mother, to be careful and cautious and sensible. 'For these and similar reasons,' she writes, 'it is very important that each sister should discuss her method of prayer quite frankly with her prioress, who in her turn must be most careful to keep in mind the temperament of that sister and her progress in

'God made me pleasing', Teresa wrote. Her extraordinary personal charm is noted by many of her contemporaries. It certainly helps to explain how she managed to get so much done. Like **Catherine of Siena** and **Josephine Butler**, two other women with complicated political vocations, she had both this quality and an immense gift for personal friendship.

Teresa wrote voluminously, including a vast number of letters. Even when travelling she wrote. Her style has a wonderful intimate quality, often slightly mischievous and *faux naïve*. She sometimes wrote in ecstasy – enormous quantities of writing, during the production of which she would appear not to be conscious.

A great deal of Teresa's writings address this question. Her main aim was – for the sake of evangelism – to make mystical prayer both accessible and safer for people, especially her own nuns. This particular four-point scheme is based, somewhat loosely, on Chapter 8 of *The Book of the Foundations* (*Complete Works of St Teresa* (3 vols), trans. and ed. E. Allison Peers). Quotation marks imply quotations – but not necessarily in the same order as the original.

Chapter 7 of *The Book of the Foundations* (see above) is about dealing with 'melancholic' (depressive? more generally neurotic?) nuns. It shows an interesting sensitivity as to how much moral control such illness leaves its victims (she is clear that the truly mad are not blameworthy). It is fascinating, modern and sympathetic.

Teresa's self-derogation and diminishment of women have received a lot of attention recently, since they are apparently so out of keeping with her life. See A. Weber, *Teresa of Avila and the Rhetoric of Femininity*, and R. Williams, *Teresa of Avila* for further discussion.

perfection, so that she may help the confessor to understand her case better and may also choose a special confessor if the one the sister has is not capable of treating such cases. We must all take great care that things like these even if they are clearly of God, or favours recognized as being miraculous, are not discussed with people outside the convent, or with confessors who are not prudent enough to keep silent about them; this is a more important point than may be realized. The sisters too should not discuss such things among themselves. The prioress must be prudent, and must tend always to praise those who are outstanding in humility, mortification and obedience, rather than those led by God along this most supernatural way of prayer, even though they possess these other virtues.'

And even as Mother writes these wise and helpful words, like a strong swift impulse, the cloud, the powerful eagle of her own rapture seizes her — and her body is left, hand still holding the pen, still seated at her writing desk, rigid; and her body grows cold, though conscious of the greatest sweetness and delight. The eagle rises and bears her up upon its wings, and she is carried she knows not where, and resistance is impossible and there is light and glory and sweetness and a yearning, a yearning to die, and pain because death is not given, but only the longing, the longing for the sweetness of God and she is crucified between heaven and earth and can gain no pleasure nor joy from either and yet pleasure and joy are perfected with her, and she resists and resistance is impossible so without consent, she consents. She consents. And she sees the face of Christ, her betrothed, her promised promise; she knows nothing, nothing, nothing except that she knows nothing.

Now her soul has grown new wings and learns to fly.

And when she comes down, comes to, comes round it is drains — drains concern her today. She is exhausted, joyful, half asleep, mourning her loss, hoping, and it is drains that concern her.

The new foundation must have sisters, must have a chapel and the sacrament reserved; it must have a competent prioress, reasonable confessors available. The foundation must have enough room, light, air. Must have good drains.

The idiotic prefecture must be charmed. There will be difficulties. There will be ruffled feathers, ruffled pride, to be smoothed with crafty love. There will be a smiling, sweet firmness and, since it is

The relationship between a nun and her confessor was, to Teresa, a key element in her spiritual progress. Confessor, for her, meant director too. Many of her closest relationships were with her confessors, and the reforms of Carmel insisted on the right of every sister to choose her own confessor and consult freely with him. Teresa was much harassed during her early years by confessors who had no sympathy at all with the state of her soul – being either nervous or indulgent about her experiences. The modern term 'soul friend' might describe the flavour of relationship she believed in.

This, generally, is the view of the Catholic Church – that spiritual phenomena are interesting only in as much as they generate a growth in grace. They are not 'proofs' of holiness.

Teresa's raptures did, by her own account, come on rather suddenly and take various different forms. The images and details here are taken from Chapter 20 of *The Life of St Teresa*, see above). I have tried here to use only those that Teresa speaks of as 'usual' or frequent for her – and have avoided some of the more extreme moments she represents. Teresa distinguished with enormous care between various types of experience (even positive ones) – rapture, visions, union and so on. She would call this particular sort of experience 'rapture' (I think), rather than a vision, although she did certainly experience those too: both of Christ himself, and of angels and saints.

All seventeen of Teresa's foundations had particular difficulties, and the sisters often suffered acutely from lack of suitable accommodation, opposition within the locality, and poverty itself. Teresa had wanted all her reform houses to be unendowed, that is, with no capital, and she planned for the sisters to be mendicant (quite literally begging). This made towns very reluctant to permit them to settle. In some cases Teresa was prepared to compromise. Although the austerity of her Carmels was pronounced, she did believe that true prayer required a certain sufficiency in food, fresh air

God's way she will get her way, but it may not be easy. She assesses the complicated political situation. Kings, bishops, duchesses, nuncios, monks do not care much about drains. They want to know about her visions, not about her drains. But she, who has been shown the wounds of Christ, knows that drains — and charity of course — are very important.

And discernment also. That is important.

Most important of all is the Incarnation — the God who needs her. Who gave up his high honour to honour her by needing her, wanting her. Christ will look after the visions, the voices, (*the psychoses*), the raptures: that is God's business. She will look after Him — and after the drains.

She would sing 'Stand by your man' if she did not happen to live four centuries too soon. It is a song Mother would have liked.

She writes:

'The withdrawal from the corporeal world must doubtless be good since it is advised by such spiritual people, but my belief is that it should be practised only when the soul is very proficient; until then it is clear that the Creator must be sought through the creatures.'

Visions are creatures. Whose creatures? All creatures are God's creatures.

In the face of so much good sense the dark angel sheaths his sword, gives an ironic salute and slouches off.

The Blessed Virgin Mary in her courtesy smiles at Teresa, Doctor of Theology, mystic and competent housekeeper, drains and all. Then she smiles at me. I am happy. I am very happy. Consoled, empowered, freed.

The Blessed Virgin Mary pulls a small brown bottle out of her pocket; she unscrews the lid, shakes something out on to her hand and holds it out to me.

'What's that?' I ask.

'Stelazine,' she says. 'Keep taking the tablets.'

We are all laughing.

and security. The internal politics of Church and State in Spain at this time were extraordinarily complex, and the position of the reform movement — necessarily dependent on Crown, local bishops and Vatican authorities all at once — was unstable and occasionally actually dangerous. Teresa's remarkable skill in negotiating this minefield was crucial: that she was so successful while still worrying about the daily needs of her rapidly expanding order and their — and her own — spiritual lives is a testament to her energy and intelligence.

A Tammy Wynette song. It does seem to reflect rather precisely how Teresa felt about Jesus.

The Life, Chapter 22 (*Complete Works of St Teresa*, see above). This paragraph shows Teresa at her most delicately sardonic.

'Martha and Mary must join together in order to show hospitality to the Lord' (*Interior Castle*, 7.4 (*Complete Works of St Teresa*, see above)). The equality of Martha and Mary was an important theme of Teresa, who repudiated the more usual superiority of Mary's (contemplative) over Martha's (active) ministry. See R. Williams (*op. cit.*, p. 138).

Stelazine is a fairly commonly prescribed modern anti-psychotic drug.

Desert Wind

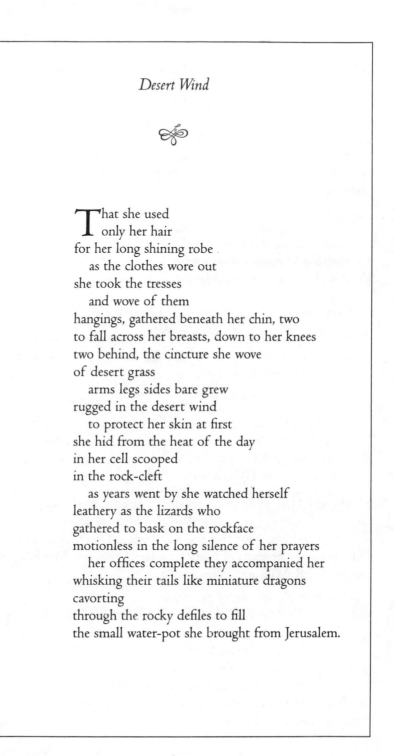

That she used
   only her hair
for her long shining robe
   as the clothes wore out
she took the tresses
   and wove of them
hangings, gathered beneath her chin, two
to fall across her breasts, down to her knees
two behind, the cincture she wove
of desert grass
   arms legs sides bare grew
rugged in the desert wind
   to protect her skin at first
she hid from the heat of the day
in her cell scooped
in the rock-cleft
   as years went by she watched herself
leathery as the lizards who
gathered to bask on the rockface
motionless in the long silence of her prayers
   her offices complete they accompanied her
whisking their tails like miniature dragons
cavorting
through the rocky defiles to fill
the small water-pot she brought from Jerusalem.

Mary of Egypt: c. 5th century
Hermit, penitent
Feast: 2 April

❧

A certain Mary lived the life of a hermit in Palestine according to John Moschus, and her tomb was visited by Cyril of Scythopolis, who in his Life of Cyriacus *related how two of his disciples had met a woman hermit in the desert beyond Jordan, and on a second visit found her dead and buried her. There is no record of a public cult.*

Oxford Dictionary of Saints

With the desert saints, it is not authority, nor succession that counts, but present charismata and the power of discernment that enables them to be the touchstones of 'true' reality: through them the world is kept in being.

Benedicta Ward, *Harlots of the Desert*

There were a number of women living as ascetics and hermits in the desert in the early centuries of the Church. The sayings of three of them are recorded amongst the sayings of the desert fathers – Amma Syncletica, Amma Theodora and Amma Sarah.

All their teachings were passed down by word of mouth by their disciples until they were written down two to three centuries later. Of all these sayings, the *Apophthegmata Patrum* (Sayings of the Desert Fathers) form the greater part; a few sayings, the *Apophthegmata Matrum*, are attributed to these women. Amma Syncletica and Amma Theodora were abbesses and well-educated. Amma Sarah, like Mary of Egypt, was a hermit and penitent.

Of the untold number of ascetics living in the desert, a number lived as solitaries and were not known to be women until they died. And some presumably were never found. The hermit way of life was one possible way for a woman to dedicate herself to God entirely in the early centuries, as long as she kept herself concealed.

Amma Sarah was a solitary but she was known; according to her sayings, she fought against the demon of lust for thirteen years, and lived her life for sixty years alone by the Nile.

As years went by she no longer missed
the sound of human voices
the desert sang
its intricate harmonies
to her the night yielded up the
many voices of beast and bird
attuned to silence she caught
the sound of migrant swifts
of moth and bat
the good God who fed her
desert herbs and manna-bread
who made the dried-up spring to flow
wrapped her sense in light in sound
each day renewed for her delight his
creation, bestowed on her for her simplicity
beauty, for all she needed, gave

For her there was no space in which it was possible to be a woman: she is reputed to have said, 'According to my thoughts I am a man, although according to nature a woman.'

They saw the period in which they lived as one of exceptional temptation – Amma Theodora said 'The present age is a storm'; temptations were valued because they were the testing fire through which experience was gained and spiritual growth made possible. Conflict and struggle were seen as an essential part of the holy life.

Amma Syncletica said, 'It is dangerous for anyone to teach who has not first been trained in the practical life.' Practical experience of life first was the basis for recognizing the demons you contended with. The demonic stood not only for that which was hostile, but also for all that was anomalous and incomplete in personal development. It is for these kinds of insights that the teachings of the desert fathers and mothers are now valued today. Mary of Egypt's story, however, was used within this context in a quite particular way.

The traditions of the desert fathers made use of the stories of women such as Mary of Egypt, Pelagia and others as models of repentance, and the Church carried on this tradition. The story of Mary was a favourite one, and many miracles were associated with her after her death.

Mary's life was considered to be an icon of the theological truths of repentance, and the text of it, composed by Sophronius, is still used in the Orthodox Lent liturgy. She is especially celebrated in the Orthodox Church, her feast day occurring on the 5th Sunday of Lent.

The life of Mary, as related by Cyril of Scythopolis, described her as a prostitute in Alexandria from the age of twelve. At the age of twenty-nine she joins a pilgrimage to Jerusalem out of curiosity, and pays for her passage by taking the sailors as her clients. In Jerusalem she is converted, experiencing an unseen force which prevents her entering the church with the other pilgrims, and receiving heavenly guidance from an icon of the Virgin to cross the Jordan and go and live in the desert. She takes three small loaves and a jar of water with her, which never fail, and lives on them and desert fruits.

She remains hidden in a remote part of the desert for some eighteen to thirty years, in penitence for her sins. One day, Abba John and his disciple Pananmon, going to visit the cell of the holy monk Kyriakos, stumble on her cave. Her body is blackened by the sun, covered only by the tangles of her long uncombed hair. She hides from them and will barely speak with them. When they press her, she tells them to return to her on their way back from Kyriakos' cell, and give her communion.

The monks go on their way, but uncertain what to do, seek Kyriakos' advice. He instructs them to return and to do as she bids. When they return they find only her corpse. They bury her with full Christian rites.

In another version there is only one monk, Zossima, who enlists the help of a lion to dig her grave.

In all its forms the story underlines the contrast between the striving monks and the repentant sinner who, full of grace, only needs to receive 'the simple gift of salvation from Christ without any acts, self-exploration, sacraments or prayers, . . . only because of her great need' (Benedicta Ward, *op. cit.*).

Because women were considered a great source of temptation, strictly to be shunned by the early monastic church, they could only occupy the positions of harlots or hearth-keepers. Only virgins and penitents were allowed in the theology of the desert, Sister Benedicta Ward points out, and they had to be 'hidden in a cave or cell, unseen even unknown' (Benedicta Ward, 'Miracles in the desert tradition' in *Signs and Wonders: Saints, Miracles and Prayers from the 4th to the 14th Centuries*.

There were many other versions of this story. In the most frequently retold one she is a disgraced canoness (a consecrated virgin) of the Church of the Holy Sepulchre in Jerusalem — the story of a nun seduced in Jerusalem was current in the fifth and sixth centuries amongst the desert fathers.

SOURCES

Benedicta Ward, *Harlots of the Desert: A Study of Repentance in Early Monastic Sources* (Mowbray, Oxford, 1987).

Benedicta Ward, *Signs and Wonders: Saints, Miracles and Prayers from the 4th to the 14th Centuries* (Variorum, Aldershot, 1992).

Virtuous Magic?

There was a time when you were not a slave, remember that. . . . You say you have lost all recollection of it, remember. . . . You say there are no words to describe this time; you say it does not exist. But remember. Make an effort to remember. Or, failing that, invent.

Monique Wittig, Les Guerillères

At the end of this writing we want to raise some of the issues that have arisen in the course of it – subjects that we have dropped into drawers or in-trays marked *come back to this later*. These are questions which still engage us and which, since we do not for the most part have any clear answers to them, we still find of interest and worthy of note.

It is the nature of a holy life, of a saint, to be open-ended; to resist the logically fixed boundaries. The saint both inhabits her mortality and presses against its limits, so that her life is always crossing through the boundaries both of this world and another that, to most of us, is the stuff of myth and fairy-tale, archetype and symbol. While, on the one hand, through martyrdom and/or renunciation she must ultimately leave this world 'for some non-assured life . . . Tearing [her]self away from the land of [her] birth to plunge [her] roots into a land still virgin. And therefore unknown' (Luce Irigaray, *L'Oubli de l'air*, in M. Whitford, *The Irigaray Reader*), on the other hand, after her departure her cult will return her to the land of her birth, a local habitation and a name. The paradox of the transcendent earthed in the local will once more be affirmed. It is this essential nature of our subjects which encourages us to resist closure, and instead end with some of the provocations, the areas that we still wish to debate.

If saints are embodied beings of extra-ordinary spiritual power, how does that power reach us, in what ways can it travel down to us today?

This is an issue about transmission: once, that communication was authentically processed through the cults of relics, through the patronage of churches and guilds, through shrines and pilgrimages and so forth, in a pattern which formed part of community. The likelihood today, however, is that knowledge of saints, in the sense of information about their lives and acts, will be consumed by individuals via the major channels of communication, appropriately enough via terrestrial and extra-terrestrial (satellite) systems. And if this is so, what kind of impact can their lives have?

Perhaps to experience their power, their friendship in our lives, we do still need authentic personal experiences, such as pilgrimage, novenas, etc., in order to be touched at first hand. Or can 'virtual reality' deliver that power through the data of lives, legends and histories, deeds, martyrdoms and teachings, visions, sayings, prayers, praises, prophecies, writings, confessions, images?

Historically, rising more to the surface at some periods than others, Christian names, wayside shrines, saints' days, names, emblems, icons and themes have provided evidence of the buried strata of the saints' contribution to our Western Christian culture. If excavated, these strata contain vital and subversive meanings from a time when sacred and profane were so closely woven together that to distinguish them made no kind of sense.

Can the saints still be a route to encounter that interfusion?

In talking about 'hagiography' is it too easy to end up talking as though there were a 'science' to be taken account of rather than an art? We need to think hard about the role of the imagination in replenishing these saintly narratives of witness, iconic empowerment and service, retelling them as something for our nourishment, along with all the other arts and fictions that sustain us in a culture where the female, if it is not subsumed, is always marginal and only ever represented as the 'Other'. These women's lives have been imaginatively, creatively, claimed over and over again. There is a conflict between trying to work out their own 'reality' and our needs.

The saints' so-called realities need to be available to the multi-levelled uses to which they may be put – from the most basic magic-working or superstition, through to the complex interpretations of theologians, artists, visionaries and pedagogues. Any study of hagiography has to be a study of representation as well as of biography. Perhaps this is the final end of radical altruism: to give those in need the right to interpret, to reinvent, to claim, to *use* one's own truth.

Do the saints offer us – women, children and men; inside and outside contemporary faith communities – the possibility of potential life-transformation? If so, how? How do the saints act as a 'conduit between the [divine] Other and ordinary existence'?

We still have a strong sense that the saints do have relevance in our lives – that their images in our churches can still possess an affective power which is more than the sum of the faded traces of their former devotions. That we can 'hear'/read/receive some of their stories today if they are recast, if they are read 'otherwise'. That patriarchal Christianity has not entirely drained them of their lifeblood.

To set that blood flowing we have used differing devices in retelling hagiography or creating through collages of sources and images, poems, which we hope can deliver a new, imagined reality, *against the grain of traditional representations*. Nonetheless hagiography is genre-coded, like any other form, and it is difficult to break free of this – especially for 'believers', Christians, ourselves.

While agreeing wholeheartedly, for example, with Elizabeth Stuart's conclusion in *Spitting at Dragons*, that the 'example, energy, and encouragement [of our 'embodied ancestors in faith'] offers us some of the friendship which enables us to flourish', and warmly saluting her call for us to be worthy of their legacy so that we can 'call forth spiritual power in each other and allow the women who have gone before us to do the same', we find ourselves in a rather less comfortable position.

This effort of living alongside the saints has enlarged our sympathies, but we do not feel we can call that 'friendship'. An awareness, an increased sense of solidarity across generations of pre-feminist women, a chain of connectedness – yes. But not friendship in the sense of intimacy, a per-sonal and substantive connection.

Perhaps these saints make us feel more secure in who we are, which might be a function of friendship, but perhaps even more one of mothering. Could the saints be seen as foremothers in our identities as Christian feminists? Sheila Rowbotham's comments on feminist history seem helpful here:

> *The writing of our history is not just an individual venture but a continuing social communication. Our history strengthens us in the present by connecting us with the lives of countless women. Threads and strands of long lost experience weave into the present. In rediscovering the dimensions of female experience lost in the tangled half-memories of myth and dream, we are uncovering and articulating a cultural sense of what it is to be a woman . . . we are heaving ourselves into history, clumsy with the newness of creation, stubborn and persistent in the pursuit of our lost selves, fortunate to be living in such transforming times.*

But this does not *feel* like friendship.

What we have discovered is friendship for each other – despite the differences which have emerged. So that for Wendy it is possible to touch the quick of an earlier religious life, a spiritual companionship amongst women, through Sara's fictions; and for Sara there is a renewed sense of another dimension, a geography of women's spiritual presence in the bedrock of the land, a spatial continuity, through Wendy's poems.

We have been pursuing the notion that the saints' exemplariness lies not so much in the virtues and moral perfection they exhibit, but in what we are calling their 'Magic' – the power to disrupt and explode traditional causal connections, accepted contexts and criteria. That they *are* examples for us because of their persistence in seeking the perfection of God in the art of living each day of one's life: in turning upside-down everyday logic, common sense and decency and flying in the face of accepted codes of good behaviour. In refusing marriage, refusing food, abandoning children and families, searching out and clinging to martyrdom, isolation, enclosure. In living in filth, following their mission, confronting the powers of state, of killing machines and torturers.

These saints demonstrate the existence of the miraculous within ordinary life – and reveal how bloody uncomfortable it is to be associated with saintliness, how threatening to our comfort.

We have had a problem with the miraculous. Crudely, you could put it like this:

Do we believe in saints? Yes.

Do we believe in miracles? Well, it depends . . .

Officially one of the requirements for canonization is the capacity or ability to work miracles. Even since the Second Vatican Council in the 1960s a post-death miracle is required as part of the evidence for sainthood.

We have, however, skirted this key issue: instead we have thought of the extraordinariness of events and acts in our saints' lives in terms of *magic* – a word which for us has positive connotations with the power of women once so harshly obliterated by the Church, rather than of miracles. There are indeed miracles associated with the greater number of the saints in this book, but we have kept pretty quiet about them. The interdependence of miracles and saints is shown at another level in the etymological connection between 'holy' and 'healing', – healing miracles traditionally make up the greater part of the miracles associated with women saints – so it is hardly an issue we can ignore. Moreover, because of our own declared interest in the saintly condition of breaking causality and rationality, imploding contemporary logics and disrupting time, we must ask why we find the miraculous such a dodgy concept. If we as twentieth-century feminists are still so heavily determined by our own shaping that we cannot suspend our disbelief in the miraculous, what are we missing out on?

Might the words liminal and/or trangressive be deployed helpfully here? Saints are necessarily boundary-transgressors: the logically fixed boundary between time and eternity was breached by the Incarnation, and this transgression is relived, represented, in the lives of the saints. If sanctity is a capacity to maintain a foot in both camps, as it were, of the *big* dualist splits – eternity v. history, God v. creation, spirit v. matter, etc. – then holiness is necessarily a liminal condition, and hagiography – the writing about saints – becomes a geography of the boundaries, of the borders and of the unboundaried. The transgressive condition of sanctity is a location of confusion, where categories will tend to break down. The sparks that fly out of such explosions may indeed be the *how* of the 'conduit between the [Divine] Other and ordinary existence' (L. Irigaray, *L'Oubli de l'air*, in M. Whitford, *The Irigaray Reader*). But it is also obvious that such a condition is inherently unstable.

Since women are held by masculinist culture to be of their nature unstable to start with, this may help to explain why the hagiography of women is so often so bizarrely stupid, blind and undiscerning. Women cannot be allowed to decategorize themselves. Therefore,

> *the chief problem in charting any history of women is the recovery and use of sources. The marginality [liminality from the point of view of those who are in the centre] of women in the Christian tradition means that few sources exist . . . those that can be found were generally recorded by males . . . material about women that does not fit the prescriptions tends to be edited out if the woman is being held up as a 'good' model, or turned into a polemic if the woman is regarded as a 'bad' example.*
>
> Elizabeth Stuart, *Spitting at Dragons*

Women in pursuit of holiness (as women *and* as saints) are doubly vulnerable to destabilization, implosion and fracture. What is remarkable then is not that so few women have been canonized relative to men, but that so many have managed this duality-smashing activity and have managed to perform as both explorers and cartographers; as both pioneers and gatekeepers. Messages have been transmitted, but it is, not surprisingly, hard to understand how.

Because of their vision of God, what the saints have in common above all else is their sheer *unreasonableness*, their intransigence and quite over-the-top dedication to chancing themselves in the unnamed game of disregarding reasonable selfish concerns and instead lavishing themselves upon a particular relationship with God and with their fellow human beings. For what is most self-defining, most significant about the saints is that, because of their vision of God, they exist given over to an Other, in a state that we have been calling 'Radical Altruism'.

We are indebted here to Edith Wyschogrod's discussion of ethics, and her introduction of the term Radical Altruism in her book *Saints and Postmodernism*. Wyschogrod argues that a new ethics, a new understanding of selfhood in this post-Holocaust age, could be based upon the lives and examples of both saints and fictional heroes, if differently read (i.e., within the context of postmodern reading strategies).

Such an altruism, however, is an extremely difficult concept to harmonize with more standard feminist ideas of autonomy, self-ownership and self-authentication. Is there an inevitable conflict between radical altruism and the being of an 'owned self', a boundaried and autonomous self? Or is the relationship dialectical? Does holiness lie in some resolution which ultimately means that the saint has a strong enough self to be able to have something to give away? Does anything in this book point towards how, as feminists, we can begin to create a balance between integrity and self-giving, between owning the self and giving it away in service? Between integrity and charity?

Might ideals of 'radical obedience' or even singleness or solitariness in the lives of women saints (once expressed symbolically in virginity, but now perhaps requiring a new mythology and iconography – chastity, voluntary poverty, or lesbianism ???) point towards sources of self-authorization and self-authentication that women might usefully explore further? And if so would this say anything to men, about their pilgrimage towards grace?

To return to the beginning: a great deal of this is about the sources and transmission of the lives of women saints, or more specifically, about the way voices from the periphery are so often not transmitted but blocked and delayed. This book is an attempt to clear out the drains a little: this channel-clearing forms part of our oppositional critique of the traditional readings of the saints. From the point of view of moral philosophy, it is a constant of all major religions and thought traditions that the past must be reinterpreted, re-patterned, in order to allow moral change, or growth. One major change that concerns us here is one that affirms the value of difference, of the Other as marginal, disempowered, non-hegemonic. Within the churches that does not only mean women, but it does importantly include them since the established authority and traditions have for so long treated women's voices as peripheral to their main concerns.

The issue is one of gender positions, but (by the same token) it is at the same time one of democracy. It is an issue about the receptiveness of the Christian churches to the experiences and voices of all humanity. One of the ways in which, in the Middle Ages, women traditionally got their voices heard was by their visionary utterance, their claim to direct unmediated experience of Christ. Their contribution to the life of the Church did not depend upon their role as religious. In the century in which women have become institutionalized as ministers within all the mainstream Protestant denominations, and as priests within the Anglican Communion, it is perhaps time to reclaim those visionary oppositional voices – or at least to make sure they are audible. We would like this book to be seen within that tradition.

Conclusion

Forty-one women saints later we have reached the end of the book.

Traditionally we should now write the conclusion and sum up what we have done and neatly encapsulate what it all means: close the text tidily, enfold the contents in a woolly blanket and put it to bed, perhaps with a lullaby, perhaps just a slammed door.

Oddly enough we don't at all feel as if we *have* come to *the* conclusion — or, indeed, conclusions. And this is in fact not a negative feeling but quite an exhilarating one. For the way it has turned out is quite other than the way we had expected. When we started work, over two years ago, we both had an image in our minds of a goal, a 'somewhere' that we would get to: like a pilgrimage, the process of rewriting these saints would lead us to a destination, if only as a point of arrival, which would be its own clarification. We would have understood the meanings of female sainthood for us as contemporary women.

These meanings would be ethical and perhaps theological, they would be about empowerment, about how we search in the material world for that something we vaguely sense eludes us, that thread of the original creative Spirit's work around us and in us, in our communities, families, workplaces, a thread linking back to the earliest marks left behind by these persons called saints. The gap between us and that mysterious, evasive quality we call 'virtue' would in some perceptible way be narrowed.

More interestingly though — and characteristically, we would say, of the work of the Holy Spirit — something rather different, more complex and baffling has occurred. The sense of certainty, of taxonomy, of precise knowledges, tabulations, has disintegrated. We have failed to clip the wings of this manifestation of the divine, to label and place on display these literally extra-ordinary women.

They have escaped us – except in so far as the creative Spirit at work in our texts sometimes re-creates them in the mind of the reader. (This seems to us perhaps even more than many books produced in the postmodernist context to be a book which depends upon its readers for its life and its answers.)

For us as outsiders the life that these women hurtle themselves into with the speed and directness of a rocket is altogether unknowable, hypothetical. It is the life of a creative fiction. To them and to the devotees who follow them it is unmapped but it is clear – luminous and vibrant with promise. They are not pinned down to our understandings, our intentions, our needs or our desires.

So how can we argue that we have reclaimed these saints for ourselves, let alone for any other contemporary women or men? This indeed was part of the project of this book, as it has been for other feminists writing about the saints in recent years. But we cannot *generalize* out from their lives, much less insert them into our pre-fabricated theoretical feminist and theological frameworks.

They defy inclusion. They remain Other.

We thought full imaginative/creative engagement with their lives would reveal *them* and, therefore, their meanings. We would look at these diverse socially constructed individuals, the saints who for various reasons appealed to us, with all the weight of their material, psychological histories, through writings, relics, representations, hagiographies – and they would yield up our conclusions. But the encounters we have engaged in with the women in this book – and many more we have had to leave out – have baffled our attempts to extract from them a theologically coherent account of saint-hood's meanings for today.

We are left with the idiosyncrasies of our own histories and the accidents of contacts and clues which have made us pervious to some of the lives to the point at which we have creatively felt driven to *write them*, to struggle our-selves to find a new way to articulate their meanings for us as individuals. It is, of course, just possible that this is in itself a theological conclusion. In the light of the Incarnation it might just be.

List of Main Works Cited

A. M. Allchin, *Celtic Christianity: Fact or Fantasy* (Inaugural Lecture, University College of North Wales, Bangor, 1993).

A. M. Allchin, *Pennant Melangell: Place of Pilgrimage* (Oswestry, 1994).

Emilie Amt (ed.), *Women's Lives in Medieval Europe: A Sourcebook* (Routledge, London, 1993).

R. J. Armstrong and I. C. Brady (trans. and eds), *Francis and Clare: The Complete Works* (Paulist Press, New York, 1982).

Clarissa Atkinson, *Mystic and Pilgrim: The Book and World of Margery Kempe* (Cornell University Press, Ithaca, NY, 1981).

Donald Attwater, *The Penguin Dictionary of Saints* (Penguin, 1965).

D. Baker (ed.), *Medieval Women* (Blackwell, Oxford, 1978).

Sabine Baring-Gould, *Lives of the Northumbrian Saints* (Llanerch Enterprises, Llanerch, 1990).

Alexandra Barratt (ed.), *Women's Writing in Middle English* (Longman, London, 1992).

Marco Bartoli, *Clare of Assisi*, trans. Sr Francis Teresa (Darton, Longman & Todd, London, 1993).

Bede, *Ecclesiastical History of the English People*, ed. B. Colgrave and R. A. B. Mynors (Clarendon Press, Oxford, 1969).

F. Beer, *Women and Mystical Experience in the Middle Ages* (Boydell Press, Woodbridge, 1992).

Nancy R. E. Bell, *The Saints in Christian Art*, 3 vols, 1901–4.

T. A. Bevis, *The Story of a Famous Fen Church: St Wendreda, March* (Chatteris, Cambs, n.d.).

Osbern Bokenham, *Legendys of Hooly Wummen*, ed. M. S. Serjeantson (Early English Text Society, 1938).

Louis Bouyer, *Women's Ministry in the Early Church* (Sheed and Ward, 1968).

E. G. Bowen, *Saints, Seaways and Settlements in the Celtic Lands* (University of Wales, Cardiff).

Fiona Bowie and Oliver Davies (eds), *Beguine Spirituality* (SPCK, London, 1990).

P. Brown, *The Cult of the Saints: Its Rise and Function in Latin Christianity* (SCM, London, 1981).

Peter Brown, *The Body and Society* (Faber & Faber, London, 1992).

Roger Brownrigg, *Who's Who in the New Testament* (Weidenfeld and Nicolson, 1973).

Anne Budge, *Annals of the Early Friends* (London, 1887).

A. S. G. Butler, *Portrait of Josephine Butler* (London, 1954).

Josephine Butler, *The Hour before the Dawn* (London, 1876).

Caroline Walker Bynum, *Fragmentation and Redemption: Essays on Gender and the Human Body in Medieval Religion* (Zone Books, New York, 1992).

P. Caraman (ed.), *Saints and Ourselves*, second series (Hollis and Carter, London, 1953).

Alexander Carmichael (ed. and trans.), *Carmina Gadelica* (1900–1971, 6 vols, various editions. Selection republished by Floris Books, Edinburgh, 1994).

Ana Carrigan, *Salvador Witness: The Life and Calling of Jean Donovan* (Ballantine Books, New York, 1984).

Sheila Cassidy, *Good Friday People* (Darton, Longman & Todd, London, 1991).

D. Chitty, *The Desert a City: Introduction to the Study of Egyptian and Palestinian Monasticism under the Christian Empire* (St. Vladimir's Seminary Press, Crestwood, NY, 1992)

Carol Christ *et al.*, *The Politics of Women's Spirituality* (Touchstone, 1982).

E. Colledge OSA and J. Walsh SJ (eds), *A Book of Showings to the Anchoress Julian of Norwich* (Pontifical Institute of Medieval Studies, Toronto, 1978).

Mary Condren, *The Serpent and the Goddess: Women, Religion and Power in Celtic Ireland* (Harper & Row, San Francisco, 1989).

Dorothy Day, *Loaves and Fishes* (Harper & Row, San Francisco, 1973).

Dorothy Day, *The Long Loneliness* (Harper & Row, San Francisco, 1981).

Dorothy Day, *On Pilgrimage* (Catholic Worker Press, 1948).

H. Delehaye, *The Legends of the Saints*, trans. D. Attwater (1962).

E. J. Dobson, *The Origins of Ancrene Wisse* (Oxford University Press, Oxford, 1976).

Peter Dronke, *Women Writers of the Middle Ages* (Cambridge University Press, Cambridge, 1984).

E. S. Duckett, *Anglo-Saxon Saints and Scholars* (New York, 1947).

E. Duffy, *Holy Maydens, Holy Wyfes: The Cult of Women Saints in Fifteenth and Sixteenth Century England*. Vol. 27 of Women in the Church. Studies in Church History (Oxford University Press, Oxford, 1990).

E. Duffy, *The Stripping of the Altars: Traditional Religion in England 1400–1580* (Yale University Press, New Haven, 1992).

Alison Elliott, *Roads to Paradise: Reading the Lives of the Early Saints* (New England University Press, 1987).

K. M. Evans, *A Book of Welsh Saints* (Cardiff, 1967).

F. W. Faber, *The Saints and Servants of God* (London, 1847).

G. Ferguson, *Signs and Symbols in Christian Art* (1954).

J. T. Fisher, *The Catholic Counter Culture in America 1933–1962* (University of North Carolina Press, 1989).

George Fox, *Journal*, ed. Norman Penney (New York, 1924).

Marie-Louise von Franz, *The Passion of Perpetua* (Spring Publications, 1980).

L. Gelber and R. Leuven (eds), *Life in a Jewish Family* (1986).

M. E. Giles (trans. and ed.), *The Book of Prayer of Sor Maria of Santo Domingo: A Study and Translation* (State University of New York Press, Albany, NY, 1990).

Lady Gregory, *A Book of Saints and Wonders*. Reprinted by Colin Smythe Ito, Gerrards Cross, Bucks, 1993. (First published 1906).

E. R. Henken, *Traditions of the Welsh Saints* (Boydell and Brewer, Woodbridge, 1987).

E. R. Henken, *Welsh Saints: A Study in Patterned Lives* (Boydell and Brewer, Woodbridge, 1991).

Waltraud Herbstrith, *Edith Stein: A Biography*, trans. B. Bonowitz (Harper & Row, New York, 1985).

G. Herzfield (ed.), *An Old English Martyrology* (Early English Text Society, 1900).

Jane Hirshfield (ed.), *Women in Praise of the Sacred: 43 Centuries of Spiritual Poetry by Women* (Harper Collins, New York, 1995).

C. Horstmann (ed.), *Lives of Women Saints of Our Contrie of England* (Early English Text Society, London, 1886).

K. H. Jackson (sel. and trans.), *A Celtic Miscellany: Translations from the Celtic Literatures* (Penguin, 1971).

M. R. James, *Norfolk and Suffolk* (Dent, London, 1930).

David Jones, *Art in Relation to War* (1942)

Francis Jones, *Holy Wells of Wales* (Cardiff, 1954).

R. Kieckhefer, *Unquiet Souls: 14th Century Saints and Their Religious Milieu* (University of Chicago Press, Chicago, 1926).

T. E. Lawrence, *Seven Pillars of Wisdom* (1926).

Jacques Le Goff (ed.), *The Medieval World*, trans. L. Cochrane (Collins & Brown, London, 1990).

Brendan Lehane, *Early Celtic Christianity*, 2nd edn (Constable, London, 1994).

Robert Llewelyn (ed.), *Julian, Woman of Our Day* (Darton, Longman & Todd, London, 1985).

Mina Loy, *The Last Lunar Baedeker* (Jargon, Corinth, USA, 1978; Carcanet Press, Manchester, 1985).

E. W. McDonnell, *The Beguines and Beghards in Medieval Culture* (New Brunswick, NY, 1954).

Sara Maitland, *A Big-Enough God* (Mowbray, London, 1995).

Sara Maitland, 'Passionate prayer: masochistic images in women's experience' in Linda Hurcombe (ed.), *Sex and God* (RKP, 1988).

S. Merrim (ed.), *Feminist Perspectives on Sor Juana Inés de la Cruz* (Wayne State University Press, Detroit, 1991).

H. V. Morton, *In the Steps of St Paul* (Methuen, London, 1979. First published 1936).

J. A. S. Morton (ed.), *The Nun's Rule, Being the Ancrene Riwle Modernised* (King's Classics, London, 1905).

N. Pevsner, *The Buildings of England: Cambridgeshire*, 2nd edn (Penguin, Harmondsworth, 1970).

Daphne Pochin Mould, *The Saints of Ireland* (Dublin, 1964).

Sylvia Mundahl-Harris, *St Hilda and Her Times* (Abbey Press, Whitby, 1985).

Margaret Murray, *The God of the Witches* (Oxford University Press, Oxford, 1952).

Margaret Murray, *The Witch-Cult of Western Europe* (Oxford University Press, Oxford, 1921).

The Northumbria Community, *Liturgy of St Hild*, reprinted in *Celtic Night Prayer from the Northumbria Community* (HarperCollins, London, 1996).

Amy Oden (ed.), *In Her Words: Women's Writings in the History of Christian Thought* (SPCK, London, 1995).

Julia O'Faiolin, *Women in the Wall* (Virago, London, 1989).

Raghnall O'Floinn, *Irish Shrines and Reliquaries of the Middle Ages* (Country House, Dublin, 1994).

L. Ouspensky, *Theology of the Icon*, Vol. I, trans. A. Gythiel (St. Vladimir's Seminary Press, Crestwood, NY, 1992).

Margaret Sayers Peden (ed. and trans.), *A Woman of Genius: The Intellectual Autobiography of Sor Juana Inés de la Cruz* (Lime Rock Press, Salisbury, CT, 1982).

E. A. Petroff, *Medieval Women's Visionary Literature* (Oxford University Press, Oxford, 1986).

W. W. Ramsay, *The Church in the Roman Empire* (Hodder and Stoughton, London, 1893).

Michèle Roberts, *The Wild Girl* (Women's Press, London, 1985).

D. Rollason, *Saints and Relics in Anglo-Saxon England* (Blackwell, Oxford, 1989).

F. Ross, *Ruined Abbeys of Britain* (n.d).

R. R. Ruether and E. McLaughlin (eds), *Women of Spirit* (Simon and Schuster, 1979).

A. Savage and N. Watson (trans. and intro.), *Anchoritic Spirituality: Ancrene Wisse and Associated Works* (Paulist Press, New York, 1991).

Mary-Lee Settle, *The Long Road to Paradise* (Collins, 1974).

Amanda Berry Smith, *An Autobiography: The Story of the Lord's Dealings with Mrs. Amanda Smith, the Colored Evangelist* (Garland Publishing, New York, 1987).

R. Spencer, *Guide to Saints of Wales and West Country* (Llanerch, 1991).

Lady Hester Stanhope, *Travels, Narrated by Her Physician*, 3 vols (John Colburn, 1846).

Edith Stein, *Edith Stein: A Self-Portrait in Letters*, trans. Josephine Koeppel OCD. Vol. 5 of *Collected Works*, ed. L. Gelber and R. Leuven (ICS Publications, Washington, DC, 1993).

Edith Stein, *Edith Stein, the Hidden Life: Hagiographic Essays, Meditations, Spiritual Texts*, trans. Waltraud Stein. Vol. 4 of *Collected Works*, ed. L. Gelber and R. Leuven (ICS Publications, Washington, DC, 1992).

Whitley Stokes (ed.), *Lives of the Saints from the Book of Lismore*, with translation notes by the editor (Anecdota Oxoniensa, Oxford, 1890).

Elizabeth Stuart, *Spitting at Dragons: Towards a Feminist Theology of Sainthood* (Mowbray, London, 1996).

C. H. Talbot (ed.), *The Life of Christina Markyate* (Oxford, 1959).

A. Vauchez, 'The saint', in J. Le Goff (ed.), *The Medieval World* (Collins & Brown, London, 1990).

Jacob de Voragine, *Legenda Aurea* [*The Golden Legend*], trans. William Caxton (London, 1878).

Helen Waddell (trans. and ed.), *Mediaeval Latin Lyrics* (Penguin, 1929).

Helen Waddell, *The Desert Fathers* (Constable, London, 1936).

Benedicta Ward, *Harlots of the Desert: A Study of Repentance in Early Monastic Sources* (Mowbray, Oxford, 1987).

Benedicta Ward, *Signs and Wonders: Saints, Miracles and Prayers from the 4th to the 14th Centuries* (Variorum Press, Aldershot, 1992).

Marina Warner, *From the Blond to the Beast* (Chatto & Windus, London, 1995).

Marina Warner, *Joan of Arc: The Image of Female Heroism* (Weidenfeld and Nicolson, London, 1981).

Marina Warner, *Monuments and Maidens* (Faber, 1987).

Maria Webb, *The Fells of Swarthmore Hall* (Philadelphia, 1884).

A. Weber, *Teresa of Avila and the Rhetoric of Femininity* (Princeton, 1990).

D. Weinstein and R. Bell, *Saints and Society: The Two Worlds of Western Christendom* (University of Chicago Press, Chicago, 1982).

C. H. Westlake, *The Parish Gilds of Medieval England* (London, 1919).

M. Whitford (ed.), *The Irigaray Reader: Luce Irigaray* (Blackwell, Oxford, 1994).

R. Williams, *Teresa of Avila* (Geoffrey Chapman, London, 1991).

K. M. Wilson (ed.), *Medieval Women Writers* (Manchester University Press, Manchester, 1984).

B. A. Windeatt (trans. and ed.), *The Book of Margery Kempe* (Penguin, Harmondsworth, 1985).

Edith Wyschogrod, *Saints and Postmodernism: Revisioning Moral Philosophy* (University of Chicago Press, Chicago, 1990).

Adomnan's Life of Columba, trans. and ed. A. O. and M. O. Anderson (Nelson, London, 1961).

The Martyrdom of Perpetua, trans. W. H. Shewring, introd. and commentary Sara Maitland (Arthur James, Evesham, 1996).

Selected Letters of Boniface, trans. E. Emerton (Oxford University Press, Oxford, 1940).

The Book of Prayer of Sor Maria of Santo Domingo: A Study and Translation, trans. and ed. M. E. Giles (State University of New York Press, Albany, NY, 1990).

The Revelations of St Birgitta, ed. W. P. Cumming (Early English Text Society, 1929).

Complete Works of St Teresa, 3 vols, trans. and ed. E. Allison Peers (Sheed and Ward, 1946).

The Voyages of Brendan the Navigator (1973).

WORKS OF REFERENCE

F. Arnold-Forster, *Studies in Church Dedications or England's Patron Saints*, 3 vols (Skeffington & Son, London, 1899).

S. Baring-Gould and J. Fisher, *The Lives of the British Saints*, 4 vols (Hon. Soc. Cymmodorion, London).

A. Bond and N. Mabin, *Saints of the British Isles* (New Horizon, Bognor, 1980).

Alban Butler, *Lives of the Saints*, 4 vols rev. 2nd edn, H. Thurston and D. Attwater (Burns and Oates, 1956).

V. Cronin, *A Calendar of Saints* (Darton, Longman & Todd, London, 1963).

J. Delaney, *Dictionary of Saints* (Kaye and Ward, 1982).

A. Dunbar, *Dictionary of Saintly Women*, 2 vols (George Bell & Sons, London, 1904).

David H. Farmer (ed.), *The Oxford Dictionary of Saints (ODS)*, 3rd edn (Oxford University Press, Oxford, 1992).

M. Gibson, *Saints of Patronage and Invocation* (Bristol, 1982).

Alison Jones, *The Wordsworth Dictionary of Saints* (Wordsworth Editions, Ware, Herts, 1994).